AMC'S BEST DAY HIKES NEAR
PHILADELPHIA

Four-Season Guide to 50 of the Best Trails in
Eastern Pennsylvania, New Jersey, and Delaware

Second Edition

SUSAN CHARKES

AMC is a nonprofit organization, and sales of AMC Books fund our mission of protecting the Northeast outdoors. If you appreciate our efforts and would like to become a member or make a donation to AMC, visit outdoors.org, call 800-372-1758, or contact us at Appalachian Mountain Club, 10 City Square, Boston, MA 02129.

outdoors.org/publications/books

Distributed by National Book Network.

Front cover photograph of Delaware Water Gap © Philip Shull/AMC Photo Contest
Back cover photograph of Schuylkill River © Montgomery County Planning Commission/Creative Commons on Flickr; back cover photograph of South Mountain area © DME1234/Creative Commons on Flickr
Interior photographs © Susan Charkes, unless otherwise noted
Maps by Ken Dumas © Appalachian Mountain Club
Book design by Abigail Coyle

Library of Congress Cataloging-in-Publication Data
Names: Charkes, Susan, author. | Appalachian Mountain Club, issuing body.
Title: AMC's best day hikes near Philadelphia : four-season guide to 50 of the best trails in eastern Pennsylvania, New Jersey, and Delaware / Susan Charkes.
Other titles: Appalachian Mountain Club's best day hikes near Philadelphia | Best day hikes near Philadelphia
Description: Second Edition. | Boston, Massachusetts : Appalachian Mountain Club Books, 2018. | Includes bibliographical references and index.
Identifiers: LCCN 2017055767 (print) | LCCN 2017057043 (ebook) | ISBN 9781628420913 (ePub) | ISBN 9781628420920 (Mobi) | ISBN 9781628420906 (pbk.)
Subjects: LCSH: Hiking--Pennsylvania--Philadelphia Region--Guidebooks. | Trails--Pennsylvania--Philadelphia Region--Guidebooks. | Philadelphia (Pa.)--Guidebooks.
Classification: LCC GV199.42.P42 (ebook) | LCC GV199.42.P42 P553 2018 (print) | DDC 796.5109748/11--dc23
LC record available at heps://lccn.loc.gov/2017055767

The paper used in this publication meets the minimum requirements of the American National Standard for Information Sciences-Permanence of Paper for Printed Library Materials, ANSI Z39.48-1984. ∞

Outdoor recreation activities by their very nature are potentially hazardous. This book is not a substitute for good personal judgment and training in outdoor skills. Due to changes in conditions, use of the information in this book is at the sole risk of the user. The author and the Appalachian Mountain Club assume no liability for accidents happening to, or injuries sustained by, readers who engage in the activities described in this book.

Interior pages and cover are printed on responsibly harvested paper stock certified by The Forest Stewardship Council®, an independent auditor of responsible forestry practices. Printed in the United States of America, using vegetable-based inks.

10 9 8 7 6 5 4 3 2 1   18 19 20 21

MIX
Paper from
responsible sources
FSC® C005010
www.fsc.org

This book is dedicated to my parents,
who first took me to the woods
and then let me go to walk on my own

and to my son,
who is on the verge

LOCATOR MAP

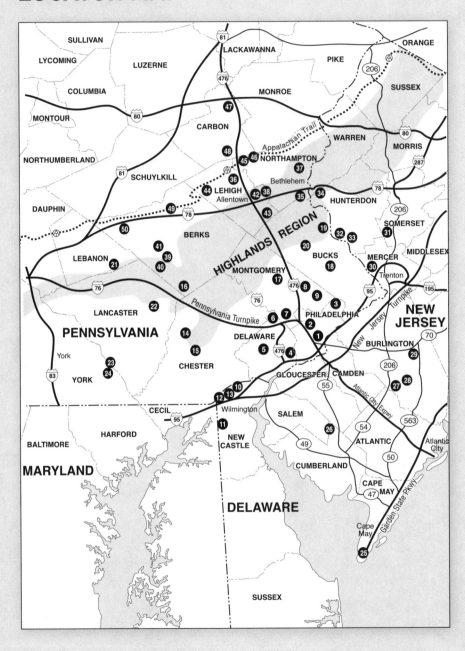

CONTENTS

NATURE AND HISTORY ESSAYS

AT-A-GLANCE TRIP PLANNER

TRIP NUMBER	TRIP NAME	LOCATION	DIFFICULTY	DISTANCE	ELEVATION GAIN
SOUTHEASTERN PENNSYLVANIA AND DELAWARE					
1	Fairmount Park Loop: Philadelphia Museum of Art	Philadelphia, PA	Moderate	9 mi	Minimal
2	Wissahickon Valley Park	Philadelphia, PA	Moderate-Difficult	7.5 mi	1,120 ft
3	Pennypack Park	Philadelphia, PA	Moderate	8 mi	50 ft
4	John Heinz National Wildlife Refuge at Tinicum	Philadelphia, PA	Easy	5.25 mi	Minimal
5	Ridley Creek State Park	Newtown Square, PA	Moderate	5.5 mi	875 ft
6	Valley Forge National Historical Park: Mount Misery and Mount Joy	King of Prussia, PA	Moderate	4.25 mi	450 ft
7	Valley Forge National Historical Park: River Trail	King of Prussia, PA	Easy	6 mi	25 ft
8	Green Ribbon Trail	Lower Gwynedd Twp, PA	Easy-Moderate	7.5 mi	Minimal
9	Pennypack Ecological Restoration Trust	Huntingdon Valley, PA	Easy-Moderate	7 mi	225 ft
10	Alapocas Run State Park	Wilmington, DE	Easy	4.5 mi	100 ft
11	Lums Pond State Park	Bear, DE	Easy-Moderate	7.5 mi	Minimal
12	White Clay Creek Preserve and White Clay Creek State Park	Landenburg, PA, and Newark, DE	Moderate	10 mi	400 ft
13	Brandywine Creek State Park	Wilmington, DE	Moderate	8 mi	275 ft
14	Hibernia County Park	Wagontown, PA	Easy	5.5 mi	365 ft
15	Natural Lands' Stroud Preserve	West Chester, PA	Moderate	5.25 mi	775 ft
16	French Creek State Park	Elverson, PA	Moderate	6.75 mi	1,100 ft
17	Green Lane Park	Green Lane, PA	Moderate	9 mi	1,250 ft
18	Peace Valley Nature Center	New Britain, PA	Easy-Moderate	7 mi	150 ft
19	Ralph Stover State Park and Tohickon Valley Park	Point Pleasant, PA	Moderate	8 mi	225 ft
20	Nockamixon State Park	Quakertown, PA	Moderate	6 mi	450 ft
21	Clarence Schock Memorial Park at Governor Dick Environmental Center	Mount Gretna, PA	Moderate	7 mi	400 ft

TIME	TRIP HIGHLIGHTS	FEE	GOOD FOR KIDS	DOG-FRIENDLY	PUBLIC TRANSPORT	X-C SKIING	SNOWSHOEING
3.5 hrs	River at the heart of the city		✓	✓	✓		
4 hrs	Rugged, wild gorge; old-growth forest			✓	✓	✓	✓
3 hrs	Picturesque wooded valley on the city's edge		✓	✓	✓	✓	✓
2 hrs	Freshwater tidal marsh and pond, great birding		✓	✓	✓		✓
2.75 hrs	Steep, forested hills along a winding creek		✓	✓			✓
2.25 hrs	Woods and hills near Washington's headquarters		✓	✓	✓		✓
2.75 hrs	Historic, placid Schuylkill River greenway		✓	✓	✓	✓	✓
3 hrs	Rail-accessible wooded creekside walk			✓	✓		
3.5 hrs	Extensive meadows		✓	✓		✓	✓
2 hrs	Urban oasis		✓	✓	✓		✓
3 hrs	Scenic forested pond	$		✓		✓	✓
4.5 hrs	Two states, one creek, many hills			✓			✓
3.5 hrs	Steep, forested, blue-rock valley	$		✓		✓	✓
2.5 hrs	Rocky, gently rolling hills		✓	✓		✓	✓
2.25 hrs	Farm fields and woods		✓	✓		✓	✓
3 hrs	Peaceful walk in a big woods		✓	✓			✓
4 hrs	Deep woods surround a quiet lake			✓			✓
3 hrs	Diverse rural landscape		✓			✓	✓
4 hrs	Spectacular High Rocks gorge			✓			✓
3 hrs	Rocky forest with lake views		✓	✓			✓
3.25 hrs	Large contiguous forest		✓	✓			✓

TRIP NUMBER	TRIP NAME	LOCATION	DIFFICULTY	DISTANCE	ELEVATION GAIN
22	Money Rocks County Park	Narvon, PA	Easy-Moderate	3 mi	275 ft
23	Kelly's Run–Pinnacle Overlook Preserve	Holtwood, PA	Difficult	7 mi	1,200 ft
24	Mason-Dixon Trail: Holtwood Dam	Slab, PA	Moderate-Difficult	7 mi	700 ft
CENTRAL AND SOUTHERN NEW JERSEY					
25	Cape May	West Cape May, NJ	Easy	5 mi	Minimal
26	Parvin State Park	Pittsgrove, NJ	Easy	5 mi	Minimal
27	Mullica River Trail	Atsion and Batsto, NJ	Moderate	9 mi	25 ft
28	Batona Trail: Carranza Memorial to Apple Pie Hill	Tabernacle, NJ	Moderate	9 mi	110 ft
29	Pakim Pond	Woodland Twp, NJ	Easy-Moderate	7 mi	240 ft
30	Ted Stiles Preserve at Baldpate Mountain	Titusville, NJ	Moderate	8.25 mi	500 ft
31	Sourland Mountain Preserve	Hillsborough Twp, NJ	Easy-Moderate	5 mi	400 ft
32	Bull's Island, Delaware Canal, and D&R Canal	Lumberville, PA; Bull's Island and Raven Rock, NJ	Moderate	9 mi	Minimal
33	Rockhopper Trail and Dry Run Creek Trail	Lambertville, NJ	Moderate	7 mi	350 ft
34	Musconetcong Gorge Preserve	Holland Twp, NJ	Easy-Moderate	4 mi	250 ft
BERKS COUNTY AND LEHIGH VALLEY, PENNSYLVANIA					
35	Natural Lands' Mariton Wildlife Sanctuary	Easton, PA	Easy-Moderate	3.5 mi	500 ft
36	Trexler Nature Preserve	Schnecksville, PA	Moderate-Difficult	7 mi	3,350 ft
37	Jacobsburg Environmental Education Center	Wind Gap, PA	Easy-Moderate	2.5 mi	200 ft
38	Monocacy Way	Bethlehem, PA	Moderate	6 mi	Minimal
39	Neversink Mountain Preserve	Reading, PA	Easy-Moderate	4 mi	525 ft
40	Nolde Forest Environmental Education Center	Reading, PA	Moderate	8 mi	500 ft
41	Blue Marsh Lake	Leesport, PA	Moderate	7.5 mi	960 ft

TIME	TRIP HIGHLIGHTS	FEE	GOOD FOR KIDS	DOG-FRIENDLY	PUBLIC TRANSPORT	X-C SKIING	SNOWSHOEING
1.5 hrs	Rugged rock formations, extensive forests		✓	✓			
3.5 hrs	Wild, rugged gorge in old-growth forest			✓			
3.5 hrs	Eagles soar above rocky riverside ravines			✓			
2.5 hrs	Ocean beach and dune forests		✓	✓			
2.5 hrs	Diverse forests on the edge of the Pinelands		✓	✓		✓	✓
4 hrs	Soft, pine-needle trails; cedar-brown river			✓		✓	✓
4 hrs	Quiet woods; view			✓		✓	✓
3.25 hrs	Pine Barrens woods; pond with pitcher plants		✓	✓		✓	✓
4.25 hrs	Mountain in miniature			✓			✓
2.25 hrs	Ridge-top boulder "amusement park"		✓	✓			✓
4 hrs	Along the wild and scenic Delaware River			✓		✓	✓
3 hrs	Gentle, rocky hillside and flat, wide creek		✓	✓			✓
3 hrs	Moist, rich, rocky woods		✓	✓			✓
2 hrs	Forested hills, river view		✓	✓			✓
4 hrs	Hilltop views, historic bridges			✓			✓
1.75 hrs	Meadows, old trees, ravine, and history		✓	✓			✓
3 hrs	Explore historic Bethlehem and its outskirts		✓	✓			✓
2.5 hrs	Rugged hike with scenic summit views		✓	✓			✓
3 hrs	Extensive conifer and hardwood forests			✓		✓	✓
4 hrs	Wooded hills around lakeshore			✓			✓

TRIP NUMBER	TRIP NAME	LOCATION	DIFFICULTY	DISTANCE	ELEVATION GAIN
42	Lehigh Parkway	Allentown, PA	Easy-Moderate	6.5 mi	125 ft
43	South Mountain Preserve	Emmaus, PA	Easy-Moderate	3.3 mi	500 ft
44	Appalachian Trail: PA 309 to Bake Oven Knob	New Tripoli, PA	Moderate-Difficult	11 mi	200 ft
45	Lehigh Gap Nature Center and Appalachian Trail	Slatington, PA	Moderate-Difficult	7.5 mi	1,000 ft
46	Appalachian Trail: Lehigh Gap East	Slatington, PA	Difficult	2.75 mi	900 ft
47	Hickory Run State Park	White Haven, PA	Difficult	12 mi	550 ft
48	Glen Onoko Falls and Lehigh Gorge State Park	Jim Thorpe, PA	Difficult	10 mi	950 ft
49	Appalachian Trail: The Pinnacle and the Pulpit	Hamburg, PA	Difficult	9.25 mi	1,300 ft
50	Sand Spring Trail and Tom Lowe Trail	Shartlesville, PA	Moderate	5.25 mi	500 ft

PREFACE

There's no such thing as a bad hike. How could there be? You're outdoors; you're walking: all's right with the world. I was raised in the western Philadelphia suburbs, where I picked up the hiking habit from my parents. On weekends we'd go day-hiking in the area, so I grew up thinking it was only natural that hiking was what you did for fun outdoors: all that beauty, all that fresh air, all those interesting things to look at for free. Unlike much of the rest of my early type-A life, hiking was noncompetitive. It didn't matter how fast you got to the end; what mattered was how you got there.

From my father, the scientist, I inherited a voracious appetite for observation, identification, classification, and contextualization. I could hardly take a step without noticing something interesting—some rock or tree or creature—and trying to figure out more about it. What's that rock saying about how the land got to be the way it is? Why is that tree growing here and not there? How did this tree get to be shaped like this? Why are birds singing in these woods and not those?

From my mother, the humanist, I inherited a craving to make stories out of what I observed. With British novelist E. M. Forster, she could say, "Only connect." There is an emotional, spiritual significance to everything in nature that goes beyond what we can see. Discovering the stories is half the joy; sharing them is the other half.

A hike is a time to enjoy the good feeling we get from propelling ourselves forward, straining against gravity going uphill, and braking against it going downhill. But a hike can be more. When we learn about a place—really learn it by walking through it and observing it—we open ourselves up to the possibility of falling in love with it. The place becomes part of our life story.

I continued hiking after I left home, got married, and formed a family. My family and I hiked on weekends and on vacations, wherever we went. After I went back to being on my own and moved to new locales, hiking led me to new friends and helped me feel like I was almost home even in a strange place. It was a familiar activity that I could apply to new ground.

Affection for the Philadelphia area drew me home after living away; hiking helped cement my determination to remain. Besides helping me nurture emotional bonds with the area's forests and parks, hiking has also helped me nurture comparable ties with my hiking companions. The strongest of these is the bond I've developed with my son as we have hiked together in the region where both of us grew up. Handing down what I am passionate about, the way my parents handed down their passions to me, has been my greatest hiking joy.

I'm still learning about new places to go—new trails, and trails new to me. The region is so full of places to hike that I could take a different hike every day of the year. But every hike is different, even if you hike the same path every day. There's always something new because every day is different.

Since the first edition of this book was published, Philadelphia and its surrounding areas have benefited from a steady proliferation of trail options. New parks and preserves have added hiking trails. There has been fervent interest in creating networks of multiuse trails to facilitate transportation, as well as recreation. Many places have modified or expanded their trails, improved the footpaths or signage, and added amenities.

So, it's a good time to take stock of the region's trails and to revise this book to make it an even more useful resource for hikers—those looking for new destinations and those seeking to discover the area's amazing diversity of hiking choices.

For the second edition, I've added several destinations (Blue Marsh Lake, Pakim Pond, Rockhopper and Dry Run Creek trails, Natural Lands' Stroud Preserve, and Trexler Nature Preserve) and eliminated others. I've also replaced some hikes with different trails at the same destinations (French Creek State Park, Nockamixon State Park) and tweaked other hikes by adding trails (Lehigh Gap Nature Center, Hibernia County Park). In many other destinations, I modified hikes to reflect changes in the trail system (some major, some minor). In some cases, I revised descriptions to reflect changes in land ownership or management or in the landscape itself. Indeed, very few of the hike descriptions have remained completely unchanged.

The hikes will keep evolving, in ways big and small. This guidebook is a snapshot of our region's best hikes. Even if you've walked them all, every hike still has the capacity to surprise and delight.

To paraphrase Ernie Banks, "It's a beautiful day for a hike—let's take two!"

ACKNOWLEDGMENTS

FIRST EDITION

This book is the product of an enormous amount of hard work, determination, and vision. Heather Stephenson, publisher of AMC Books, has been the guiding force behind the project from the beginning. Books editor Dan Eisner made sure that what needed to get done did, and always maintained a calm, centered presence. Kristen Sykes, Mid-Atlantic project manager for the Appalachian Mountain Club and vice chair for the Highlands Coalition—a can-do person if there ever was one—has tirelessly spearheaded Highlands protection initiatives. Without her encouragement I would never have considered this project. Jennifer Heisey, AMC's Mid-Atlantic recreation planner, has devoted countless hours to promoting hiking in the Highlands. She was indispensable to the creation of this book, having spent countless hours on the trails and having written ten of the trips.

When gathering background information, I was delighted to meet and speak with numerous public servants who are engaged in park and trail management, as well as volunteers who spend their spare time working to preserve, protect, and share the places they love. Among these were Claire Mickletz (Brandywine Creek State Park); Steve Heitzer (Delaware Canal State Park); David Bartoo (Delaware State Parks); David Long (Durham Township, Bucks County); Laurie Goodrich and Mary Linkevich (Hawk Mountain Sanctuary); Kevin Blair (Hickory Run State Park); Karen Ament and Lissette Santana (Holtwood Environmental Area); Bill Clother (Hunterdon County Parks); Gary Stolz and Bill Buchanan (John Heinz National Wildlife Refuge); Dan Kunkle (Lehigh Gap Nature Center); Lisa Frittinger (Mercer County Parks); Tim Ciotti (Montgomery County Parks); Brent Burke (The Nature Conservancy, Cape May); Gretchen Ferrante (New Jersey Audubon Society, Cape May); Martin Rapp (New Jersey Natural Lands Trust); Alan Hershey (New Jersey Trails); Daniel Hewko (Nolde Forest State Park); Craig Olsen and Gail Hill (Peace Valley Nature Center); David J. Robertson, Ph.D. (Pennypack Ecological Restoration Trust); Drew Brown (Philadelphia Water Department, Fairmount Waterworks Interpretive Center); Claire Adair (New Jersey Audubon Society, Rancocas); Roger McChesney (Ridley Creek State Park); Phil Richard and Dave Dendler (Somerset County Park Rangers); Mike Wilson (Trout Unlimited); Deirdre Gibson (Valley Forge National Historical Park); Jeannie Ford (Wharton State Forest, Batsto); Barbara Woodford (Wilmington State Parks); and Carol DeLancey (Wissahickon Valley Watershed Association).

To a great degree the book reflects input from AMC's Delaware Valley Chapter (AMCDV) hike leaders and volunteers. The AMCDV Chapter—of which I am a member, hike leader, and former conservation chair—hikes regularly throughout the Philadelphia area and beyond. To select and map the best hikes from the hundreds possible around the area, I depended heavily on the expertise of many people who cheerfully offered their advice, including Al Schwartz (also of Allentown Hiking Club), Pete Jarrett, Charlie Phy, Kathy Kelly-Borowski, Rich Wells (R.I.P.), Seth and Sue Bergmann, Lennie and Bill Steinmetz, Dan and Noelle Schwartz, Phil Mulligan, Tom Sherwood, Bill Lotz, Jerry Goldstein, Jeff Lippincott, Pat McGill, Alan and Bette Male, Mike and Tina Lawless, Cliff Hence, Dwayne Henne, Terry Stimpfel, and Kevin Burkman. There are other fine hiking clubs in the Philadelphia area, and I also appreciated the input of Mike Hughes and Milt Cannan of the Batona Hiking Club, and Jim Hooper of the York Hiking Club and Mason-Dixon Trail System.

Special thanks go to those hikers who not only helped with selection and routing but also accompanied me on hikes, including AMCDV's Jim Sayne (also of Chester County Trail Club), Dave Stein (also of Batona Hiking Club), Joan Aichele, Ron Phelps, Dale Brandreth, and Rich Benningfield, as well as Batona's Allen Britton, Lisa Sandler, and Paul Piechowski. Many happy hiking hours were spent in the company of my son Nick Stevick and my cousin Ann Summer. My father, David Charkes, a longtime AMC member, hikes with me now vicariously. Finally, my intrepid companion Ref deserves the most prominent mention for never ending a hike without a smile.

SECOND EDITION

In addition to those mentioned in the first edition, many of whom were kind enough to assist me in updating this book, thanks to the AMC volunteers John Garner and Greg Bernet and to Tricia McCloskey of AMC's Mid-Atlantic office. Kevin Cronin and Jan King were stalwart hiking companions. Thanks to Barbara Wiemann, a legend in the Pennsylvania hiking comunity, for reviewing the book. Thanks to Shannon Smith and Jennifer Wehunt of AMC Books and (again) to editor Dan Eisner. Special thanks to Stuart Fineman for encouragement and support, as well as many happy hiking hours.

INTRODUCTION

Why hike? Why not just stay home?

We hike, in the first place, to leave home, in the sense of "home" as the place we're used to. People are hardwired to seek novelty. We want to use our senses, to learn, to develop our skills, and to adapt to change. Hiking is an activity: We take action, engaging our minds as well as our bodies—not passively receiving experience but actively creating it.

And we hike, also, to go home, in the sense of "home" as the outdoors. People evolved outdoors: tramping through forests, scrambling along riverbanks, surveying grassy valleys, climbing mountains, kicking sand along the shore, listening to birds, spotting fish, avoiding snakes. When we hike, we reconnect with what we gave up for the comforts of indoor life: the body in nature.

The Philadelphia area—southeastern Pennsylvania, central and southern New Jersey, and northern Delaware (what residents call the Delaware Valley)—is home to millions of people. Hiking in the area offers an astonishingly diverse array of experiences. No matter where you live in the region, a one- to two-hour drive in any direction will result in a completely different landscape. That's because the area is where two very different pieces of Earth's crust meet. The meeting is not entirely peaceful—not at all like Edmund Hicks's iconic painting of the treaty between William Penn and the Lenape Indians. No, here the flat Atlantic coastal plain encounters hard rock and breaks it up into pieces. The meeting place is called the "fall line" because innumerable waterfalls cascade down the dislocated rocks along it. It roughly parallels Route 1 in New Jersey, cuts across the Delaware River at Trenton, and runs southwest across the Susquehanna River south of the Conowingo Dam.

Philadelphia lies on the fall line where the meeting place crosses the Schuylkill River. To the southeast of the city, the sandy, flat coastal plain stretches like a table. Northwest of the city, the ridges and valleys of the Appalachian Mountains ripple like folds in a tablecloth. The area in between—a mosaic of rolling hills, open fields, small woods, and meandering streams—is the Piedmont, literally, from the French, the foothills of the Appalachians.

This variety of terrain creates a multiplicity of hiking opportunities. You could hike in the morning on a flat, pine needle–strewn trail along a boggy pond and in the afternoon climb by a boulder-strewn creek cascading down a rugged ravine. In between, you could hike through butterfly-bedecked meadows or sit on a low stone and watch falling leaves drift into a shallow stream.

Diversity, too, can be found in the region's trails. National, state, county, and local parks; state game lands; and nonprofit nature centers abound, all crisscrossed with trails that can be hiked in a day.

Also within easy driving reach of the Philadelphia area are great long-distance trails. The most famous, the Appalachian Trail, runs more than 2,000 miles between Maine and Georgia. In southeastern Pennsylvania, it traverses the crest of Kittatinny Ridge (Blue Mountain), the southernmost mountain of the Appalachian Plateau. Hikes in this area provide some glorious valley views and access to deep, rich woods full of wildlife. To hike any portion of the Appalachian Trail is to join a unique community: hikers and trail maintainers fiercely committed to preserving its legacy as the premier long-distance trail in the eastern United States. Other, lesser-known long-distance trails are also hiked and maintained by avid volunteers, including the Batona Trail in the New Jersey Pine Barrens (50 miles long); the Horse-Shoe (140), Mason-Dixon (193), and Conestoga (63) Trails in Pennsylvania's Chester and Lancaster counties and in Delaware; and the Highlands Trail, the newest of the region's long trails, still being laid out and developed in New Jersey and Pennsylvania, with the goal of connecting four states within a forested region just south of the Appalachians.

Other long-distance trails are those along canals and old railbeds, which are just as numerous in the region as wilderness trails. These trails, remnants of nineteenth-century industries, remind us that one way to leave home is to travel back in time and to discover that what we know now as home was not always this way. The Philadelphia area is as rich in history as it is in habitat. The nation was born here, and you can hike in some of the now-venerated sites of the American Revolution. The area was also an economic engine for the new nation, due in part to its countless rushing waterways.

There are numerous opportunities to hike in or near sites that were once communities centered on mills and forges, the industrial parks of their day, or through farms that once fed families and villages. Now preserved as parkland, these sites have largely reverted to nature. Old stone walls, crumbling foundations, charcoal hearths, dam stub ends, millrace trenches, fencerows marking onetime fields, and trees lining disused roads are all traces—fading but not yet disappeared—of what once was modern life. They, like the hikers who pause to contemplate the passage of time and the stubborn persistence of wild nature, are going home.

HOW TO USE THIS BOOK

With 50 hikes to choose from, you may wonder how to decide where to go. The locator map at the front of this book will help you narrow down the trips by location, and the At-a-Glance Trip Planner that follows the table of contents will provide more information to guide you toward a decision.

Once you settle on a destination and turn to a trip in this guide, you will find a series of icons that indicate whether the hike is good for kids, whether dogs are permitted, whether snowshoeing or cross-country skiing is recommended, whether the location is accessible via public transportation, and whether fees are charged.

Information on the basics follows: location, rating, distance, elevation gain, estimated time, and maps. The ratings are based on the author's perception and are estimates of what the average hiker will experience. You may find hikes to be easier or more difficult than stated. The estimated time is also based on the author's perception. Consider your own pace when planning a trip.

The elevation gain is calculated from measurements and information obtained from U.S. Geological Survey (USGS) topographic maps, landowner maps, and Google Earth. Each hike identifies the relevant USGS maps, if any, as well as where you can find additional trail maps. The boldface summary provides a basic overview of what you will see on your hike.

The directions explain how to reach the trailhead by car and, for some trips, by public transportation. GPS coordinates for parking lots are also included. Enter these coordinates into your own device for driving directions. Whether or not you own a GPS device, it is wise to consult an atlas before you leave home.

In the trail description, you will find instructions regarding where to hike, the trails on which to hike, and turn-by-turn directions. You will also learn about natural and human history along your hike, as well as information about flora, fauna, and any landmarks and objects you will encounter.

The trail maps that accompany each trip will guide you along your hike, but it would be wise to take an official trail map with you. They are often—but not always—available online, at the trailhead, or at the visitor center.

Each trip ends with a section titled "More Information" that provides details about restroom locations, access times and fees, the property's rules and regulations, and contact information for the place where you will be hiking.

TRIP PLANNING AND SAFETY

While elevations in and around Philadelphia are relatively low, and the hikes detailed in this guide aren't particularly dangerous, you'll still want to be prepared. Some of the walks traverse moderately rugged terrain along rocky hills, while others lead to sandy beaches, ponds, and fields where you'll have extended periods of sun exposure and slow walking in soft sand. Many places in the region have complex trail networks, some of which are unmarked. Allow extra time in case you get lost.

You will be more likely to have an enjoyable, safe hike if you plan ahead and take proper precautions. Before heading out for your hike, consider the following:

- Select a hike that everyone in your group is comfortable taking. Match the hike to the abilities of the least capable person in the group. If anyone is uncomfortable with the weather or is tired, turn around and complete the hike another day.

- Plan to be back at the trailhead before dark. Before beginning your hike, determine a turnaround time. Don't diverge from it, even if you have not reached your intended destination.

- Check the weather. Spring and fall bring unstable air masses to the area; summer features late-afternoon thunderstorms. If you are planning a ridge or summit hike, start early so you will be off the exposed area before the afternoon hours, when thunderstorms most often strike. Temperatures at higher elevations, including the ridges of the Lehigh Valley, are often significantly lower than they are in the city and suburbs and tend to fall quickly after sunset. Storms are a potential hazard throughout the area. If rain is in the forecast, bring waterproof gear.

- Bring a pack with the following items:
  - ✓ Water: Two quarts per person is usually adequate, depending on the weather and the length of the trip.
  - ✓ Food: Even if you are planning a one-hour hike, bring some high-energy snacks, such as nuts, dried fruit, or snack bars. Pack a lunch for longer trips.
  - ✓ Map and compass: Be sure you know how to use them. A handheld GPS device may also be helpful but is not always reliable.
  - ✓ Headlamp or flashlight, with spare batteries

- ✓ Extra clothing: rain gear, wool sweater or fleece, hat, and mittens
- ✓ Sunscreen
- ✓ First-aid kit, including adhesive bandages, gauze, nonprescription pain-killers, and moleskin
- ✓ Pocketknife or multitool
- ✓ Waterproof matches and a lighter
- ✓ Trash bag
- ✓ Toilet paper
- ✓ Whistle
- ✓ Insect repellent
- ✓ Sunglasses
- ✓ Cell phone: Be aware that cell phone service is unreliable in rural areas. If you are receiving a signal, use the phone only for emergencies to avoid disturbing the backcountry experience for other hikers.
- ✓ Binoculars (optional)
- ✓ Camera (optional)

- Wear appropriate footwear and clothing. Wool or synthetic hiking socks will keep your feet dry and help prevent blisters. Comfortable, waterproof hiking boots will provide ankle support and good traction. Avoid wearing cotton clothing, which absorbs sweat and rain, contributing to an unpleasant hiking experience. Polypropylene, fleece, silk, and wool all wick moisture away from your body and keep you warm in wet or cold conditions. To help avoid insect bites, you may want to wear pants and a long-sleeved shirt.

- When you are ahead of the rest of your hiking group, wait at all trail junctions until the others catch up. This avoids confusion and keeps people from getting separated or lost.

- If you see downed wood that appears to be purposely covering a trail, it probably means the trail is closed due to overuse or hazardous conditions.

- If a trail is muddy, walk through the mud or on rocks, never on tree roots or plants. Waterproof boots will keep your feet comfortable. Staying in the center of the trail will keep it from eroding into a wide hiking highway.

- Leave your itinerary and the time you expect to return with someone you trust. If you see a logbook at a trailhead, be sure to sign in when you arrive and sign out when you finish your hike.

- Poison ivy is always a threat when hiking. To identify the plant, look for clusters of three leaves that shine in the sun but are dull in the shade. If you do come into contact with poison ivy, wash the affected area with soap as soon as possible.

- Snakes, common in many hiking areas, are cold-blooded. Their body temperature rises and falls with the ambient temperature, and they hibernate during cold months. In summer, snakes may bask on exposed rocks or on open trails, although you also may find them near stone walls, brush piles, or fallen logs. Snakes usually avoid confrontation and are not aggressive toward humans; when surprised or provoked, however, they may bite. Most snakes in the Philadelphia region are harmless, but northern copperheads and timber rattlesnakes have venomous bites that can be painful or, in rare cases, fatal. To reduce the chance of an unpleasant encounter for both parties, use proper snake etiquette, especially when hiking around rocky areas in the warm seasons: Look before taking a step or reaching in between rocks; if you see a snake, leave it alone. If you are bitten by a snake, seek medical attention as quickly as possible.
- Wear blaze-orange items in hunting season. Hunting seasons vary. Check with state game commissions:
  - Pennsylvania: pgc.state.pa.us
  - New Jersey: state.nj.us/dep/fgw/hunting.htm
  - Delaware: dnrec.delaware.gov/fw/hunting/pages/wildlife.aspx
- Ticks, which can carry diseases, are common in many wooded and grassy areas in suburbs and exurbs, though uncommon on mountain ridges, and are active year-round in the greater Philadelphia region. To reduce the chance of a tick bite, you may want to wear pants and a long-sleeved shirt. After you finish your hike, check for ticks on your clothes and body. The deer tick, which can carry Lyme disease, can be as small as a pinhead. Run a lint roller over your clothes. Take a shower when you get home and check for ticks again.
- Mosquitoes can be common in the woods in summer and fall. Although some carry diseases, their bite is mostly annoying. As with ticks, you can reduce the chance of bites by wearing long sleeves and pants. A variety of options are available for dealing with bugs, ranging from sprays that include the active ingredient diethyl-meta-toluamide (commonly known as DEET), which potentially can cause skin or eye irritation, to more skin-friendly products. Head nets, often cheaper than a can of repellent, are useful in especially buggy conditions.

LEAVE NO TRACE

The Appalachian Mountain Club (AMC) is a national educational partner of Leave No Trace, a nonprofit organization dedicated to promoting and inspiring responsible outdoor recreation through education, research, and partnerships.

The Leave No Trace program seeks to develop wildland ethics, or ways in which people think and act in the outdoors to minimize their impact on the areas they visit and to protect our natural resources for future enjoyment. Leave No Trace unites four federal land management agencies—the U.S. Forest Service, National Park Service, Bureau of Land Management, and U.S. Fish and Wildlife Service—with manufacturers, outdoor retailers, user groups, educators, organizations such as AMC, and individuals.

The Leave No Trace ethic is guided by these seven principles:

1. *Plan ahead and prepare.* Know the terrain and any regulations applicable to the area you're planning to visit, and be prepared for extreme weather or other emergencies. This will enhance your enjoyment and ensure that you've chosen an appropriate destination. Small groups have less impact on resources and the experiences of other backcountry visitors.

2. *Travel and camp on durable surfaces.* Travel and camp on established trails and campsites, rock, gravel, dry grasses, or snow. Good campsites are found, not made. Camp at least 200 feet from lakes and streams, and focus activities on areas where vegetation is absent. In pristine areas, disperse use to prevent the creation of campsites and trails.

3. *Dispose of waste properly.* Pack it in, pack it out. Inspect your camp for trash or food scraps. Deposit solid human waste in cat holes dug 6 to 8 inches deep, at least 200 feet from water, camps, and trails. Pack out toilet paper and hygiene products. To wash yourself or your dishes, carry water 200 feet from streams or lakes and use small amounts of biodegradable soap. Scatter strained dishwater.

4. *Leave what you find.* Cultural or historic artifacts, as well as natural objects such as plants and rocks, should be left as found.

5. *Minimize campfire impacts.* Cook on a stove. Use established fire rings, fire pans, or mound fires. If you build a campfire, keep it small and use dead sticks found on the ground.

6. *Respect wildlife.* Observe wildlife from a distance. Feeding animals alters their natural behavior. Protect wildlife from your food by storing rations and trash securely.

7. *Be considerate of other visitors.* Be courteous, respect the quality of other visitors' backcountry experiences, and let nature's sounds prevail.

AMC is a national provider of the Leave No Trace Master Educator course. AMC offers this five-day course, designed especially for outdoor professionals and land managers, as well as the shorter two-day Leave No Trace Trainer course at locations throughout the Northeast. For Leave No Trace information and materials, contact the Leave No Trace Center for Outdoor Ethics, P.O. Box 997, Boulder, CO 80306; 800-332-4100 or 302-442-8222; lnt.org. For information on AMC's Leave No Trace Master Educator training course, see outdoors .org/education/lnt.

SOUTHEASTERN PENNSYLVANIA AND DELAWARE

Southeastern Pennsylvania and Delaware have the most diverse geography of the regions described in this book. The Atlantic coastal plain meets the rocky foothills of the Piedmont at the fall line, which crosses the Delaware River close to Trenton, New Jersey, and continues southwest,

crossing the Susquehanna River below the Conowingo Dam. This flat, sandy coastal plain includes some of Philadelphia and all of Delaware south of the Christina River. Hikes in the coastal plain include Fairmount Park Loop (Trip 1), John Heinz National Wildlife Refuge at Tinicum (Trip 4), Lums Pond State Park (Trip 11), and Bull's Island, Delaware Canal, and D&R Canal (Trip 32).

The fall line, or the change in elevation between the Piedmont and the coastal plain, is marked by dislocations in the bedrock, creating a cliff or scarp. Not so much a bright line as a zone of varying width, it is called the fall line because waterfalls and rapids form where streams cross the boundary between the soft, sandy soils and the harder rocks of the Piedmont. All that falling water proved an irresistible source of power for mills and other early waterwheel-based industries; the Wissahickon Creek alone was home to more than 70 mills. Philadelphia, located on a bluff along the Delaware River formed by piled-up sediment from the coastal plain, was a port city to which the mill products could be shipped for export.

Thomas Mill Bridge is the only covered bridge in Philadelphia located in Wissahickon Valley Park.

The fall line also marks the point at which major rivers—including the Delaware, Schuylkill, and Susquehanna—cease to be navigable. The falls of these rivers (at Trenton, East Falls, and Conowingo) are rapids formed by huge rocks displaced from the scarp. It is virtually impossible to hike anywhere along a stream or river near the fall line and not encounter reminders of the power of water as it drops down the scarp. Old mill dams, millraces, and mills themselves abound, and even though the structures are gone, the names cling to the places and roads they once occupied. The only hike in the book that directly crosses the fall line is the Fairmount Park Loop (Trip 1), most of which is in the coastal plain, but others, including the Pennypack Ecological Restoration Trust (Trip 9), go very near it.

North of the fall line to Blue Mountain, which marks the southern edge of the ridge and valley section, the Piedmont's varying character is illustrated by the diverse topography of its landforms, and these in turn are determined by the dominant bedrock—typically sedimentary rock, such as shale or sandstone, or metamorphic rock, such as schist or gneiss. In turn, the landforms are shaped by the effects of wind, water, and weather on the rock. There are swampy lowlands, floodplains, dry woods, hills, bluffs, ravines, and diabase ridges. Piedmont hikes typically include a variety of terrain, which not only makes the hikes more fun but also helps support a diverse population of wildlife, and thus makes it more likely the hike will continue to be enjoyable for years to come.

1

FAIRMOUNT PARK LOOP: PHILADELPHIA MUSEUM OF ART

Art and architecture, boats and bridges, history and nature: All converge along the river that has been at the heart of Philadelphia since the city's founding.

DIRECTIONS

To the Philadelphia Museum of Art: Take the Benjamin Franklin Parkway west from Center City; Kelly Drive or Martin Luther King Jr. Drive east; or take I-676 west to Benjamin Franklin Parkway exit and turn right onto 22nd Street, then left onto the left outer lanes of Benjamin Franklin Parkway and continue to art museum; or take I-676 east to Spring Garden Street exit. Park on street or in the art museum's public garage. (Alternatively, since this is a loop, you can park on the Martin Luther King Jr. Drive side for free, except on weekends April–October, by crossing the river at Spring Garden Street.) *GPS coordinates:* N 39° 58.090′ N, 75° 11.031′ W.

For detailed directions see philamuseum.org/visit/12-453-3.html.

To reach the museum area by public transportation, use SEPTA bus routes 7, 32, 38, 43, or 48; or Regional Rail lines to 30th Street Station (walk east on Market Street to the steps down to the Schuylkill Banks and continue west). May through August, the Philly PHLASH Downtown Loop shuttle provides direct service between Center City and the museum between 10 A.M. and 6 P.M; at other times of year, check the website.

TRAIL DESCRIPTION

This hike features one of the glories of Philadelphia: the Schuylkill River waterfront. While this is the most urban hike in the book, it is surprisingly close to nature. The hike

LOCATION
Philadelphia, PA

RATING
Moderate

DISTANCE
9 miles

ELEVATION GAIN
Minimal

ESTIMATED TIME
3.5 hours

MAPS
USGS Philadelphia; myphillypark.org/explore/map/

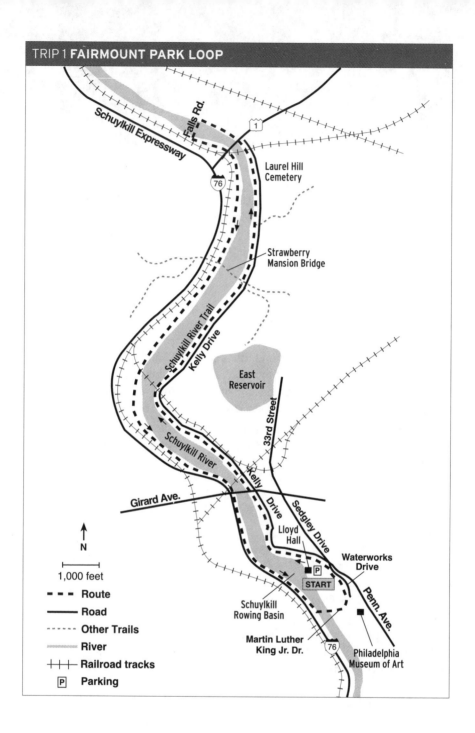

N

1,000 feet

- - - Route
——— Road
-------- Other Trails
░░░░ River
+++ Railroad tracks
P Parking

Schuylkill Expressway

Falls Rd.

1

76

Laurel Hill
Cemetery

Strawberry
Mansion Bridge

Schuylkill River Trail

Kelly Drive

East
Reservoir

33rd Street

Schuylkill River

Kelly Drive

Girard Ave.

Sedgley Drive

Lloyd
Hall

Waterworks
Drive

START

P

Penn. Ave.

Schuylkill
Rowing Basin

Martin Luther
King Jr. Dr.

76

Philadelphia
Museum of Art

is virtually all paved and level; the only elevation gain is the climb up Fairmount to the Water Works scenic overlook at the hike's end.

The route follows a portion of Schuylkill River Trail, a planned riverside trail well on its way to completion that will eventually extend 130 miles between the river's source at Pottsville, Pennsylvania, and its mouth at the Delaware River. In addition to the segment near the Philadelphia Museum of Art that you'll hike, other completed parts of the trail now include a 20-mile leg from Philadelphia's Center City district up to Valley Forge (see Trips 6 and 7).

This loop hike stays within Fairmount Park, which, at 9,200 acres, is one of the largest urban parks in the world. Beginning on the east bank at the Fairmount Water Works, the route proceeds upstream toward the East Falls neighborhood, crosses the river, and returns on the west side. Some of Philadelphia's most distinguishing features—its ethnic and cultural diversity, passion for athletics, and embrace of arts and history—are on display. The trail is popular not only with walkers but also with runners, cyclists, dog owners, and families. It is crowded on weekends, particularly during special events, such as regattas.

Begin at the parking area near the Fairmount Water Works, below the Philadelphia Museum of Art. A stroll through the Fairmount Park Azalea Garden, adjacent to the parking lot, makes for a grand prelude in spring. Start the hike itself at SRT trail marker 086 on the corner of Waterworks Drive and Kelly Drive. Follow the paved path west past Boathouse Row, a cluster of diverse Victorian-era rowing clubhouses; at night their lit outlines shimmer, reflected in the river.

Proceed along the riverbank to the left. To the right is Kelly Drive—formerly East River Drive, and still known as such to many local residents—named for Jack Kelly, the Olympic rower, city councilman, and father of actress Grace Kelly. Look for his sculpture farther down the trail. This section contains many examples of Fairmount Park's renowned collection of public art, honoring both the famous and the obscure.

The trail bends right along the roadway, but a sidewalk continues along the riverbank. Take the sidewalk. The riverside walk is quieter and provides a superior view of the large sculpture garden devoted to American history. Past the sculpture garden, the sidewalk rejoins the trail and passes under the Girard Avenue Bridge then around Promontory Rock, which hosts innumerable tiny plants that have gained a roothold in its crevices. Notice the rock's wavy layers of gneiss and Wissahickon schist with shiny mica flakes.

After Promontory Rock, the trail meanders by a mile-long grove of cherry trees (many of which were gifts from Japan) that burst with pink and white flowers in early spring. Pass under several bridges, each with a historical marker. The stone-arched Pennsylvania Railroad Connecting Railway Bridge, built from 1866–67, was featured by Thomas Eakins in his 1871 painting *Max Schmitt in a Single Scull*.

Rowers spill out from the boathouses in profusion. Rowing is a longtime Delaware Valley tradition; it's a rare hike on this trail that doesn't include a glimpse of the powerful, graceful rhythm of a crew team.

Past the cherry trees, the riverfront landscape returns to its natural state and becomes crowded with floodplain trees: silver maple, box elder, sumac, slippery elm. Across Kelly Drive are looming bluffs covered with plants typical of steep river slopes: oaks, dogwoods, and rhododendrons. If you squint and cover your ears, it is possible to imagine the wild landscape that flourished before the roadway was built and the Schuylkill dammed, when the river had the Lenape names of Manayunk ("where we drink") and Ganshowahanna ("falling waters").

From here to East Falls, the trail alternately rises above the riverbank and returns to it. On the bluffs are the ornate mausoleums of Laurel Hill Cemetery. East Falls itself is an old commercial district, marking the end of the naturalistic walk. It's a short trek along sidewalks to Falls Bridge, a steel-truss bridge built in 1895. Cross the bridge, pausing to look in the river for the partially submerged boulders that give the East Falls of the Schuylkill its name. The boulders mark the fall line, the zone where the continental shelf collides with the Piedmont. These are the easternmost natural falls on the river.

Leaving the bridge, turn left into West Fairmount Park. This side of the route is less urban and usually less crowded. On weekends from April through October, Martin Luther King Jr. Drive (formerly West River Drive) is closed to vehicles. Hidden inlets along the river attract fish and anglers; birds sing among the trees that throng the riverbanks; and water spills from the bluffs on the far side

Scullers ply the Schuylkill River along Boathouse Row in Philadelphia.

of the road. On the west side are grassy lawns and picnic areas. In other ways, the west bank mirrors the east, albeit on a smaller scale: a few sculptures, a smaller grove of cherry trees. Regularly placed signposts show the distance to the art museum.

About 2.5 miles from the museum, past the Belmont Water Intake, the Schuylkill Expressway emerges from above. Traffic noise increases measurably unless the drive is closed. A fine distraction comes into view at just this moment: the classic view of Boathouse Row and the Fairmount Water Works. Lines are strung over the Water Works dam to help stop runaway boats. Cormorants— big, dark diving birds—often sit atop the lines, drying their wings.

Cross the river by the pedestrian bridge, continue along Martin Luther King Jr. Drive to the marked Schuylkill River Trail Connector pedestrian crossing; once across the street turn right at the entrance to Schuylkill Banks. (To extend your hike, turn left and enjoy a walk along the river in this recently constructed section of the SRT.) Follow the paved walkway under the overpass, up a slight incline and finally up the bluffs via a steep path to one of several viewing gazebos atop Fairmount; the coastal plain, stretching to the Atlantic Ocean, is to the east of this rocky knob. This is a good place to sit and have a snack; the bird's-eye view of the Schuylkill ("hidden creek") here is dramatically different from the view you've just left behind.

MORE INFORMATION

Schuylkill River Trail is open 24 hours a day and is well lit at night, however, the west side is not. Restrooms are located in Lloyd Hall, the only public athletic facility on Boathouse Row, open from 7 A.M. to 9 P.M. The Philadelphia Museum of Art's collections are world-renowned; the Fairmount Water Works also houses a water museum. City of Philadelphia Parks & Recreation, phila.gov/parksandrecreation. Schuylkill River Trail, schuylkillrivertrail.com. Fairmount Park Conservancy, myphillypark.org.

2

WISSAHICKON VALLEY PARK

This is a strenuous, varied hike through a rugged creek gorge within the city of Philadelphia; shorter routes are available. It also features old-growth forests, extensive meadows, rock formations, and historic stone structures.

LOCATION
Philadelphia, PA

RATING
Moderate to difficult

DISTANCE
7.5 miles

ELEVATION GAIN
1,120 feet

ESTIMATED TIME
4 hours

MAPS
USGS Germantown; fow.org/visit-the-park/maps/

DIRECTIONS

Take Germantown Avenue to Chestnut Hill Avenue. From Chestnut Hill Avenue, turn right onto Crefeld Street. The Wissahickon Valley Park entrance is just ahead on the left behind an unlocked gate. Park on the street, where you will find room for eight to ten cars. *GPS coordinates: 40° 04.614′ N, 75°12.990′ W.*

To get to the trailhead by public transportation, take the SEPTA Chestnut Hill West Regional Rail line or bus route 23 to the Chestnut Hill West Station. Walk downhill from Germantown Avenue, turn left onto Chestnut Hill Avenue and right on Crefeld Street.

TRAIL DESCRIPTION

Casual visitors and well-informed hikers alike may be amazed that Philadelphia is home to a park sporting 50 miles of hiking trails, many of which are as challenging and scenic as any in the mountains hours away: the rocky, 1,800-acre gorge known as Wissahickon Valley Park, surrounding the Wissahickon Creek.

The circuit hike described here is deliberately challenging, designed to satisfy the hiker who desires a strenuous workout in a rugged landscape within reach of public transportation. It provides encounters with the valley's history, the creek (the park's central feature), and the many shapes of Wissahickon schist. For several shorter options, see the description below.

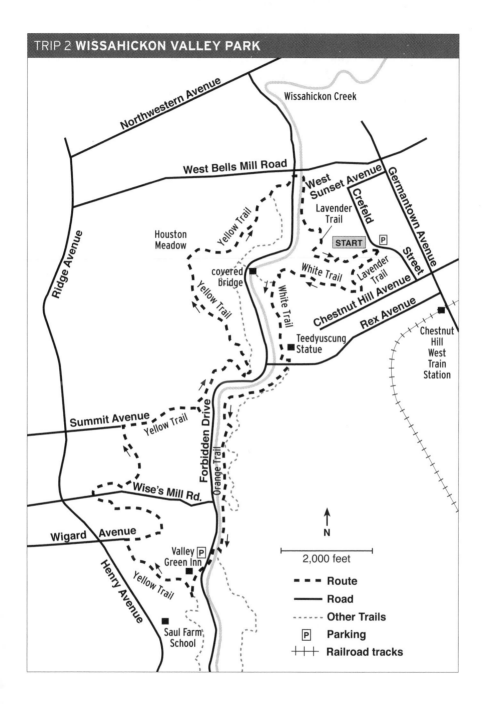

People have been enjoying the Wissahickon's resources for centuries. Lenape Indians fished and hunted here. The name "Wissahickon" is derived from the Lenape word "wisameckhan" meaning "catfish stream." The eighteenth and nineteenth centuries brought industry: Water-powered mills were built, and the hillsides were logged. Roads were laid for commerce, then for recreation, bringing tourists to the scenic gorge. Inns and taverns sprang up to serve travelers.

The city acquired much of the parkland in the late nineteenth century to safeguard sources of drinking water. Protected for more than a century, the valley is a rich natural environment. It hosts an enormous variety of breeding birds, troves of spring wildflowers, and an incredible variety of habitats ranging from large meadows to hemlock ravines.

The hike begins at the Crefeld Street trailhead, where you will see an information kiosk and a simplified trail map. Signage and trail marking throughout the park are excellent, thanks to efforts by Friends of the Wissahickon, the nonprofit organization that manages the trails. At most trail intersections, posts indicate mileage and arrows to features, roads, or intersections, as well as which trails are open to bikes and horses. Trails are either named after colors or are unnamed connectors; named trails are marked with circles in that color. Connector trails are typically unmarked.

Follow Lavender Trail. Start by taking the left fork, heading into an imposing forest of huge old oak, beech, walnut, and tulip trees. This is one of many areas of old-growth forest in the Wissahickon Valley, preserving trees that have grown in the 150 years since the valley was last logged.

Head downhill, crossing a stream over a stone bridge. At the next intersection, continue straight onto the connector trail. Turn right onto White Trail, a gravel road. Head downhill to a three-way fork, where there is a park bench. Take the left fork (the right fork drops down sharply to the creek), staying on White Trail, which becomes a rocky footpath and heads uphill.

Here and on some other steep hillside trails, the soft rocks are eroding into sand from the impact of trail traffic and storms. Ongoing projects in the park aim to rebuild and fortify the trails, both for safety and to reduce the amount of sediment flowing into the creek.

Go downhill, cross a stream, and turn uphill, passing by massive schist outcrops on the left. Stone steps make the path easier. About 0.2 mile after the stream, look right: A statue of the Lenape chief Teedyuscung gazes out from a slab of schist known as Council Rock, where the Lenape supposedly gathered—an oft-repeated myth of dubious veracity. Regardless, John Massey Rhind's 1902 sculpture commemorates the passing of the Lenape from this region; the chief looks westward toward his departing people.

White Trail makes a sharp right downhill then turns left toward the crossing at Rex Avenue, a gravel road closed to traffic. Turn right toward the creek and make a left onto Orange Trail just before the stone bridge.

Follow Orange Trail. This trail is only intermittently marked but is generally easy to follow, as it stays along the creek. You will be clambering along rocks for much of the next mile. In inclement weather, exercise special caution; an alternative is to follow White Trail, which parallels Orange Trail higher up on the

Wissahickon meadows in winter display the stark beauty of tree forms and standing native grasses.

ridge. Orange Trail provides close-up views of the creek and its constantly changing shapes, sounds, and colors. You'll pass the Magargee Dam, a remnant of one of the nineteenth-century mills that once stood along the creek but now exist only in the names of the roads that led to them.

After about 1 mile, the trail turns left and uphill to climb a set of wooden steps that leads to Valley Green Road. Turn right to follow the road over the stone bridge (built in 1832) to Valley Green Inn at Forbidden Drive. (To shorten the hike by approximately 3.5 miles, turn right and follow Forbidden Drive for about 1.5 miles until you reach West Bells Mill Road. Continue the hike from that point.)

Forbidden Drive is a nineteenth-century turnpike that is now closed to motor vehicles, except for the parking area at Valley Green. It's a flat gravel drive that is popular with families. While this hike does not use Forbidden Drive, it's a great route to explore the many historic features in the park, including the much-photographed Thomas Mill Covered Bridge (the last remaining covered bridge within Philadelphia).

Turn left onto Forbidden Drive. Immediately after passing the inn, take a sharp right onto a connector trail that leads uphill on a steep, rocky footpath. Turn right at the T intersection onto the flatter, yet still rocky, Yellow Trail. Keep straight at the next intersection then make the second left onto a connector trail heading toward Henry Avenue. Turn right at the T intersection, passing the fields of W. B. Saul High School of Agricultural Sciences.

At the end of the field, turn right at Wigard Avenue and continue past the trailhead kiosk on Yellow Trail and into an old-growth forest of tall trees. Just after the gate is a large deer exclosure, a fenced-in area that is the focus of a study on how keeping deer out of the woods may help to encourage the regrowth of trees, shrubs, and wildflowers. You'll also see many umbrella magnolias, abundant here but uncommon throughout most of the region. Take a sharp left, continuing on Yellow Trail and passing through a gate to cross Wise's Mill Road. Continue on Yellow Trail, crossing a stream, then head uphill to the residential Summit Avenue. Make a right to follow the road downhill and into the woods, where Yellow Trail becomes a dirt road.

Turn left at the T intersection, following the connector trail toward Houston Meadow. Pass below Courtesy Stables and Houston Playground before reaching the winding paths through Houston Meadow. The 48-acre meadow was restored in 2013 through the removal of small shrubs and trees and the planting of native warm-season grasses and wildflowers. It has a year-round beauty that changes with every season.

Follow the trail around the meadow and back into the woods. At the intersection with Yellow Trail, turn left to follow it steeply downhill to Forbidden Drive, crossing a stream on a concrete footbridge. At Forbidden Drive, turn left and walk a short distance to West Bells Mill Road. Turn right and cross the creek via the stone bridge (built in 1820), watching for traffic as you go. Immediately turn right onto Orange Trail. Go uphill into the woods and take a sharp left onto Lavender Trail, still uphill. This is the last leg. After the second of two footbridges, turn left at the fork and follow Lavender Trail back to the Crefeld Street trailhead and your car.

MORE INFORMATION

There are restrooms adjacent to Valley Green Inn and on West Bells Mill Road. The park is open for hiking 24 hours a day, 7 days a week, although a seasonal curfew may be imposed to allow deer management efforts (typically December through March, 8 p.m. to 6 a.m.). With the exception of Lavender and Orange trails' creekside segments, all of the trails on this hike are open to bikes. Horses are permitted on many trails. Dogs must be on a leash no longer than 12 feet. Friends of the Wissahickon (fow.org) maintains trails, sells maps, organizes hikes, and provides educational programs. The park is administered by the Philadelphia Parks and Recreation Department (phila.gov/parksandrecreation).

3
PENNYPACK PARK

Smaller and under less stress from human impact than the Wissahickon Valley, Pennypack Park is an underutilized natural area within the city's borders. This hike takes you on trails that wind through a forested valley and alongside the wide, picturesque Pennypack Creek.

DIRECTIONS

Take US 1 (which becomes Roosevelt Boulevard) to Bustleton Avenue. After 3.4 miles, turn left onto Benton Avenue; the Pennypack Park entrance is immediately on the right. Park across the street, where there is space for ten cars along the road. *GPS coordinates: 40° 04.550′ N, 75° 02.797′ W.*

To reach Pennypack Park via public transportation, take SEPTA bus routes 58 or 67.

TRAIL DESCRIPTION

Tucked into the far northeast section of Philadelphia, Pennypack Park doesn't get the same attention as Wissahickon, its larger city park sibling. Pennypack deserves to be better known, as it boasts everything a hiker could ask for: rich woods, a scenic creek, a variety of terrain, and diverse wildlife.

Pennypack Creek begins in Horsham, Pennsylvania, and empties into the Delaware River coursing beneath the Frankford Avenue Bridge in Philadelphia's Holmesburg neighborhood. The 1697 bridge is the oldest surviving bridge in the United States. Pennypack Creek, whose name derives from the Lenape word meaning "slow-flowing creek," is no longer so slow; its densely developed 57-square-mile watershed deluges the creek with stormwater. But watershed restoration initiatives abound, including planting meadows and trees (at Pennypack

LOCATION
Philadelphia, PA

RATING
Moderate

DISTANCE
8 miles

ELEVATION GAIN
50 feet

ESTIMATED TIME
3 hours

MAPS
USGS Frankford; friendsofpennypackpark.org/greenway.pdf

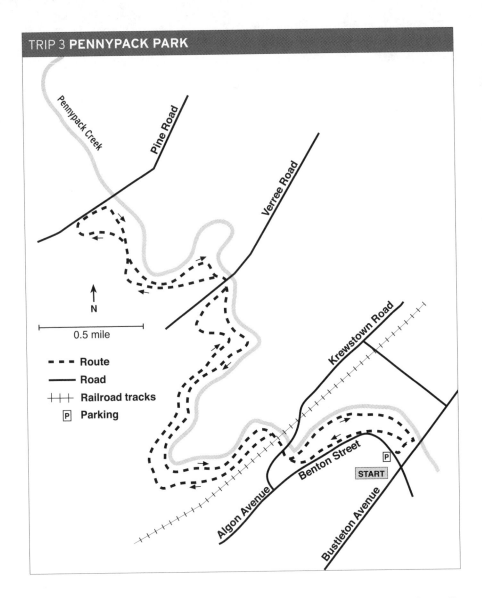

Ecological Restoration Trust, Trip 9, for example), removing dams, and install-ing fish passages.

Pennypack Park's 1,334 acres stretch 9 miles along the creek valley from the Montgomery County line to the Delaware River. This hike focuses on trails in the northernmost, and prettiest, section. The circuit goes out on a natural sur-face trail in the hills and returns on a paved multiuse path along the creek; you can also hike it in the opposite direction.

Begin at the Benton Avenue entrance, heading downhill on the paved path. Don't go all the way down to the creek; take a left after about 0.2 mile, onto the dirt path into the woods. This is a moist woods that hosts tall, old trees (ash,

With its thick forest and network of streams, Pennypack Park is a hidden gem in Philadelphia.

maple, tulip) and a dense understory. There are deer in the park, but controlled hunting is reducing the damage they have caused. As a result, the condition of the woods in this northern section is as good as that in more remote areas. In winter there are delightful views of the creek below; in other seasons the forest envelops the trails in green. Horses use this trail, so it can get muddy, but their tracks make it easier to follow. After about 0.5 mile, the trail approaches Krewstown Road. Cross the road by going downhill to pass under the stone bridge, along the paved creekside path; continue on the paved path under the railroad bridge and take the next left to return to the dirt path going uphill.

The trail is rocky; underfoot are crumbled bits of the bedrock that underlies the valley and occasionally outcrops along the creek (see "Wissahickon Schist," page 17). Cross the trail, heading left toward the power line that parallels the railroad tracks; stay on the main (horse) trail, gently bearing right at the next four-way intersection. The trail is unmarked, but at all crossings the horse trail can be identified by heavy, squared wooden beams placed across it to protect it from water damage. Continue going straight through the next intersection, heading downhill to the creek and crossing the multiuse trail. Cross the iron bridge over a stream. Black walnut trees thrive in the moist, rocky soil of this area. Go straight through the next two intersections, crossing another stream in between and keeping the creek below and to your right. You'll enter a steep gorge with tall canopy above and ferns and wildflowers, such as jack-in-the-pulpit, below.

The trail bears left and up the hill then back down toward the multiuse path. At this point, about 3 miles into the hike, you'll reach Verree Road. At the intersection with the paved multiuse path is a wetlands area (to the right on Verree Road) created by the Pennypack Environmental Center's planting of native scrub-shrub vegetation in what used to be a parking lot.

Cross Verree Road by following the multiuse trail under the bridge. You may see some blue-brown, fork-tailed birds zipping out from under the bridge and back to catch insects on the wing. These are barn swallows, which build nests under the span.

Again, bear left up the hill along the dirt path. This wooded area, closer to major parking areas, is more heavily trafficked and not quite as rich or healthy as the forest to the south, but it affords creek views even during the height of summer. There are extremely large, old trees in this section. One of them, at 4 feet in diameter and about 200 years of age, used to be a prominent landmark signaling a turn; although the tree has now fallen, it continues to mark the turn. Head downhill alongside the remains of the tree, cross a stream, and take the macadam path across a wide lawn with a sunflower meadow; 4 miles into the hike, you'll reach Pine Road. There is a United States Geological Survey (USGS) gaging station here to measure the stream flow.

Turn around and follow the multiuse trail back along the creek. There are no turns to worry about. The path does have ups and downs, given the schist upwellings and outcrops in the terrain. At outcrops, you can look closely at cross sections of the rock to see its flat, platelike structure and multiple color variations. The creekside trail also allows an intimate appreciation of the creek's flow, which is a relatively recent development. Between 2005 and 2009, four of the seven major dams were removed and two fish passages were installed in the lower reaches, eliminating stagnant, sediment-trapping pools and creating a healthier habitat for fish and other aquatic life. You will pass under the same five bridges as on the outward leg; at the fifth bridge, immediately after the railroad bridge, turn right to go uphill and make a right on the dirt path to exit the park at Benton Avenue.

MORE INFORMATION

Pennypack Park is open 24 hours a day, 7 days a week. From May to October, a portable toilet is located at the turnaround point on Pine Road. There are bathrooms at the Pennypack Environmental Center (8600 Verree Road), which is also worth a visit to view three outdoor sculptures designed by Ed Levine to embody the conservation ideals of Henry David Thoreau. The trails are maintained by Friends of Pennypack Park (friendsofpennypackpark.org), and the park is administered by the Philadelphia Parks and Recreation Department (phila.gov/parksandrecreation).

WISSAHICKON SCHIST

If a rock could be said to define Philadelphia, it woud be Wissahickon schist, first studied along the city's Wissahickon Creek (see Trip 2). From a distance, this schist appears dark gray-black, like the garments worn by Quaker settlers. On closer inspection, it's composed of multiple layers of colors and textures, much like the diverse community that Philadelphia's founder, William Penn, sought to create: silvery mica; ruby-colored garnet; black tourmaline; ribbons of white quartzite; and splotches of gold, umber, gray, green, and tan. It is the bedrock that supports the city's skyscrapers, and similar schist varieties underlie much of southeastern Pennsylvania, southern New Jersey, and Delaware. Schist is a metamorphosed sedimentary rock, with layers of minerals originally deposited by inland seas. The minerals were transformed and recrystallized by heating and cooling, resulting in a hard rock that flakes into flat plates. Schist's beauty and variety, as well as its strength, made it a favorite building stone in the masonry era of the nineteenth and early twentieth centuries. In situ, the rock resists erosion from wind and water, forming vertical cliffs and ravines; its tendency to fracture into plates creates horizontal outcrops—such as Council Rock, the slab on which the Wissahickon Indian statue sits—and wide, flat boulder debris from rocks that break off cliffs.

4

JOHN HEINZ NATIONAL WILDLIFE REFUGE AT TINICUM

Transport yourself to Pennsylvania's coastline without leaving the city. This level walk winds around a pond and through a tidal marsh.

DIRECTIONS

From I-95 south, take Exit 14 (Bartram Avenue) and, at the fifth light, turn right onto 84th Street. At the second light, turn left onto Lindbergh Boulevard and follow it until you reach the first stop sign. Just past it, on the right, is the refuge entrance. Follow the road as it bends to the left, and you will find ample parking.

From I-95 north, take Exit 10 (PA 291) and, at the first light, turn left onto Bartram Avenue. At the fifth light, turn left onto 84th Street and follow directions above to the refuge entrance. *GPS coordinates: 39° 53.570′ N, 75° 15.446′ W.*

To reach the refuge via public transportation, take SEPTA Regional Rail to Eastwick Station or bus routes 37 or 108.

TRAIL DESCRIPTION

In the center of a triangle formed by I-95, Philadelphia International Airport, and dense residential neighborhoods, a pair of bald eagles soar silently over the placid waters of Tinicum Marsh. They glide beneath electric lines and above a pipeline, wheel slowly with wings spread flat, then drop onto a tree. They gaze north toward downtown Philadelphia, the city whose football team is their namesake.

The John Heinz National Wildlife Refuge at Tinicum, the nation's first urban wildlife refuge, remains its most urbanized one. Despite its location, it is a haven for wildlife, especially birds, because of its varied habitat.

LOCATION
Philadelphia, PA

RATING
Easy

DISTANCE
5.25 miles

ELEVATION GAIN
Minimal

ESTIMATED TIME
2 hours

MAPS
USGS Lansdowne Quadrant; fws.gov/refuge/John_Heinz/map.html

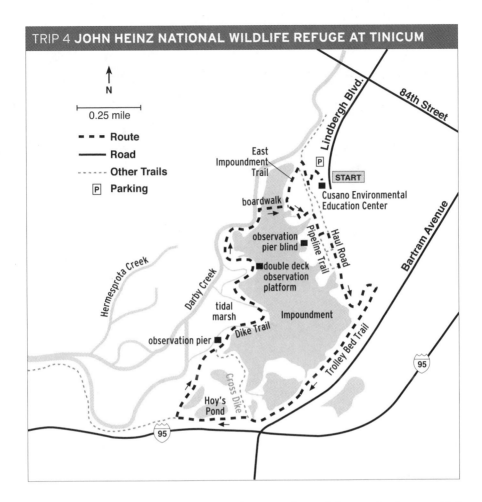

Within the refuge lies Tinicum Marsh, Pennsylvania's largest freshwater tidal marsh. Although the state has no coastline, it does have creeks and rivers that receive an influx of tidewater twice a day from Delaware Bay, creating a unique habitat of mudflats and aquatic vegetation. Tinicum's marshes were drained and filled over the course of 300 years, reducing the 6,000 acres the marsh covered in the seventeenth century to a mere 200 today. In the early 1970s, concerned citizens working with U.S. Representative (and later Senator) John Heinz succeeded in establishing a federal refuge to protect and restore 1,200 acres around the marsh.

The Cusano Environmental Education Center is certainly worth visiting. Not only does it boast outstanding exhibits detailing the nature and history of Tinicum Marsh, but the building itself, made of renewable materials and designed to be energy efficient (geothermal and solar powered), is an award-winning example of green construction.

John Heinz is a haven for birds whose habitats include marshes, woods, and shores. Photo by David Kauffman.

Hiking trails begin behind the Cusano Center. The short hike detailed here traverses the refuge's three main habitats: tidal marshland, woods, and nontidal diked impoundment (a confined body of water). You can stretch out the trek by stopping at wildlife observation points along the way.

From the parking lot, follow the paved path around the center to the rear, where the path winds toward the woods, and cross Haul Road, a multiuse gravel trail. The entrance to the woods is marked by a large metal sign indicating a 0.6-mile accessible trail. Follow this paved trail for about 0.1 mile, passing the impoundment, until the trail meets a long boardwalk over the impoundment. Do not continue onto the boardwalk but instead turn left into the woods and onto a natural-surface trail.

This trail winds through Warbler Woods, a low-lying, often flooded area thick with sweetgum and other young trees and shrubs: an early succession floodplain forest. The trail is unmarked but easy to follow as it passes in and out of woods and thickets; keep the impoundment on your right. The trail crosses a wide inlet over a long bridge, where you'll pass a bird blind on your left. Continue, crossing Pipeline Trail, a wide grassy area marked by metal posts, and a small footbridge then immediately turn right onto Haul Road. From here on, look for blazed posts placed at trail intersections, featuring blue triangles that indicate "toward visitor center" and yellow circles that signify "toward PA 420" (the opposite direction from the visitor center). Follow the yellow circles.

Haul Road continues in a straight line for about 0.4 mile, winds left into an aspen grove, then turns sharply right, where it becomes the dirt-surfaced Trolley Bed Trail. Look for excellent views to the north, up the length of the impoundment. The reed domes that dot the water near the shore are the roofs of muskrat dens.

The trail approaches I-95 above and to the right; as the views of the impoundment become more dramatic, the road noise increases. After about 0.75 mile, the trail approaches the highway. Bear left at the fork to go around the shallow Hoy's Pond.

After 0.25 mile more, there is another fork, with a bench along the fork to your right. With the highway to your left, continue straight, approximately 0.25 mile to the next intersection. Turn right. Now you are in the midst of the tidal marsh area. Containing low mudflats, shallow trickling streams, and open areas of reeds and grass, it is dramatically different from the woodsy impoundment area. Whereas the nontidal impoundment attracts birds that grab fish from deeper water, such as cormorants, kingfishers, and gulls, this section is home to shorebirds that probe the mudflats and shallow waters. In these tidal flats, refuge managers and biologists are working to restore wetlands by replacing exotic invasive plants with native species.

Continue about 0.25 mile more until you reach a small footbridge. This is an ideal spot to peer across the marsh in all directions. Darby Creek and its tributaries form an intricate network of channels, perhaps even as complex as the flight paths of the jets taking off next door.

Turn around here. (If you wish to extend your hike, you can continue on the trail for another 1.5 miles through the marsh, until you reach the parking area at PA 420.) Retrace your steps to the second Y intersection and turn left (toward the visitor center), away from I-95 and past Hoy's Pond on your right.

After about 0.2 mile from Hoy's Pond you'll pass a 0.25-mile boardwalk to your left, offering another opportunity to observe the tidal marsh. Just past it, join Impoundment Trail and bear left. The tidal marsh is on your left and impoundment on your right, offering continuous contrast, with low shore-loving trees, such as box elders, lining the pathway. The trail hugs the shoreline of the impoundment, passing several shallow coves. This is a rich habitat for frogs of various species, including wood frogs, which can be heard in great numbers in early spring "quacking" like ducks (which also abound here). Also in spring, look for bald eagles, which have been breeding on an island across the impoundment since 2010.

A two-level observation deck provides long-distance views of the impoundment about 0.3 mile from Hoy's Pond. After another 0.25 mile, turn right onto the long boardwalk over the impoundment. Numerous resting spots and interpretive signs describe the birds you're likely to see, encouraging you to walk slowly and stop along the way. The boardwalk meets the paved accessible trail on the other side of the impoundment; follow it out of the woods and past the Cusano Center to the parking lot.

MORE INFORMATION

The refuge is open from sunrise to sunset every day of the year; however, the Cusano Environmental Education Center is closed on federal holidays. Bikes are permitted. There are restrooms in the center, as well as a portable toilet in the main parking lot. Trails are maintained by Friends of Heinz Refuge at Tinicum (friendsofheinzrefuge.org). For more information, contact John Heinz National Wildlife Refuge at Tinicum, 8601 Lindbergh Boulevard, Philadelphia, PA 19153; 215-365-3118; fws.gov/refuge/John_Heinz.

5

RIDLEY CREEK STATE PARK

Ridley Creek is a hidden gem with year-round surprises. With its steep, forested hills and rocky streams, this hike demonstrates you don't need to go far to get away.

DIRECTIONS

Take I-476 to Exit 9 for PA 3 (West Chester Pike) west. Drive about 0.6 miles, turn left onto Bishop Hollow Rd.; travel 1.8 miles; turn right on Gradyville Rd. Continue about 2.6 miles to the park entrance on the left. Follow signs to Picnic Area 9. You will find ample parking. *GPS coordinates: 39° 57.228' N, 75° 26.479' W.*

TRAIL DESCRIPTION

Ridley Creek State Park is a testament to the power of terrain. Driving along West Chester Pike through densely developed Delaware County, you'd never guess this gem of a hiking park, with miles of wooded hillside trails and picturesque creeks, lies just off the road. Even many of the park visitors walking or biking on the paved paths that wind through the park are unaware that trails traverse the hills above and below.

The hilltops of the park are at the same elevation as the surrounding roads, hiding the internal topography. Ridley Creek itself lies at the bottom of a steep valley, while smaller tributary streams meander through shallower valleys. From any of these, it is difficult to get a sense of the whole park. Hiking Ridley Creek State Park is an experience of coming upon surprise after surprise.

Although the hike described here can be done in an afternoon, it provides beauty, challenge, and interest at almost every step along the way. This is a four-season hike: In spring, wildflowers carpet the woods and streambanks; cool, shaded woods relieve summer's heat; autumn leaves

LOCATION
Newtown Square, PA
(Delaware County)

RATING
Moderate

DISTANCE
5.5 miles

ELEVATION GAIN
875 feet

ESTIMATED TIME
2.75 hours

MAPS
USGS Media; dcnr.pa.gov/
StateParks/FindAPark/
RidleyCreekStatePark/
Pages/Maps.aspx

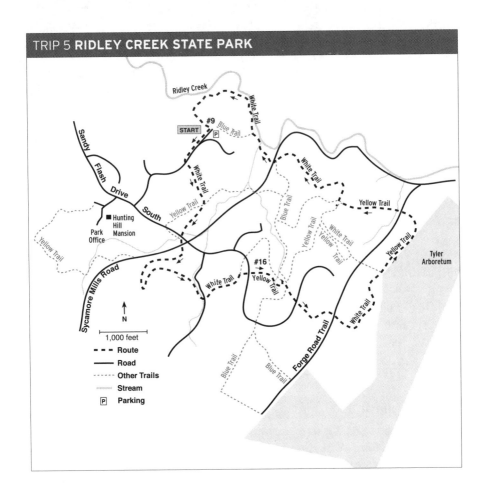

burnish the treetops in brilliant colors; and winter provides icy, clear views of hills, creek, and sky.

The hike starts at Picnic Area 9. Near the comfort station, look for a post marked "To White" and follow that trail slightly downhill to a post on the left, marked with a white blaze. The trails are well marked at intersections and road crossings, blazed with colors along the way, with occasional painted arrows at turns. Turn left to follow White Trail as it parallels the roadway above about 750 feet, following a natural footpath through mature oak-beech woods. The trail ascends, crossing the roadway. After a short open section, the trail enters successional woods—trees and shrubs that have grown up in formerly open areas over recent decades. When the state bought the land for the 2,606-acre park in the 1960s, it was the Hunting Hill estate of the wealthy Jeffords family, with many cleared farm fields, pastures, and drives. Hunting Hill's extensive grounds included not only a historic gristmill and associated structures but also a mansion designed by the noted architect Wilson Eyre and built in 1918 around a farmhouse dating to 1773. Today, a wing of the mansion houses the park's main office. (The mansion is worth a peek; in addition to its architectural interest and formal gardens in season, there is a large wall-mounted relief map of the park on display.)

The trail through the young woods is a natural-surface footpath that starts out relatively flat, climbs the side of the hill, then descends steeply into a ravine. The rock comprising most of the park's hills and ravines is gneiss: billion-year-old metamorphic rock created when colliding plates of Earth's crust crushed and heated existing sedimentary rocks, causing them to deform and recrystallize like taffy. Although the gneiss isn't visible here, outcrops appear along the creek later in the hike.

White Trail bends right as it crosses Yellow Trail; continue on White Trail as the hill grows even steeper. This section can be slippery. As the trail descends, it dodges large, old oak trees. (Steeper hills were more difficult to log, so you'll often find mature forests on ravine slopes.) At the bottom of the hill, the trail bends left to cross a small stream, which can be wet in spring and icy in winter. Follow White Trail into a round-arched culvert that passes under Sandy Flash Drive South.

On the other side, White Trail crosses a paved multiuse trail then ducks back into the woods, ascending a steep hill by fits and starts: up, down, and around. The woods are of oak, hickory, and tulip trees. Descend the hill, cross a wooden footbridge over a stream, ascend to cross Sandy Flash Drive South again, then climb the hill on the other side. As the trail descends once more, it crosses a pipeline section; follow the trail diagonally downward, where it reenters the woods. At the bottom, it crosses the drive again, skirts the rear of the restroom facilities at Area 16, and winds back around the hill. White Trail briefly meets up with Blue Trail, crosses Yellow, and continues as Blue peels off to the right. (From here, a level loop on Blue can add another mile to your hike, but it's not especially interesting.)

As you cross Sandy Flash Drive South (again!), note the high banks on either side of the trail and the locust trees at the corners. White Trail follows a centuries-old, long-abandoned roadbed, wide enough for an oxcart. Within the park are the remains of 25 eighteenth-century farmsteads and four roads; the process of historical succession (farm community to estate to park) is a counterpoint to natural succession (mature woods to cleared land to young woods), also observable here.

About 0.1 mile after the drive crossing, watch carefully for a trail marker and follow White Trail up several wooden steps to the left. Pass through a shrubby area then cross a paved multiuse trail as it goes over an old stone culvert. (White used to go under the culvert; the remnants may be confusing at this point, but no harm done if you follow the old trail to its junction with the new White Trail.) After about 0.35 mile, White Trail meets Yellow Trail at a Y intersection that is not well marked. Bear right and say goodbye to White Trail for a while as you follow the yellow blazes. This section borders Tyler Arboretum on the right. To your left is a white pine plantation—not a naturally occurring woods, although the eastern white pine is native to the area. The sounds of the wind, the fragrance of the trees, and the needle-covered footpath are sweeter and quieter in the pine forest than in the hardwood forest you've been walking through.

In another 0.25 mile, Yellow Trail turns left and descends into the pines. After it crosses the paved multiuse trail 500 feet later, you're back in the deciduous forest. Pass by a large boulder marking the trail as you ascend the next hill. Yellow Trail climbs a long, steep hill that falls away to Ridley Creek. At the top, turn right onto White again at the intersection. Continue uphill, level off, and head downhill, passing trailer-size boulders that suggest hideaways for gneiss gnomes. Blue Trail meets White Trail; continue on Blue-White Trail as it crosses the multiuse paved trail and nears the creek, where there are inviting benches, then a footbridge.

This section along Ridley Creek is one of the loveliest trails in the book, with the wide, rushing creek on one side and craggy boulders on the other. The terrain flattens out into a floodplain forest that's rife with wildflowers in spring and lush greenery in summer, and as wild as southeastern Pennsylvania gets any time of year. Gneiss outcrops, with their distinctive light-and-dark alternating bands, occur along the creek. Follow White Trail along the creek when Blue Trail turns up the hill. After about 1,500 feet, White Trail turns and ascends. The sounds of the creek gradually fade, and the trail ends at the parking lot where you started.

MORE INFORMATION

Restrooms are located at the main office parking area and at the trailhead. Bow-hunting is permitted in some areas; check with the park office during deer season. The trails are maintained by Friends of Ridley Creek State Park (friendsofrcsp .org). For more information, contact Ridley Creek State Park, 1023 Sycamore Mills Road, Media, PA 19063; 610-892-3900; dcnr.state.pa.us/stateparks/parks/ ridleycreek.aspx.

Mayapples and other wildflowers blanket the hillsides along Ridley Creek in early spring.

6

VALLEY FORGE NATIONAL HISTORICAL PARK: MOUNT MISERY AND MOUNT JOY

Climb rocky hills and traverse meadows alongside a meandering creek in a rural landscape imbued with American history.

DIRECTIONS

Take I-76 (Schuylkill Expressway) west to Exit 328A; stay right and merge onto US 422 west to the Valley Forge exit (PA 23 west). Turn left at the exit ramp. If you are stopping first at the visitor center, stay in the center lane and, when you reach the traffic light at the intersection of North Gulph Road, continue straight into the park. If you are going directly to the trailhead, get in the right lane and turn right at the traffic light then follow PA 23 west approximately 2.2 miles to another traffic light. At the light, turn left onto PA 252 (Valley Creek Road) and follow it approximately 1.3 miles to the Knox parking area on the right. There is ample parking. *GPS coordinates:* 40° 05.177' N, 75° 27.066' W.

To use public transportation, take SEPTA bus route 125 to the visitor center. (You will have to walk approximately 2.25 miles from the visitor center to the trailhead via Joseph Plumb Martin Trail.)

TRAIL DESCRIPTION

Valley Forge hiking? Philadelphians often think of Valley Forge as a vast, open grassy area, where paved roads circumnavigate scattered stone memorials and clusters of log huts—not as a hiking destination.

But Valley Forge contains two essential Philadelphia-area hikes: a pleasant riverside walk along the Schuylkill (River Trail, see Trip 7) and this hike, a trek through a part of Valley Forge that retains a sense of the countryside in which the Continental Army endured a winter of privation during the encampment of 1777–78.

LOCATION
King of Prussia, PA (Chester and Montgomery counties)

RATING
Moderate

DISTANCE
4.25 miles

ELEVATION GAIN
450 feet

ESTIMATED TIME
2.25 hours

MAPS
USGS Valley Forge quadrant; trail map available onsite; nps.gov/vafo/planyourvisit/maps.htm

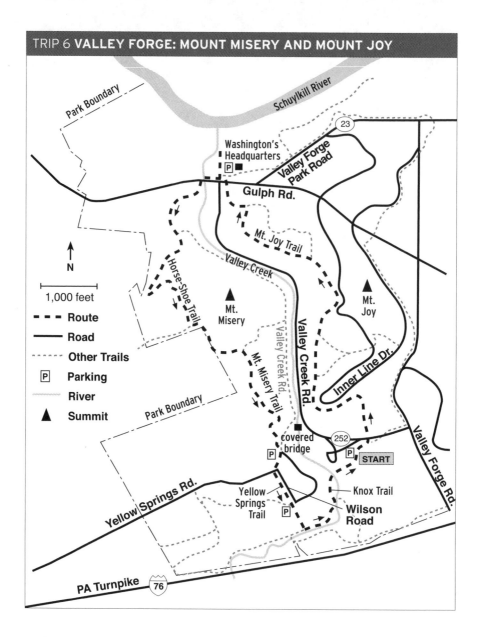

The northwest corner of the park surrounds Valley Creek and preserves a landscape similar to that of the Delaware Valley during the Revolutionary War: stone farmsteads with small fields checkering the steep, wooded stream valleys. Ironically, the encampment devastated much of the landscape, as soldiers tore up fields and felled trees. Muddy farm fields—not emerald lawns—provided the ground for the encampment. To travel any distance was either to go on foot over rugged, unlit dirt traces or to navigate through thick, forbidding woods.

This hike, a circuit between two summits with a level walk in between, can be done in either direction; the counterclockwise version described here climbs the shorter summit first.

Mount Misery (577 feet) on the west and Mount Joy (402 feet) on the east flank Valley Creek, which has cut a gorge through the sedimentary quartzite rock of the hills. The "mountains" loom over a plateau to the east composed of dolostone, a soft rock similar to limestone that dissolves easily in water. Quartzite, easily recognizable by its large, white crystals, weathers slowly but fractures easily when water freezes in its crevices. Boulders split off from exposed surfaces and slide downhill, creating slopes of rock debris.

Tradition offers several explanations for the mountains' names, first mentioned in a seventeenth-century deed from William Penn. In Governor Samuel Whitaker Pennypacker's colorful 1872 version, two lost settlers wandered overnight on one mountain, bruising themselves on the numerous rocks and feeling "continual dread of being devoured by . . . wild beasts." The next morning, they crossed the creek to climb the opposite peak and discovered their settlement below—thus the "misery" of the first mountain and the "joy" of the other.

From the kiosk at the Knox parking lot, cross PA 252 at the pedestrian crosswalk, heading north. Once across, a footpath through a meadow begins ascending Mount Joy. Ahead is a rocky woods; to your right are replica huts. Feel free to climb slowly: The view on this approach embodies the essence of Valley Forge.

Past the huts, the trail enters the oak woods and soon intersects with Mount Joy Trail; turn left. From here the trail continues along the hillside, alternately ascending and descending, with occasional views back along the valley. (Ignore all options that go off to the right, as none of them offers superior views. Do not be fooled by the "Observatory" trail marker; that structure was long ago dismantled.) Outcrops of exposed quartzite along the trail also provide fine viewing platforms. The trees through which you peer are primarily drought-tolerant chestnut oak, black oak, and black gum. The trail briefly skirts Inner Line Drive then returns to the woods. On its final 0.5 mile, it descends into a floodplain forest with sweetgum, box elder, silver maple, red maple, and spicebush shrubs. The trail becomes a gravel road then ends at the corner of PA 252 and PA 23.

Across PA 23 is Washington's Headquarters. During the encampment, Washington lodged in the home of Isaac Potts, whose family owned the iron forges that gave Valley Forge its name. The headquarters and other historical structures in this complex are worth a visit, either at this point or after your hike.

Proceed west across PA 252. A bronze plaque at the bridge over Valley Creek marks the trailhead of the Horse-Shoe Trail, which heads northwest 140 miles to the Appalachian Trail at Stony Mountain. Follow its yellow blazes over the creek then go left along a gravel road, past a small complex of old stone buildings, to a gate with a kiosk. The trail begins to climb Mount Misery.

Fields, wooded hills, and history: Mount Misery, with its reconstructed soldier cabins, is quintessential Valley Forge.

About 0.29 mile from the start, you'll cross a wide road with signs indicating Valley Creek Trail to the left. Horse-Shoe Trail becomes a rocky footpath, following a stream; it passes the ruins of an old water-bottling plant then turns left and continues up the hill. As you pass through these dry, open oak woods, it is possible to imagine the storied lost settlers wandering at night among these boulders, hearing—instead of the noise from PA 23 below—the cries of wolves and bobcats, unable to see the stars through the thick canopy overhead.

After another 0.6 mile, Horse-Shoe Trail meets the white-blazed Mount Misery Trail. Turn left (Horse-Shoe Trail turns sharp right) and follow the white blazes along the ridge. After 0.25 mile, the trail reaches a junction with Valley Creek Trail. Continue along Mount Misery Trail and hike along the hillside, descending 0.5 mile until you reach a small parking lot near a covered bridge.

The next part of the hike provides a respite between the two summits: a pleasant walk along peaceful meadows by a shaded fishing stream. Exit the parking lot and turn right onto Yellow Springs Road then left onto Wilson Road (open to traffic). Follow Yellow Springs Trail along the right side of Wilson Road, past meadows of native grasses and wildflowers, to the Yellow Springs parking area. You may detour into the meadows by following seasonal mown paths. From these meadow trails, you can see a cluster of old stone farm buildings along Yellow Springs Road identified as Lord Stirling's Quarters.

From the parking area, follow Wilson Road a short distance as it descends to Valley Creek. To your left, a spur trail follows the creek along the banks, which have been restored with native trees and shrubs to reduce erosion and increase the shade that aquatic wildlife need.

Retrace your steps uphill along Wilson Road then turn right onto Knox Trail across from the Yellow Springs parking area. To your left is a beautiful view across a field behind the nineteenth-century P. C. Knox estate, with Mount Misery and Mount Joy in the background and the creek running between them—certainly worth a long pause.

Follow the stream then cross it over a wooden footbridge. You'll pass between several buildings of the estate that served as General Henry Knox's quarters before ending back at the parking area.

MORE INFORMATION

The park is open year-round from 7 A.M. to dark (30 minutes after sunset). The visitor center—which has extensive exhibits and information on the history of Valley Forge, as well as on the American Revolution—is open daily from 9 A.M. to 5 P.M. Restrooms are located at the Yellow Springs Road parking area. Hunting may be permitted; check with the visitor center during deer hunting season. Dogs are permitted and must be leashed at all times. Washington's Headquarters houses restrooms, as well as a number of exhibits; parking is restricted to two hours, but faster hikers (or those opting for shorter versions of this hike) may choose it as an alternative starting point. There are about 20 miles of hiking trails in the park. The Mount Misery trails are maintained by the Appalachian Mountain Club's Delaware Valley Chapter (amcdv.org). For more information, contact Valley Forge National Historical Park, 1400 North Outer Line Drive, King of Prussia, PA 19406; 610-783-1000; nps.gov/vafo.

7

VALLEY FORGE NATIONAL HISTORICAL PARK: RIVER TRAIL

Follow a placid greenway along the Schuylkill River through a historic landscape.

DIRECTIONS

Take I-76 west (Schuylkill Expressway) to US 422 west; follow US 422 to the exit for PA 363 (Audubon/Trooper exit), immediately after the bridge over the Schuylkill River. At the top of the exit ramp, turn left onto Trooper Road and continue to the end of the roadway. Turn right onto Sullivan's Lane. The Betzwood parking area is just ahead on your right; there is ample parking. *GPS coordinates:* 40° 06.576′ N, 75° 25.289′ W.

To reach Valley Forge via public transportation, take SEPTA bus route 125 to the visitor center and walk down to the pedestrian-only Sullivan's Bridge over the Schuylkill River then bear left into the Betzwood parking area.

TRAIL DESCRIPTION

A delightful benefit of the preservation of Valley Forge National Historical Park is that several miles of the lower Schuylkill River are largely undeveloped or have been restored to green space. Within 10 miles of Philadelphia, this river—so much a part of the early history of the city and its countryside—can be enjoyed for its natural scenery and placid qualities, characteristics that were fast disappearing even during the Continental Army's encampment. (See "Valley Forge: The Encampment of 1777–78," page 36.)

At this point, the Schuylkill River is 105 miles from its headwaters in Schuylkill County and 28.5 miles from its mouth at the Delaware River. Although the Schuylkill generally flows southeast, there is a great bend just north of this hike's turnaround point, where the river joins the Perkiomen Creek and arcs westward briefly at the erosion-resistant rocks that form Mount Misery and Mount Joy on

LOCATION
King of Prussia, PA (Chester and Montgomery counties)

RATING
Easy

DISTANCE
6 miles

ELEVATION GAIN
25 feet

ESTIMATED TIME
2.75 hours

MAPS
USGS Valley Forge; trail map available onsite; nps.gov/vafo/planyourvisit/maps.htm

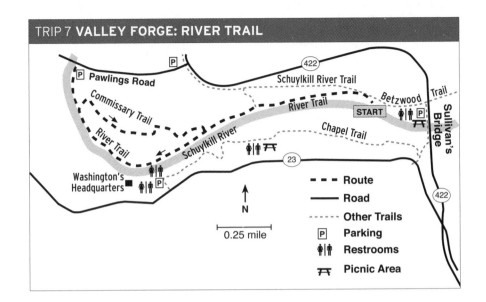

its southwestern banks. The river again curves east where Valley Creek comes in on the opposite bank, at Washington's Headquarters. The point of land bordered by the bend is known as the Perkiomen Peninsula.

This hike is an easy walk among riverside woods, with a foray into the surrounding fields and wetlands. It follows the park's River Trail from the Betzwood parking area to the River Trail parking area. River Trail is also locally referred to as Betzwood Trail to distinguish it from the Schuylkill River Trail (SRT), the paved multiuse trail that parallels it for a short distance (see Trip 1).

Begin the hike at the Betzwood parking area. At the eastern end of the parking area is a pedestrian bridge over the Schuylkill that connects the park's northern and southern trail systems. Constructed in 2016 and named Sullivan's Bridge after the original (described below), it's worth visiting to appreciate the river from a height, but the hike begins at the opposite (western) end of the parking lot. Head west and upstream away from the SRT trailhead, past the restrooms, to the trailhead. The packed-dirt River Trail is usually a quiet haven for pedestrians, since most bikers are happier on the paved SRT. From the trailhead entrance, the wide, flat trail follows the river upstream about 3 miles. Side trails, including a connection to the SRT, branch off to the right; keep left at these intersections.

The trees and other vegetation are typical of a southeast Pennsylvania floodplain forest. Tall silver maples and sycamores arch over the river and shade the trail; basswoods and slippery elm populate the understory. Look for the beautiful (albeit unflatteringly named) bladdernut tree, with its compound leaves of three leaflets, dainty white flowers, and distinctive three-sided seed cases. Bladdernut seed cases first appear in spring and persist through the winter, hanging

The delicate bell-like spring flowers of the unfortunately named bladdernut tree turn into seed pods that last into winter.

like miniature lanterns from the branches, and darkening from light green to brown as they dry, the seeds rattling as the cases tremble in the wind.

After about 1,000 feet, you will pass the long, narrow Catfish Island; catfish, along with bass, sunfish, walleye, carp and other species inhabit the lower Schuylkill. After another 0.25 mile, you will pass an oxbow, where a small tributary winds toward the river's banks. Cross this stream on the footbridge.

At about 1 mile, the trail passes the site of the original Sullivan's Bridge, marked by a sign on a large boulder. During the Continental Army's encampment, food and supplies were stored on the north bank of the river, and this bridge, built by Major General John Sullivan, enabled goods to be transported to the soldiers on the other side. Constructed from timber, it was the only bridge built by the Continental Army during the American Revolution. Primarily a natural area today, the peninsula formed by the bend in the Schuylkill was the center of activity for soldiers who loaded and unloaded the horse-drawn wagons that carried supplies and livestock to and from Pawling Farm.

Around the 2-mile mark, the trail passes opposite the site of Washington's Headquarters, clearly visible across the river through the trees. Here, Valley Creek meets the Schuylkill River. Just upstream of this point, the river rushes over an obstacle course of large rocks. The trail terminates approximately 1 mile later at the River Trail parking area.

Turn around and head back, bearing left at the fork after 0.3 mile. This trail (Commissary Trail) heads uphill through a grassy area. After about 1,000 feet, the trail intersects with a gravel road; turn right and continue heading east on this road. The upland forest here contrasts with the floodplain woods along the riverbank. Numerous unofficial trail turnoffs head over a network of berms, mounds of coal sediment dredged from the river between 1947 and 1951 in one of America's first environmental remediation projects.

At 0.5 mile from the turnaround, the trail bends left to enter the historic Commissary site. This was one of the main structures used during the Colonial Army encampment. Watch the trail carefully here, as it veers sharply to the right just past the Pawling Farm trailhead kiosk. Commissary Trail then heads across a meadow and down into a moist woods dotted with pools and seeps. Not long after, the trail bends left and uphill a short way, turns right onto a rutted road, and bears right and downhill to meet River Trail again. Turn left and follow the riverbank another 1.5 miles to the parking lot.

MORE INFORMATION

Restrooms can be found at the trailhead and at the welcome center. The park is open year-round from 7 A.M. until dark (30 minutes after sunset). Bikes are permitted. For more information, contact Valley Forge National Historical Park, 1400 North Outer Line Drive, King of Prussia, PA 19406; 610-783-1077; nps.gov/vafo.

VALLEY FORGE: THE ENCAMPMENT OF 1777-78

In late December 1777, the Continental Army, under the command of General George Washington, had just suffered defeats at the battles of Brandywine, Paoli, and Germantown, and the British had captured the colonial capital of Philadelphia. As was customary at the time, Washington decided to establish a winter camp for his 12,000 soldiers. He selected a site along the Schuylkill River, 20 miles northwest of the city: Valley Forge, an easily defensible location high in the hills with a view of the valley.

Ill-shod, poorly fed, sick, and weary, the citizens-turned-patriots marched into Valley Forge through icy wind and over snowy ground. The thriving iron-works settlement was situated on a creek and surrounded by farmland. Washington's soldiers felled trees and dragged them out of the woods to construct shelters, dug forts and trenches into the frozen earth, built a bridge over the Schuylkill, and laid out roads. Food was constantly in short supply, illness rampant. Of the 2,000 deaths during the encampment, most resulted from disease.

The hiatus became a transformative experience with the arrival of the Prussian army officer Baron Friedrich von Steuben in February 1778. Von Steuben trained the encamped soldiers and organized them into a mature fighting force. In June 1778, the troops marched out of Valley Forge to Monmouth, New Jersey, where they crushed the British army and began the long road to decisive victory.

A movement to protect what was viewed as sacred ground began in the late nineteenth century. The area around Washington's Headquarters was established as the first Pennsylvania state park in 1893. Over the next 100-plus years, a great effort was made to preserve much of the land where the soldiers were encamped; the site became a national park in 1976. Historic buildings (a handful dating back to the encampment) have been preserved and some (including Washington's Headquarters) restored. Scattered around the grounds are reconstructed log huts similar to those built by the soldiers.

The park has preserved neither the industry that occupied the valley at the time of the encampment nor the community it sustained, although visitors can still see ruins of the two forges along Valley Creek, along with remnants of other industries that occupied the site in the years since. The expanse of open space invites visitors to contemplate history from the vantage point of those who lived it and to ponder how choices made in the present may profoundly affect the future.

8
GREEN RIBBON TRAIL

Take a train to a hike! Leave the driving to SEPTA and walk along and over Wissahickon Creek in quiet woods and sunny thickets.

DIRECTIONS

Take I-276 (Pennsylvania Turnpike) to Exit 339 (Fort Washington). Follow PA 309 north to Norristown Road (Spring House); make a left at the bottom of the ramp. Take Norristown Road west to Bethlehem Pike, turn left, and immediately turn right onto Penllyn Blue Bell Pike. After 0.2 mile, turn left onto Old Penllyn Pike; bear left and park on the street. Penllyn Station is ahead; parking is limited to commuters. Neighborhood street parking is available at Penllyn Woods Park. *GPS coordinates:* 40° 10.178′ N, 75° 14.624′ W.

To get to the trailhead by public transportation, take SEPTA Regional Rail to the Penllyn stop.

TRAIL DESCRIPTION

A model of sustainable thinking, the 20-mile-long Green Ribbon Trail winds between regional rail stations from Fort Washington to North Wales along upper Wissahickon Creek. (The creek's hikable lower reach, through a gorge, runs through Philadelphia; see Trip 2). The Delaware Valley is served by an extensive hub-and-spoke network of commuter rail stations that link neighborhoods and suburbs to Center City, but to connect a great day hike in a natural area directly to public transportation is extremely difficult. From its beginnings in the late nineteenth century, the regional rail network has been used for economic development—not for bringing people closer to nature. Wissahickon Valley Watershed Association's (WVWA) Green Ribbon Trail is a visionary effort to change this approach. This linear hike begins at SEPTA Regional Rail's Penllyn Station and ends at North Wales

LOCATION
Lower Gwynedd Township, PA (Montgomery County)

RATING
Easy to moderate

DISTANCE
7.5 miles

ELEVATION GAIN
Minimal

ESTIMATED TIME
3 hours

MAPS
USGS Ambler, USGS Lansdale; wvwa.org/greenribbontrail

Station, meaning you can take the train, hike, and take another train home. You can shorten this hike by ending one station earlier, at Gwynedd Valley.

To reach the Green Ribbon Trail, exit from the southbound side of Penllyn Station (signs: "To Center City") and walk down Old Penllyn Pike. The street sign may be absent, but the pike is the middle of the three residential streets that intersect at the station. You can see the Wissahickon Creek through the woods on the left.

After about 600 feet, you'll pass by a sign where the southbound Green Ribbon Trail (GRT) goes into the woods. You are now on the northbound GRT. The Green Ribbon Trail is easy to follow through natural areas, and most entrances are indicated by a GRT sign. Continue on the road to the intersection with Penllyn Blue Bell Pike, turn left, and walk alongside the road another 1,000 feet to Township Line Road; turn right and cross the street to enter WVWA's Penllyn Natural Area. Note the stub of a stone bridge that used to cross the creek, next to an old one-room schoolhouse that has been converted into a water-quality monitoring station.

The Lansdale-Doylestown Regional Rail line passes over Wissahickon Creek and Green Ribbon Trail via a stone bridge.

After about 50 feet, the trail ducks left into the woods along the creek, becoming a natural footpath. These are typical Philadelphia-area flat, wet, suburban floodplain woods: mostly old or middle-aged trees (oak, beech, hickory) with an understory of spicebush and multiflora rose. The woods are often frequented by deer. While it is no wilderness, it a pleasant natural area, and the sight and sound of the flowing creek are quite peaceful. Note the green blazes here; they are not consistently placed along the trail but are useful where they do occur.

The GRT leaves the woods, follows a street briefly, and returns to the woods over a footbridge, entering a very wet area with pools and braided channels, with some boardwalks over the swampy spots; black walnut trees thrive here. A sign indicates "GRT mile 5" (meaning 5 miles to the terminus from here). The GRT exits the wooded area at a power-line clearing, becoming a gravel path then a grassy path. Continue past a maintenance shed to a fork. Take the left-hand path, closer to the creek, and note the blue blazes and signs identifying this as a horse trail. Green blazes appear only occasionally in this section; continue to follow the wide grassy trail with the horse tracks in the middle, taking care not to veer off to other blue-blazed horse trails. This wet thicket, with the creek unseen to the left and woods to the right, is a good birding area. After another 0.75 mile, the trail reaches the creek and follows its banks under a stone railroad bridge. Use caution, as the path becomes quite rocky and slippery.

Bear right at the next Y intersection, following the horse track. After another 500 feet, the trail crosses the creek at the 4-mile mark. The creek is quite wide here, but it can be forded via concrete stepping-stones. Continue straight uphill to Plymouth Road, cross the road, turn left, and cross the grade-level tracks to the Gwynedd Valley train station parking lot. Note the GRT directional signs here. Turn right and go to the rear of the parking lot, where the trail parallels the tracks for a few hundred feet before skirting tree-lined backyards. Eventually the trail slopes downward to follow the creek's wooded banks, passing by a dam and old foundations for a skating hut (note the fireplace). Just 50 feet past mile marker 3, you'll cross PA 202. (Be careful. This is a very busy road.)

You'll enter a swampy, open thicket with occasional boardwalks; the creek is below and to the right. After a little less than 1 mile, there is an unmarked Y intersection. Take the left fork going away from the creek and, after another 750 feet, you'll reach the intersection of Swedesford Road and Township Line. (WVWA's historic Evans-Mumbower Mill, restored to water-powered operation, is over the stone-arched bridge; it's visitable during scheduled open houses.)

Cross Swedesford Road and enter a lightly wooded area next to a tree-planting and restoration project; huge, old sycamore trees tower over the newly planted saplings. The trail continues behind houses for a while; cross the road at mile marker 2 then follow the thicket diagonally right, toward the creek. The trail continues to traverse an open wet area replete with thick brush. Cross the creek several times using the concrete stepping-stones. Just after a pipeline clearing, you'll come to a four-way intersection; turn left (note the opposite-facing sign).

At North Wales Road, the trail angles 45 degrees to the right along the thickets. (To shorten the hike by about 1.5 miles, turn right here and follow the road to the train station.) Now the trail wends through an open freshwater marsh and ponds, where you might spot unusual birds, such as bitterns. Keep an eye out for stinging nettles along the trail.

After another stream crossing, turn left at the next Y intersection; at the power-line clearing, turn right and follow the meadow's edge to a paved path behind a housing development. Then turn right again and follow the path to the GRT's terminus, in Upper Gwynedd Township's Parkside Place Park.

To get to North Wales Station, follow the paved path to the right on Sumneytown Pike then take a left on Walnut Street and continue to the station (about 1 mile from the GRT terminus). Return to Penllyn via the southbound side ("To Center City").

Station-to-station, the hike takes about 3 hours; on the train, it takes about 5 minutes. Through the speeding train window, the green ribbon is a green blur.

MORE INFORMATION

Restrooms are at the trail's end (Upper Gwynedd Township's Parkside Place Park) and Penllyn Woods; there are portable toilets at Evans-Mumbower Mill. Dogs must be leashed. Hunting is not permitted in these largely residential areas. Green Ribbon Trail is maintained by the Wissahickon Valley Watershed Association: 12 Morris Road, Ambler, PA 19002; 215-646-8866; wvwa.org.

9

PENNYPACK ECOLOGICAL RESTORATION TRUST

This hike provides a rare opportunity to experience extraordinary expanses of meadowland in a dense suburban area. These meadows, along with upland and floodplain forests, continue to be restored and managed to provide habitat and improve the Pennypack Creek watershed. The trust lands also include an old-growth forest, riparian areas along the creek, and farm fields.

DIRECTIONS

From the Pennsylvania Turnpike (I-276), take Exit 343 for PA 611 south (Easton Road). At the end of the off-ramp, turn left and follow Easton Road 0.7 mile. Turn left onto Fitzwatertown Road and continue 0.6 mile until it becomes Terwood Road. Continue on Terwood Road another 1.7 miles and turn left onto Edge Hill Road; in 0.4 mile, turn right into the park. Just up the road, you will find ample parking on your left. *GPS coordinates:* 40° 08.569′ N, 75° 05.008′ W.

TRAIL DESCRIPTION

A meadow is the botanical equivalent of a photograph. Both are the products of human efforts to stop time. Left to its own devices, a cleared site in the Delaware Valley will turn into a forest. It will quickly be colonized by grasses, flowers, and small trees. Then shrubs and larger trees will take root in the field, eventually shading out the grasses and wildflowers. But if disturbed regularly, by mowing or controlled burning, a meadow will stay a meadow. Preserving grasslands has become a high priority among the region's conservationists. One of the largest publicly accessible meadow habitats in the area is at the Pennypack Preserve of the Pennypack Ecological Restoration Trust. Of the trust's 832 protected acres, more than 160 are meadows, many

LOCATION
Huntingdon Valley, PA
(Montgomery County)

RATING
Easy to moderate

DISTANCE
7 miles

ELEVATION GAIN
225 feet

ESTIMATED TIME
3.5 hours

MAPS
USGS Hatboro; trail map available onsite; pennypacktrust.org/map/trails

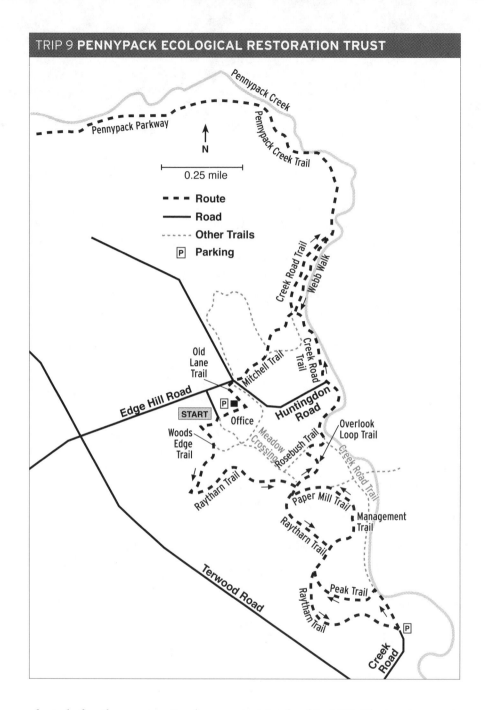

planted after the organization began acquiring land in 1976. The trust prevents woody plants from taking over by periodically mowing the fields.

This hike goes around many meadows, offering expansive views of the landscape, with distinct colors and textures in every season. But the preserve is more than meadows. It also contains streams, creeks, and wetlands; farmhouses and historic structures; and hundreds of forested acres that are being restored to improve wildlife habitats. The trails are well marked with signs bearing the trail names. Take care, though, not to confuse maintenance paths cleared around field edges for groomed trails.

From the northwest corner of the visitor center parking area, follow Woods Edge Trail. The wood-chip path leads down through trees about 500 feet to Raytharn Trail, marked by a large sign at the edge of a field (the old Raytharn Farm). Turn right, crossing the meadow of milkweed and summer-blooming wildflowers; you can see Bryn Athyn Cathedral peeking over the hilltops to the east.

Follow the trail downhill, bending left and then right. Pass through a fencerow and continue uphill through more grassland. When you enter a small woodlot, Meadow Crossing Trail will intersect from the left; turn right and cross Paper Mill Trail, continuing straight as Raytharn Trail passes between meadows of native grasses. Where Management Trail intersects from the left, turn right (uphill), following Raytharn Trail into the woods. Climb gradually uphill and emerge from the woods at a hilltop between two magnificent grassy meadows with 360-degree vistas. The trail winds through the hilltop meadows then goes downhill, skirting the woods at the bottom. Pass through a gap in the fence at Creek Road.

Turn left onto Creek Road Trail, an old road along the wide, rocky Pennypack Creek. After 0.2 mile, turn left up Peak Trail, a narrow footpath steeply ascending a rocky knoll under a canopy of towering, centuries-old oak and tulip trees. After beginning to descend, backtrack along Raytharn Trail about 1,000 feet, turning right onto Management Trail, where you'll pass through a very young woods.

Make the next left to ascend via a shady, old unpaved road, Paper Mill Trail. (Downhill to the right, a historic stone bridge, built in 1817, crosses the creek where it connects with Pennypack Trail, a 5-mile creekside rail trail.) At the top of the hill, turn right onto Raytharn Trail briefly to Meadow Crossing Trail. Follow Meadow Crossing Trail for 75 feet then turn right onto Overlook Loop Trail, which winds around the top of the ridge and offers good winter views of the Pennypack Creek valley. Turn right at the T intersection, taking Rosebush Trail back down to Creek Road Trail, and turn left.

Remain on Creek Road Trail, traversing a floodplain forest of river birch, sweetgum, and sycamore, passing by old stone foundations. These are remnants of the mill and farming community once centered here. The trail remains generally flat along old roads and passes through four gates near a small but active Swedenborgian stone church and through a small residential area by a rocky waterfall. The trail can be muddy after rain. The trail's name changes to Pennypack Creek Trail and then to Pennypack Parkway after Mason's Mill Road. At the end of the trail is the fifth gate and a five-car parking lot.

Turn around and retrace your steps, but when you return to Creek Road Trail, cross it and follow Webb Walk to go down to the creek along the bridge abutment. Pass through wetlands marked by skunk cabbage colonies, an eighteenth-century

Several varieties of milkweed are common in the Philadelphia region; most thrive in meadows and other sunny open areas. The pods burst open to reveal seeds with silken filaments that float in the wind.

stone springhouse, and beautiful boulder outcrops. Rhododendrons crowd the trail, which, dense with roots, can be slippery, although boardwalks cover some of the wettest spots.

Webb Walk rejoins Creek Road Trail. Turn left and, just 50 feet later, turn right to take Mitchell Trail up a steep, rocky hill then into a mixed woods. At the top of the hill, cross Huntingdon Road (opposite the June Fete fairgrounds). Pass through a gap made in the post-and-rail fencing. Bear left just inside the fence then go straight onto Old Lane Trail, walking between a double row of alternating silver maples and red cedars. Turn right at the bird blind and maintenance garage to return to the visitor center.

MORE INFORMATION

Restrooms are located at the visitor center and are open during business hours (Monday through Friday, 9 A.M. to 5 P.M.; Saturday 10 A.M. to 2 P.M.; Sunday, 1 to 4 P.M.). Pennypack Trust is open from 8 A.M. to dusk daily. Except for Creek Road Trail, Pennypack Creek Trail, and Pennypack Parkway, trails within Pennypack Ecological Restoration Trust are for hikers only; no bikes, dogs, or horses. Where permitted, dogs must be leashed. For more information, contact Pennypack Ecological Restoration Trust, 2955 Edgehill Road, Huntington Valley, PA 19006; 215-657-0830; pennypacktrust.org.

SPLENDOR IN THE GRASS: MEADOWS AND GRASSLANDS

If you have ever experienced the rattle of wind coursing through a canopy of dried grass stems; felt dizzy looking out at a rippling sea of amber seedheads; watched a kestrel hover high in the sky and plunge straight down to snare a vole; followed a monarch butterfly as it flits from milkweed flower to milkweed flower (and, later in the year, chased the fluffy seeds from the milkweed pod); or breathed in the sweet magical fragrance of goldenrod then count your blessings. If you have never done any of the above, meadows have been missing from your life.

Fields of native grasses and wildflowers are among the rarest of habitats in the Delaware Valley, just as they are elsewhere in the Northeast. The reason for their scarcity is trees. Forests thrive in the Northeast due to the region's abundant rainfall, the moderate temperatures afforded by the Gulf Stream (the warm current of the Atlantic Ocean), and the shelter from winds provided by Piedmont foothills.

But trees can fall, burn, or be cut down. Any area cleared of trees is a potential meadow. Grass and wildflower seeds buried in the forest floor, with no chance of sprouting in the shade, suddenly have an opportunity to do so without trees overhead. Seeds blow in from nearby meadows or are carried in on animal fur or human clothing. In a new opening, plants quickly sprout and drink in the sunlight. Native grasses appear, their roots stabilizing the soil and preventing other plants from proliferating. Suddenly, the opening is a field.

Meadows do not last long, though. Trees and woody shrubs colonize the fields, their tough roots breaking through those of the grass. Eventually taller growth shades out the sun-loving meadow plants, and the meadow disappears.

Aside from its beauty, the meadow is an important habitat for vulnerable pollinators, such as bees and butterflies; grassland birds, such as the kestrel and meadowlark; and other wildlife. Grasslands provide food, shelter, and cover for distinctive species year-round. Birds hide their nests and fledglings under dense grass clumps. In spring and summer, they eat the insects that are attracted to flowers; in fall, they eat the flower seeds. In late winter and early spring, the meadows warm up more quickly than woods and therefore can be a critical source of food for hibernating wildlife. In the larger sense, habitat diversity in a region is critical to the long-term sustainability of the web of life.

Prior to extensive human settlement in the Delaware Valley and its surroundings, the landscape was a mosaic of habitats: Meadows were created, either naturally by wildfire or intentionally by native peoples, then reverted to forest over time. With the rise of agriculture, meadows were created by farmers as a side effect of rotating crops and leaving fields fallow. But as cities and suburbs replaced farms and fires were suppressed, meadows vanished.

Today meadows are rare in the wooded Piedmont. (In the coastal plains of New Jersey and Delaware, meadows are more common, especially on the coast, because the dry, sandy soil and windy conditions are inhospitable to trees.) Wildlife conservation managers in the region target the restoration and preservation of grasslands as a high priority. Meadows need disturbance to get established and regular disturbance to persist. To establish a meadow as a habitat, a land manager must first clear woody vegetation from a field or clear a woods. To ensure the meadow is composed of native plants and not weeds, the land manager will plant grasses or wildflowers using specialized machinery that plants seeds at just the right depth. After a meadow is established, it must be mowed regularly (or, less often, burned in a controlled manner) to keep trees from encroaching upon the field. Maintaining a meadow is an intensive operation, another reason why grasslands are so rare. Nature's services are free, but human labor is not.

Meadows have been extensively restored and protected at Pennypack Ecological Restoration Trust (Trip 9). Other meadow restoration areas are located in Wissahickon Valley Park (Trip 2), Green Lane Park (Trip 17), Peace Valley Nature Center (Trip 18), and Jacobsburg Environmental Education Center (Trip 37).

Almost anyone can create a meadow in a backyard, even a tiny one. Many grassland birds require at least several acres, but bees and butterflies can benefit from smaller "pocket meadows." The more small meadows there are in a landscape, the less the pollinators need to roam. Ask your county agricultural extension agent for specific planting guidance for your yard. Whether you go out and find a meadow or make your own, there is no excuse for missing out on the grassland experience.

10

ALAPOCAS RUN STATE PARK

Take an easy walk through lush woods along the Brandywine Creek and through a huge pawpaw patch, right next to historic mills and the remains of a quarry.

DIRECTIONS

Take I-95 south in Delaware to Exit 8 for US 202 north. Remain in the right lane and take the first exit for DE 141 south/DE 261 north. Take a left at the end of the exit ramp for DE 141 south. At the light, turn left to go under US 202. At the next light, turn left onto West Park Drive. In about 0.25 mile, turn left at the sign for Blue Ball Barn. *GPS coordinates: 39° 46.617′ N, 75° 32.735′ W.*

To reach the park via public transportation, take SEPTA R2 or Amtrak to Wilmington then take bus routes 2, 11, 12, 21, or 35 to the Brandywine Zoo and from there walk 1 mile along the Northern Delaware Greenway to an informational sign complex. With this approach, you will hike in the opposite direction from what's described below.

TRAIL DESCRIPTION

The small city of Wilmington, Delaware, boasts an impressive and growing network of trails connecting numerous parks, all centered on the Northern Delaware Greenway. One of those, the 230-acre Alapocas Run State Park, offers a short, pleasant hike combining waterside walks with views of a historically significant quarry and mills, plus a plunge into a lush Piedmont woods. It is, as the promotional material says, an urban oasis.

Like Brandywine Creek State Park (Trip 13), Alapocas Run is, in part, a legacy of two wealthy families of the Brandywine Valley: the du Ponts and the Bancrofts. Structures related to each bookend the hike. The Blue Ball Barn, built in 1914 by Alfred I. du Pont, has been adapted into a

LOCATION
Wilmington, DE

RATING
Easy

DISTANCE
4.5 miles

ELEVATION GAIN
100 feet

ESTIMATED TIME
2 hours

MAPS
USGS Wilmington North; trail maps available at Blue Ball Barn; destateparks .com/park/alapocas-run/ maps/

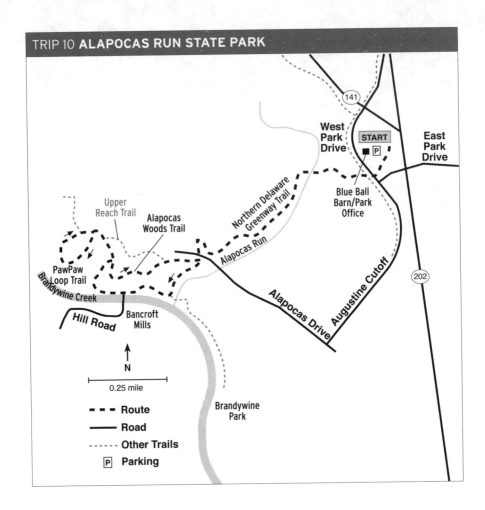

stellar example of environmentally friendly architecture. Now housing the Delaware Folk Art Collection, it's the first public building in Delaware to receive a Leadership in Energy and Environmental Design (LEED) certification and is worth a stop.

To reach the Northern Delaware Greenway trailhead, follow a short trail downhill from the Blue Ball Barn parking lot. The Greenway is a wide, paved, well-marked trail. Turn right at the trailhead and cross West Park Drive and an open area. After another 0.1 mile, you'll enter the woods.

The trail bridges the Alapocas Run—a rocky, wild-looking stream—and continues through an oak-hickory woods with the stream to the left. After a hairpin turn, it crosses Alapocas Drive and shortly intersects with Alapocas Woods Trail. Take this trail, which goes off to the right. Trail intersections are well posted in this park. In any case, the trails are short enough that getting lost is unlikely.

Follow the narrow, natural footpath as it descends the wooded, rocky hillside. The predominant tree in this woods—and the main natural attraction in this

Pawpaw Woods at Alapocas Run is an immense colony of these broadleaved members of the custard apple family.

park—is the pawpaw, a bottomland understory species that grows up to 30 feet high and has large, dark-green, teardrop-shaped leaves that are glossy when wet and fan out around the end of the branches. Dense colonies of these trees cover the hillsides here. The pawpaw is a member of the custard apple family—the only such member, in fact, native to North America. Its leaves are the sole source of food for caterpillars of the dramatically striped zebra swallowtail. The trees bear cup-shaped, dark-purple flowers directly from the branches, with fragrant mango-shaped fruits ripening in early fall. Although you may see fruits here, leave them alone. Picking pawpaws is illegal in Delaware state parks and would endanger the plant's continued survival in the state, as they grow naturally only in the tiny Piedmont section north of the fall line.

The trail winds up and down through the woods; after about 0.5 mile, PawPaw Loop branches off to the left. Take this trail downhill into a virtual forest of pawpaws; they seem to have taken over every square inch of ground. Or perhaps "they" should be "it": Pawpaws spread, in part, by cloning themselves, so what seems like many trees are, genetically, a small number of individual trees.

Alapocas Run is very close here; an unofficial spur trail takes you down to its rushing waters. Follow PawPaw Loop another 0.3 mile to its intersection with Alapocas Woods Trail and turn right.

Alapocas Woods Trail passes PawPaw Loop on the right and a left-hand turn-off for Upper Reach Trail; at the next right, turn onto the unnamed connector trail that heads straight downhill to Brandywine Creek then continues left along the creek's banks to the paved Greenway, opposite Bancroft Mills.

Built on the site of an eighteenth-century paper mill, Bancroft Mills began operating in 1831 and, by 1930, had become the world's largest textile finishing complex. Despite its status as the longest-running complex on the Brandywine, subsequent owners of Bancroft Mills went bankrupt. The old mill buildings now house a number of condominiums. Alapocas Run State Park opened in 2007, 97 years after William Poole Bancroft and the chemical company DuPont donated 123 acres to the city of Wilmington for parkland.

Continue on the Northern Delaware Greenway, passing through yet another historic site: an old quarry. High, sheer cliffs of blue rock, or 570-million-year-old gneiss, tower over the trail, seemingly carved out of the ground—and indeed they have been. The trail follows the back wall of the quarry that operated here from the 1870s through 1938. Brandywine blue gneiss, Wilmington's bedrock, is royal blue when freshly broken and turns dark gray after weathering. This hard rock forms a 4-mile-long gorge through which the creek flows, dropping 120 feet and generating enormous energy—the power source for much of the Wilmington area's early industry—on its route.

Past the complex of informative signs, the Northern Delaware Greenway forks left and right. The right fork continues along the creek to Brandywine Park (site of the zoo); turn left to return to the Blue Ball Barn.

MORE INFORMATION

Restrooms are located at the Blue Ball Barn, which is open daily from 8 A.M. to 4 P.M. Delaware State Parks fees are in effect from March 1 to November 30. Trails are open from 8 A.M. to sunset. Dogs must be on a leash no more than 6 feet long. Hunting is not permitted. The trails are maintained by Delaware State Parks, with support from the Northern Delaware Trail Stewards. For more information, contact Alapocas Run State Park, 1914 West Park Drive, Wilmington, DE 19803; 302-577-1164; destateparks.com/park/alapocas-run.

11

LUMS POND STATE PARK

Walk along a level path through rich, cool, moist forests and wetlands, taking in scenic pond views throughout the hike.

DIRECTIONS

From I-95 south, take Exit 1A (Middletown) to DE 896 south. Continue 5.6 miles then take a left onto Howell School Road. The park entrance will be on your right; drive 1 mile more to reach Area 2.

From DE 1/US 13, take Exit 152 to DE 72 and turn right at the end of the off-ramp onto Wrangle Hill Road. Drive 2.1 miles and take a left onto Porter Road. After 2.2 miles, take another left onto US 301 and continue 1.2 miles then turn left again onto Howell School Road. The park entrance will be on your right; drive 1 mile more to reach Area 2. *GPS coordinates*: 39° 33.739′ N, 75° 43.256′ W.

TRAIL DESCRIPTION

A hike around Lums Pond—at 200 acres, the largest freshwater pond in Delaware—is an easy, level walk in diverse woods and wetlands, with views of the pond at many points. The route recommended here adds a loop through neighboring fields for variety.

Much of the park's 1,790 acres is wooded. The pond was created in the early 1800s, when the Chesapeake & Delaware Canal was built to connect the Delaware River and Chesapeake Bay. St. George's Creek was dammed, forming the pond, and water from the pond was used to fill the locks of the canal to the south. Today the canal has been transformed into a sea-level waterway, carrying 40 percent of all shipping traffic to and from the Port of Baltimore. The locks were removed, but the pond remains. The combination of woods and water draws a variety of wildlife, including beavers and birds. Waterfowl, such as herons

LOCATION
Bear, DE (New Castle County)

RATING
Easy to moderate

DISTANCE
7.5 miles

ELEVATION GAIN
Minimal

ESTIMATED TIME
3 hours

MAPS
USGS Saint Georges; destateparks.com/park/lums-pond/

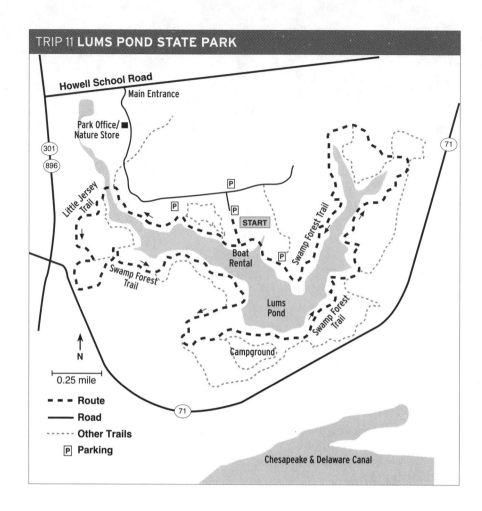

Howell School Road
Main Entrance

Park Office/■
Nature Store

301
896

71

Little Jersey Trail

P

P

P

START

Swamp Forest Trail

Boat
Rental

P

Swamp Forest
Trail

Lums
Pond

Swamp Forest
Trail

Campground

N

0.25 mile

- - - Route
—— Road
----- Other Trails
P Parking

71

71

Chesapeake & Delaware Canal

and egrets, fish along its shores, and songbirds populate the surrounding woods and fields.

The state of Delaware acquired the land around Lums Pond and established the park in 1963. There are many parking areas, picnic tables, and campgrounds, as well as a boat rental and a dog run. Two main trail systems are in place, with connectors between them: an outer loop (the blue-blazed Little Jersey Trail) and an inner shoreline loop (the yellow-blazed Swamp Forest Trail). Both trails are easy, but Swamp Forest, fittingly, can be muddy in spots, so wear either water-proof shoes or hiking boots. Ongoing projects continue to improve trail surfaces. The trails are well-maintained natural paths with good footing, although not all intersections are marked.

Begin at Parking Area 2. Head for the docks, where boats are available for rent, and find the sidewalk at the water's edge. Turn right and follow the shoreline. The sidewalk gives way to a natural-surface trail, which can get muddy. Oaks and willows shade the pond; ferns and wildflowers spread on either side of the trail; and bluebells abound here in early spring. Just past the entrance to Mile-Long Loop, cross a bridge and find your way along the gravel trail, skirting the parking lot and heading to the woods, where a trail marker indicates the yellow-blazed Swamp Forest Trail.

Swamp Forest Trail continues along the shoreline for about 0.25 mile then turns inland toward Parking Area 5. Immediately after the parking lot, Swamp Forest and Little Jersey trails intersect and cross a bridge. Once over the pond, the trails diverge. Bear right, following the blue-blazed Little Jersey Trail for a short distance. (Note that horses and bikes are permitted on Little Jersey Trail but not on Swamp Forest Trail.) Little Jersey Trail moves out of the floodplain forest of willow and sweetgum and into a successional woods (an area where young trees are colonizing a cleared area) of pine and cherry then into a grassy, open area. Turn right at the T intersection and follow the grass-lined path around a meadow and a farm field. You'll want to watch out for ticks in this edge area, especially in summer and fall. In spring and summer, look for bluebirds and flycatchers darting back and forth between woods and field.

Three-quarters of the way around the field, the trail intersects unobtrusively with the purple-blazed Swamp Forest Connector Trail off to the right, just past a gap in the split-rail fence. Follow Swamp Forest Connector Trail about 1,000 feet to Swamp Forest Trail, which enters a moist hardwood forest. Note the abundant wide leaves of skunk cabbage that indicate this as a wetland.

At each of the next two unblazed intersections, bear left, keeping the pond to your left. For 0.5 mile, the trail hugs the shore, shaded by large oaks and tulip trees. Scarred and fallen trees provide evidence of beaver activity.

The trail turns inland, joins with Little Jersey Trail for another 0.25 mile, then bears left after a footbridge. Blazes in this area may be absent. Bear left at the next two intersections. These woods are especially rich with warblers in spring and fall.

Cross a bridge over a muddy stream and turn left, following the yellow blazes; a campground is up the hill to your right. After 0.25 mile, you pass a pier on the left. These woods are acidic and full of blueberries and fragrant native azaleas, which bloom in spring. Pass the parking lot for the boat launch after another 0.3 mile then cross the ramp. Red-winged blackbirds call *conk-a-ree* in the reeds; watch for the male's bright red-and-orange epaulets. The drab female is harder to spot as she quietly goes about the business of building and provisioning the nest.

Swamp Forest Trail bends inland again into woods. Look for fresh beaver activity in the forms of chewed tree trunks with V-shaped gouges at their bases, piles of shavings, and perhaps a dome-shaped lodge at the pond's edge.

At the next three junctions with Little Jersey Connector Trail, continue to follow Swamp Forest Trail's yellow blazes. The trail climbs slightly uphill and inland. At the third junction, note the sign for the parking area. The trail becomes a flat, gravel tunnel between two narrow, claustrophobia-inducing rows of autumn olive shrubs. Fortunately, after 0.25 mile, this path ends at the parking area for the dog run and reenters the woods as a natural trail.

Look for the pink lady's slipper, a native orchid, in acidic soil near decaying wood.

This moist woods has many small streams and footbridges, as well as one very deep ravine. Look for colonies of pink lady's slipper, a native orchid with a single sack-shaped flower, which likes acidic soil and decayed wood. Savor any sighting. Each plant expends so much capital producing a flower that it may be four years before another one appears.

The trail continues close to the shoreline, passes a tiny viewing pier with split-log benches, then turns right and inland again; just over a bridge it skirts a disc golf course. In another 0.25 mile, you'll pass below Parking Area 1 and then over a large bridge. Turn left (the trail is unmarked) and follow Swamp Forest Trail for a little more than 0.1 mile to Parking Area 2, where you began. This is a great spot for an end-of-hike picnic by the pond.

MORE INFORMATION

Restrooms can be found at the park office and at the trailheads for all parking areas. Delaware State Parks fees are in effect March 1 through November 30. The perimeter trails (including Little Jersey and Swamp Forest) are closed during shotgun season, typically a week each in November, December, and January; check dnrec.delaware.gov/parks/information/pages/parkalerts.aspx for specific dates.

The trails are maintained by Delaware State Parks with support from the Friends of Lums Pond. For more information, contact Lums Pond State Park, 1068 Howell School Road, Bear, DE 19701; 302-368-6989; destateparks.com/park/lums-pond/park-office.asp.

SIGNS WITHOUT WORDS

The signs are everywhere. Some serve as labels, indicating wet ground or deer country. Others give advice, such as, "Breathe deep." These are not the numbered or lettered signs on a nature walk. These are plants. They tell you about the landscape because they thrive under specific conditions. They're called indicator plants.

Skunk cabbage, for example (which grows only in marshes, swamps, and bogs), says, "wetlands." Its enormous, thick-stemmed, bright-green leaves—each 1 to 2 feet in diameter—appear in spring, last all summer, and smell skunky when bruised. Moreover, skunk cabbage can live for a century or more, so it's really saying, "old wetlands."

Both sycamore and Atlantic white cedar indicate the presence of water. With its striking white bark, which turns mottled brown-green at the base of its trunk, the graceful sycamore stands out in a deciduous woodland. It grows in a floodplain, the area alongside a waterway that fills up during the rainy season. A line of sycamores tells you that a stream or river flows along that same line. The sycamore's seeds float downstream in spring floods, land in mud, and grow to become the next floodplain sycamore. The Atlantic white cedar grows in the Pine Barrens and on the coastal plain. Tall and straight, with a dark blue-green foliage crown and reddish shredded bark, it is an instantly recognizable tree. Cedars, too, thrive near water. A cedar line indicates a stream; a stand indicates a bog.

The white-tailed deer has become the Eastern forest's nemesis: Deer eat young plants faster than the woods can regenerate them. But plants that deer find distasteful flourish. A healthy forest would contain deer-scorned plants and many others; by contrast, a forest that has been damaged by deer is not diverse. Signs of overbrowsing by deer include wide patches of beech trees, with few other tree species present; a shrub layer of mostly spicebush, multiflora rose, or Japanese barberry; and groundcover of primarily hay-scented or New York fern.

Lichens, which arise from symbiotic fungi-algae partnerships, can say, "clean air." Certain species are sensitive to specific pollutants, such as sulfur and nitrogen. If you see many tree trunks covered with patches of scaly, leaf-like lichens, you know the air is relatively clean. In the Philadelphia area, you're more likely to see these indicators in lowlands, because air pollutants blown east are deposited on the higher-altitude mountain ridges.

12

WHITE CLAY CREEK PRESERVE AND WHITE CLAY CREEK STATE PARK

Two states, one creek: This hike begins and ends in a lovely wooded creek valley; in between, it goes up, down, and around the surrounding hills, through woods, and across meadows, providing nice hilltop views.

DIRECTIONS

To get to the Pennsylvania entrance (where no fee is charged), take US 1 South to the Toughkenamon exit. Turn left onto Newark Road, go 5 miles; turn right onto Buttonwood Road; go 0.6 miles; turn right onto Broad Run Road. After 0.5 mile continue onto London Tract Road, go 0.7 miles and turn left onto Sharpless Road. After 0.7 mile arrive at the park office on the right, where you will find ample parking in the lot. Note that a parking fee is charged in all Delaware state lots; pedestrian entry is free. *GPS coordinates:* 39° 44.813′ N, 75° 46.442′ W.

TRAIL DESCRIPTION

White Clay Creek winds through the hills of southern Chester County, Pennsylvania, and New Castle County, Delaware. It has been designated a National Wild and Scenic River for the high quality of scenery and natural resources throughout its 107-square-mile watershed. The White Clay Creek Preserve in Pennsylvania and White Clay Creek State Park in Delaware protect the main stem from encroaching development and provide access to the creek and the surrounding land. Trails on the Pennsylvania side are in the creek valley; on the Delaware side, they spiral around wooded hills and across open meadows that overlook the valley. Together, the two parks encompass more than 5,000 acres.

The hike begins on the Pennsylvania side at the main office parking lot. On foot, head south along Sharpless Road. Turn left onto South Bank Road and cross the

LOCATION
Landenberg, PA (Chester County), and Newark, DE (New Castle County)

RATING
Moderate

DISTANCE
10 miles

ELEVATION GAIN
400 feet

ESTIMATED TIME
4.5 hours

MAPS
USGS Newark West, USGS Newark East; trail maps available onsite; dcnr.pa.gov/StateParks/FindAPark/WhiteClayCreekPreserve/Pages/Maps.aspx

destateparks.com/park/white-clay-creek/maps/index.asp

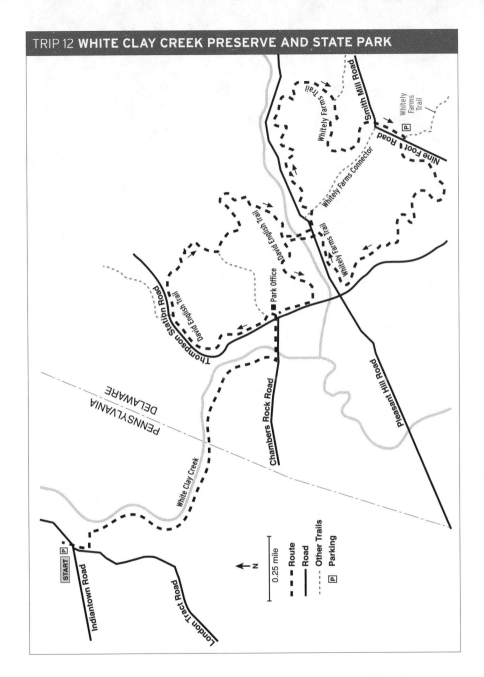

bridge, turning left again onto an old gravel road at the sign for the hiking trail. Shortly, you'll reach an intersection with the Mason-Dixon Trail and PennDel Trail. Continue straight, following the blue blazes of the Mason-Dixon Trail (M-DT). The M-DT—which, despite its name, does not follow the Mason-Dixon Line—is a long-distance trail through Delaware, Pennsylvania, and Maryland (see Trip 24).

Hikers make tracks on a snowy trail in White Clay Creek Preserve.

The flat, wide trail runs along the west bank of White Clay Creek, which is broad, clear, and swift-running at this point. The lovely surrounding woods are lush with tall old oak, beech, and sycamore trees, as well as various ferns and shrubs. Birds—notably wood warblers and forest-interior-dwelling species, such as veeries, scarlet tanagers, and pewees—are abundant along this corridor. As the M-DT rises and falls, it passes through wet patches dotted with skunk cabbage, wood nettle, and jewelweed. The trail is also lovely during winter, when the creek glistens as it snakes past snow-covered banks.

After 1 mile, the trail crosses into Delaware. Follow the M-DT as it heads left around a bridge ruins into the woods. The creek is quieter here: slow, wide, and stately.

After another 0.6 mile, you'll reach a parking lot; continue to Chambers Rock Road and turn left. (Be careful: This is an actively traveled road.) Cross the creek via a bridge and then cross active Thompson Station Road into the park office parking lot. At the far end of the lot, past a picnic table, pick up David English Trail. In the White Clay Creek State Park, look for posts at intersections identifying trail names and GPS coordinates; the trails are not marked or blazed. David English Trail is open to hikers and mountain bikers. Follow this trail, bearing left at the next fork. It is a narrow footpath through more rich woods rife with songbirds. In summer these birds sing even during the heat of the day, happy to be in such a cool, moist, shady forest.

Pass Charles Bailey Trail, continuing on David English Trail as it turns right, skirting the base of a hill and passing Boundary Line Trail. David English Trail climbs slowly, emerging from the woods intermittently to traverse meadows.

Continue past David English Cutoff Trail (which returns to the park office) to cross more meadows, these offering views of nearby ponds. Returning to the woods, the trail follows an old farm road marked by a line of Osage orange trees. These living fences were planted along boundaries by rural landowners all over the Delaware Valley due to the species' resistance to rot. You can see an old track, lined with these trees, continuing on where David English Trail turns left.

Follow David English Trail to Whitely Farms Trail Connector and turn left. This connector trail passes through bottomland forest, crosses a stream and a road, and connects to Whitely Farms Trail in about 300 feet. Turn right on Whitely Farms Trail then bear left, following it. The trail passes through shady woods as it ascends and descends, crossing many streams as it does so. (Whitely Farms Trail is open to mountain bikers.)

Continue following this trail to its intersection with the paved, multiuse Tri-Valley Trail. Follow the combined trail a short distance north to the Nine-Foot Road parking area then continue on the combined trail until Whitely Farms Trail splits off. (Just before this point is Whitely Farms Trail Cutoff, a 0.5-mile trail you can use to shorten the hike by about 1 mile, returning to the Whitely Farms Connector afterward.) Follow Whitely Farms Trail to its intersection with David English Connector; take this to David English Trail and follow it back to the Delaware park office. Backtrack from here to the Pennsylvania park office through the parking lot, across Thompson Station Road and along Chambers Rock Road, the creek, the Chambers Rock Road parking lot, back along the creek via M-DT, and the roads to the parking lot where you started.

Note: This hike can be shortened by about 3 miles if you do only one of the two Delaware trails—either by following the entire David English Trail to loop back to the office or by turning right instead of left at the initial David English trailhead and heading toward Whitely Farms Trail Connector.

MORE INFORMATION

There are restrooms outside the White Clay Creek Preserve office, in Pennsylvania, and portable toilets at the Nine-Foot Road parking area along Whitely Farms Trail. White Clay Creek Preserve is open from sunrise to sunset. White Clay Creek State Park, in Delaware, is open from 8 A.M. to sunset. Trails are maintained by the respective state parks with assistance from Friends of White Clay State Park (whiteclayfriends.org). The east end of the Mason-Dixon Line falls within in the preserve, at the Tri-State Marker. The line's theoretical intersection with Delaware's border also falls within the state park, at the Arc Corner Monument. Both points are easily reached via multiple trails, including the Mason-Dixon Trail. See Friends, park, preserve, and M-DT maps.

For more information on Pennsylvania's White Clay Creek Preserve: 404 Sharpless Road, Landenberg, PA 19350; 610-274-2900; dcnr.state.pa.us/stateparks/findapark/whiteclaycreek. For more information on Delaware's White Clay Creek State Park: 880 New London Road, Newark, DE 19711; 302-368-6900; destateparks.com/park/white-clay-creek.

EIGHT LEGS, ONE ORB

If you're the first person on the trail in the morning, a hike through the woods can be downright ticklish: You may find your face, arms, and hands covered in sticky spiderwebs. But neither you nor the spiders whose webs you're displacing are likely to find the situation laughable.

Spiders are the consummate environmental opportunists of the wildlife world, and a standard 4-foot-wide footpath is the ideal infrastructure for an orb web. An orb-weaver spider starts at the end of a branch and plays out a line of silk, letting the breeze carry the line to another branch across the trail. After strengthening this bridge, the spider draws another line and drops down from its center, making a Y-shape. The spider then secures this line at its base and creates radial lines from the center. Spiraling from the center outward, the spider connects the radials with a silken line then spirals back to the center, replacing the silken line with a stickier one.

Now it sits and waits. The linear tunnel created by a trail also serves as a highway for zooming insects. When the web vibrates, the spider rushes out to wrap the prey in silk. If the prey is a tiny, tasty fly, the spider kills it and eats it. If the prey turns out to be a hiker swatting at sticky threads, the spider spins out a quick dragline and gets out of the way, fast.

If you walk carefully, you may be able to avoid destroying webs and you might even spot the weavers. The most commonly seen Philadelphia-area woodland orb weaver is the spined micrathena. Only half an inch long, the dark brown-black spider is nonetheless visible in the center of her web (males of this species don't weave webs). What appears to be a hard, glossy backpack is actually her abdomen. Sharp black spines run along her outside, presumably protecting the spider from predators.

Spiders have been around for 380 million years, but it wasn't until about 200 million years ago, after flowering plants arose, that spiderwebs evolved from simple ground-hugging catchments to sticky orbs that fill the space between stems—space that happened to be newly populated with all kinds of pollinating insects, flying from flower to flower. And then along came people and with them, trails—all that space, all those zooming insects. Next time you take an early morning hike, you'll understand why spiders choose to share the trails with you.

13

BRANDYWINE CREEK STATE PARK

Hike through the steep, forested, blue-rock valley of Brandywine Creek and the ebullient Rocky Run.

DIRECTIONS

Take I-95 south to the I-495 south exit, just before the Pennsylvania–Delaware border. From I-495 take Exit 6 for DE 92 (Naamans Road). At the end of the off-ramp, bear right onto DE 92 west. Follow it for 4.8 miles then turn left onto US 202, heading south. After 1.6 miles, turn right onto Mount Lebanon Road and, 1.4 miles later, turn right onto Rockland Road. In 0.2 mile, bear right onto Adams Dam Road. Continue 0.5 mile to the park entrance on the right. There is ample parking at the end of the entrance road. *GPS coordinates:* 39° 48.463′ N, 75° 34.757′ W.

TRAIL DESCRIPTION

The Brandywine Creek was the source of great wealth before it became the centerpiece of a great hiking area. Prior to its acquisition by the state of Delaware in 1965, the 933-acre Brandywine Creek State Park was a dairy farm owned by a member of the du Pont family—one of the many such du Pont family sites in the Brandywine Valley that are now parks, museums, or public gardens. The origin of the family's vast fortune was E. I. du Pont's 1802 gunpowder works, a site on the Brandywine now occupied by the Hagley Museum.

Abutting Brandywine Creek State Park are 1,100 acres of First State National Historical Park, created in 2013; the acreage was acquired from land owned by Woodlawn Trustees, which still owns 900 adjacent acres. William Poole Bancroft, a prominent Delawarean whose family wealth came from cotton mills on the Brandywine, founded Woodlawn Trustees in 1901, in part to preserve

LOCATION
Wilmington, DE

RATING
Moderate

DISTANCE
8 miles

ELEVATION GAIN
275 feet

ESTIMATED TIME
3.5 hours

MAPS
USGS Wilmington North; trail map available onsite; destateparks.com/park/brandywine-creek/maps/index.asp

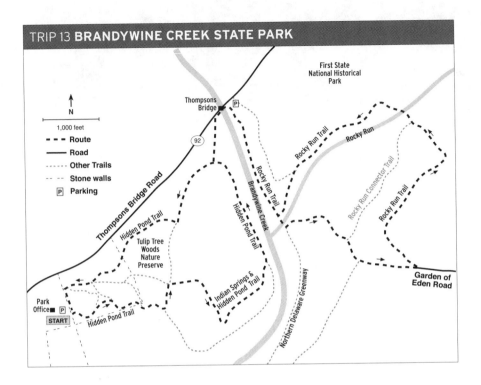

natural open space in the valley. A network of trails, with more planned, connects the three areas.

On this hike, trail intersections are clearly marked, and trails are regularly identified by blazes or posts. There are a number of side trails, but you won't be following any trail without an official marker on this hike.

Begin behind the park office, following the red-blazed Hidden Pond Trail (which coincides at times with the yellow-blazed Indian Springs Trail) into Tulip Tree Woods. This nature preserve hosts a number of enormous trees, some as old as 225 years, including tall, straight tulip trees and majestic oaks. Stone walls made of dark gray, fine-grained gneiss (locally referred to as "blue rock") snake through the woods. When this area was farmland, the walls marked boundaries between landholdings or between fields and pastures. Some of the largest and oldest trees grow along the walls and at corners. These remain today because property-marking trees, especially those mentioned on surveys, typically weren't logged when forests were cleared.

Follow Hidden Pond Trail as it descends to the Brandywine. The grade becomes steeper as you near the creek. Turning left, the trail follows the creek's banks through a moist and occasionally muddy floodplain forest. The creek is quite wide and swift here.

The trail curves left, away from the creek, and comes to a T intersection. Turn right. After about 50 feet, you'll cross a bridge over a small stream that empties into Hidden Pond. The trail climbs uphill and leaves the woods at Thompson Bridge Road (DE 92), turning right and going alongside the road. It then crosses the bridge over the Brandywine and turns right into the creekside parking area.

At the far end of the parking lot, pick up a paved, red-blazed trail that follows the creek's bank across a wide, forested floodplain. To your left are steep, blue-rock-studded hills. This is a section of the 10-mile Northern Delaware Greenway, a multiuse trail that connects Brandywine Creek, the Christina River (in downtown Wilmington), and the Delaware River. (See Trip 10.)

After about 0.4 mile, Northern Delaware Greenway crosses Rocky Run. The massive footbridge over it, completed in 2016, is designed to withstand the severe flooding that took out an older bridge, the remnants of which can be seen below. Rocky Run lives up to its name, leaping and frolicking over big rocks, cascading in falls and pools. In the park, the courses of the Brandywine Creek and Rocky Run trace boundaries between different types of bedrock, following alongside faults, or fractures where two sides of the earth's crust have shifted past each other. This has resulted in dramatic topography and numerous boulders littering the hillsides.

The blue-blazed Rocky Run Trail goes up the slope beyond the footbridge. Unofficial trails create a three-way fork; take the right fork, nearest the blue-blazed post. The trail, though wide, becomes steep and rocky. It is an old road; you'll see evidence of former human habitation, including white pines planted in lines and clumps of hostas.

The pine plantation eventually turns into beech-oak woods. Pass a T intersection marking the intersection of Rocky Run Connector Trail, to the left. Continue straight on Rocky Run Trail. At the top of the hill, you'll reach a three-way intersection marking a connector trail to the Garden of Eden Road parking area. Turn left to continue on Rocky Run Trail. Here the footpath is level and much less rocky. Marvel at the many large, old trees as you traverse a boulder-scattered woods en route to the boundary with the national park, marked by a post. Continue on Rocky Run Trail to a posted Y intersection and bear left to follow the blue-blazed trail downhill. Past the intersection with Rocky Run Connector Trail on your left, you'll shortly come to a wetland area at the bottom of the hill.

Follow the trail to Rocky Run. The trail fords the stream here. A trekking pole comes in handy to provide balance on the rocks. (If passage is not feasible, as may be the case after heavy rains, backtrack uphill and turn right onto Rocky Run Connector Trail to return to Rocky Run Trail the way you came.) After crossing, follow Rocky Run Trail up a short hill and turn left onto a level path. Enjoy the sight and sound of Rocky Run below you as the trail follows the stream through the woods, briefly emerging into an open, successional area before turning back toward the footbridge. Instead of taking the paved path, continue straight to follow the unmarked footpath that curves along the Brandywine, back toward the parking area.

Go through the parking area to Thompsons Bridge Road; turn left to cross the Brandywine. After the bridge, turn left into the woods to follow Hidden Pond

When waters are high in Brandywine Creek State Park's Rocky Run, enjoy the drama from its banks then take the alternate trail.

Trail for the remainder of the hike. The trail goes uphill, steeply at times, through the woods. You'll reach an open meadow with a Y intersection; take the right fork along the edge of the meadow and reenter the woods. Bear right at the next Y intersection as well, continuing along a small stream. The trail eventually leaves the stream; continue until you reach a stone wall dividing the woods from a meadow then turn left and follow the wall to the park office and parking area.

MORE INFORMATION

Restrooms are located at the main office; you will also find portable toilets at the DE 92 (Thompsons Bridge Road) parking area. Dogs must be on a leash no more than 6 feet long. The park is open daily from 8 A.M. to sunset. The parking fee is $4 for Delaware residents and $8 for nonresidents from March through November. Hunting is permitted in season in designated areas in the state park; there is no hunting on national park lands. The park office has a small store and a helpful staff. Other trails in the park traverse different habitat, including meadows, a freshwater marsh, and a hawk watch. Visitors to Delaware state parks can take part in the Delaware Trail Challenge, a program in which hikers receive prizes for hiking certain trails. For more information on Brandywine Creek State Park: 41 Adams Dam Road, Wilmington, DE 19807; 302-577-3534; destateparks.com/park/brandywine-creek. For more on First State National Historical Park (Beaver Valley section), visit nps.gov/frst/planyourvisit/beaver-valley.htm.

14

HIBERNIA COUNTY PARK

Hike in varied terrain: creekside, woods, lakeshore. Historical remnants along the trail reveal the park's past as an ironworks.

DIRECTIONS

Take I-76 west to Exit 328B (US 202 south), followed by US 30 west (toward Downingtown). Continue on US 30 for 13.5 miles and take the exit for Coatesville. At the end of the off-ramp, turn left onto US 82 north, toward Elverson, and take a quick left onto PA 340. (Do not follow signs for the park, which will direct you to the main entrance.) Continue on PA 340 for 1.3 miles, and turn right onto Wagontown Road. Continue to Hatfield Road, turning left followed by a quick right onto Camp Stewart Road. Continue 150 feet and turn right into the parking lot, which accommodates 40 cars. *GPS coordinates*: 40° 00.865' N, 75° 50.724' W.

TRAIL DESCRIPTION

From busy industrial site to country estate and now to peaceful natural area, Hibernia County Park encapsulates the history of many of the area's best suburban hiking spots. From 1793 to 1876, Hibernia was the site of an iron-works. A self-sustaining community, by 1850 it had two forges, two furnaces, a rolling mill, a gristmill, the iron-master's mansion, employee housing, a farm, and gardens and orchards. Many historic buildings, including the Hibernia Mansion, are still standing; others remain as ruins. Today, Hibernia County Park encompasses more than 900 acres of diverse habitat, including the West Branch of the Brandywine Creek and 90-acre Chambers Lake. The park is of particular interest to families, and this easy hike can be made shorter or longer.

LOCATION
Wagontown, PA
(Chester County)

RATING
Easy

DISTANCE
5.5 miles

ELEVATION GAIN
365 feet

ESTIMATED TIME
2.5 hours

MAPS
USGS Wagontown; trail map available onsite; chesco.org/1784/Trails

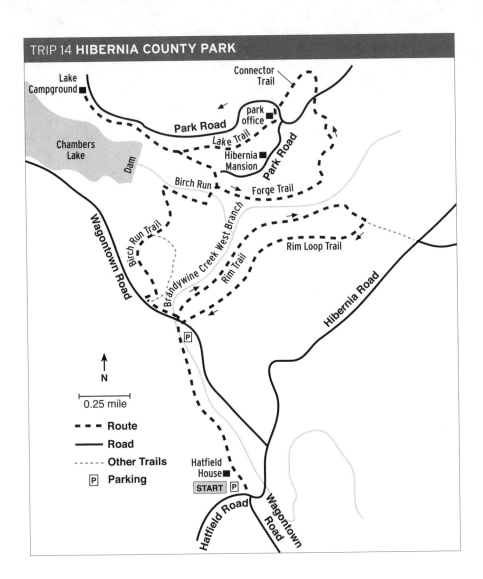

Lake
Campground

Chambers
Lake

Dam

Connector
Trail

park
office

Park Road

Lake Trail

Hibernia
Mansion

Park Road

Birch Run

Forge Trail

Birch Run Trail

Brandywine Creek West Branch

Rim Trail

Rim Loop Trail

Wagontown Road

Hibernia Road

N

0.25 mile

- - - Route
—— Road
----- Other Trails
P Parking

Hatfield
House

START P

Hatfield Road

Wagontown Road

The hike begins at the parking lot for Hatfield House, which was used as a convalescent home from 1920 until it was acquired by the county in 1980. From the house's porch, follow the steps down to the yellow gate at the road's edge. The dark blue–blazed Rim Trail, which begins here, has a stone-dust surface covering a stretch of old railbed. In the mid-1800s, trains traversed the railroad, carrying both soft and hard coal to the iron forge and transporting ice to nearby cities.

The first part of the hike follows the West Branch of Brandywine Creek. Here Rim Trail is flat and smooth, with jewelweed appearing in abundance from May through October. Growing on creek banks and moist woods, jewelweed reaches heights of 3 to 5 feet and features oval, round-toothed leaves and trumpet-shaped orange or yellow flowers that attract ruby-throated hummingbirds in summer. In fall, its seedpods jump from the plant at the slightest provocation.

Cross over Brandywine Creek on the remains of the Wilmington and Northern Railroad Bridge. In less than 25 feet, Rim Trail intersects with busy Wagontown Road. Use caution when crossing. Pass through a yellow gate and follow Rim Trail into the woods. Brandywine Creek runs to the left of the trail before it bends away. After another 0.5 mile, look for the remains of ice houses to your left. These stored harvested ice blocks waiting to be delivered to cities by railroad. Before refrigerators were invented, ice blocks were used to preserve food.

After passing the ice houses, Rim Trail ends at another yellow gate. Just before the gate, turn right at a blue diamond-shaped sign to take Rim Trail Loop. Head uphill on this natural-surface trail for 200 feet, until you reach a fork. Bear right to continue on the loop trail.

Rim Trail Loop traverses young woods of tulip and beech trees, goes up and down gentle rolling hills, and ultimately descends to Wagontown Road. Use caution, as there are many loose rocks. At Wagontown Road, turn right, proceed about 500 feet, and turn right onto Lions Head Drive (marked by two white gateposts with lion heads).

After another 400 feet, you'll come to another yellow gate, this one opposite a private residence. Turn left here onto the orange-blazed Birch Run Trail. This grassy path winds uphill along meadows of wildflowers and native grasses. It then turns sharply right into the woods and descends to Birch Run, below the Hibernia Dam. Follow the trail along Birch Run until the trail ends at a private residence. Ahead, you will see a children's fishing pond.

Turn left and follow a paved path around the pond to the post marking the yellow-blazed Forge Trail. This trail follows the West Branch of the Brandywine Creek to the Old Dam area, passing many historic structures on the way. At the Old Dam area, turn left to go up the paved road and make a quick right onto a footbridge, where the white-blazed Forest Hill Trail begins. As its name suggests, this trail ascends gradually into rocky woods. Follow the trail, bearing left at the fork. Cross Park Road. Just before the trail reaches Kaolin Road, which you can see ahead, turn sharply left into the woods to take an unnamed connector trail that goes downhill, crosses a wet area via boardwalks, and goes over Forge Run via a footbridge. The connector trail ends at the park office, which is across a field from Hibernia Mansion.

Follow the paved road around the office to a map kiosk and a post marking the purple-blazed Lake Trail; take it across the field. The gravel-surfaced trail is accessible and mostly level. Once it reenters the woods, you will see informative labels on many trees and you'll come across several wildlife observation areas. Views of Chambers Lake appear through the trees; there's an overlook just off the trail. When the footpath meets an old gravel road, bear left and follow it to Lake Campground. This is your turnaround point. (To add about 1.5 miles to

A century ago, the scenic West Branch of Brandywine Creek provided power for a thriving iron forge at Hibernia.

the hike, continue about 0.25 mile through the campground to pick up Cedar Hollow Trail, a red-blazed loop through the northern, wooded section of the park.) Start down Lake Trail, but about 500 feet past the dam overlook, turn right where Forge Trail intersects. Go steeply downhill for about 500 feet, and you'll be back at the fishing pond. Cross the bridge over Birch Run, continue down Lyons Head Drive, and return via Rim Trail to the parking area at Hatfield House.

MORE INFORMATION

There are restrooms at the park office, as well as at campgrounds and pavilions; portable toilets can be found at parking areas. Dogs are allowed but must be leashed. The park contains picnic sites, multiuse trails (for hiking, biking, horseback riding, and cross-country skiing), and campgrounds, as well as a lake and a fishing pond. Hunting is permitted in season. The park is managed by Chester County Parks and Recreation. For more information, contact Hibernia County Park, 1 Park Road, Coatesville, PA 19320; 610-383-3812; chesco.org/1743/Hibernia-Park.

15

NATURAL LANDS' STROUD PRESERVE

Walk fields, hills, and woods along the East Branch of Brandywine Creek, with views of the Chester County countryside.

DIRECTIONS

Take I-76 west to US 202 south; take the Boot Road exit and turn right at the end of the off-ramp. Continue 0.5 mile and turn left onto Phoenixville Pike; travel about 2 miles and turn right onto US 322 west. After 2.3 miles, continue through the intersection with Downingtown Pike and take a slight left onto Highland Road; travel 0.5 mile and turn right onto PA 162 west (Strasburg Road). Drive 1.1 miles and turn left onto North Creek Road immediately after the sign for Natural Lands' Stroud Preserve, which will be on your left. In 0.3 mile the entrance to the preserve will be on the right. There is parking for about 40 cars. For GPS or online directions, use the street address 454 North Creek Road, West Chester, PA 19382. *GPS coordinates:* 39° 57.166′ N, 75° 38.848′ W.

TRAIL DESCRIPTION

Chester County has retained more of its countryside than the other four suburban counties just outside Philadelphia. A landscape of rolling hills, old stone houses, meandering horse trails, and clear streams, its continued existence is due largely to preservation efforts by the county, townships, and nonprofits such as Natural Lands, whose Stroud Preserve is quintessential Chester County countryside.

Surrounding a historic farmhouse and its curtilage, or associated structures, are 571 acres with 9 miles of hiking trails. A hallmark of this area is its extensive network of horse trails. You're as likely to encounter equestrians at this preserve as you are to see other hikers.

LOCATION
West Chester, PA
(Chester County)

RATING
Moderate

DISTANCE
5.25 miles

ELEVATION GAIN
775 feet

ESTIMATED TIME
2.25 hours

MAPS
USGS Unionville; trail map available onsite; natlands.org/ stroud-preserve/

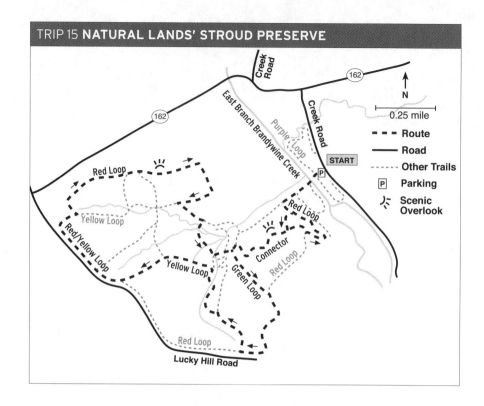

The hike begins at the trailhead kiosk at the parking area. Follow the path to the historic stone arch bridge over the East Branch of Brandywine Creek. The farm lane—still used by farm and tenant vehicles—that crosses this bridge is the central spine of the preserve. Follow it a short distance to a post on your left indicating the start of Red Loop Trail. All trail intersections are well marked and clearly blazed. The first turn, up the hill to your right, takes you onto a trail that is frequently rerouted to prevent erosion. Look for a mowed trail before you get to the woods (usually marked by a sign with a gray blaze indicating a connector trail) and wind your way up the short, steep hill. After the aerobic workout, pause to enjoy the expansive vista overlooking the farmstead below and the hills surrounding West Chester beyond. Turn right and follow the trail over the ridge, passing or resting at an inviting bench, and turning right as the trail descends the hill to the gravel lane. Turn left then left again at the post indicating the start of Green Loop Trail.

Follow this straight trail, a former farm lane, along a hedgerow on your left and a small patch of woods on your right, where you will see a number of water-collection stations dotting the banks of the wooded stream. Natural Lands' Stroud Preserve is a working farm, a wildlife habitat preserve, and a scientific study area for Stroud Water Research Center, headquartered in Chester County. Data gathered here gives researchers insights into the effect of various agricultural and land management practices on water quality.

A trek through Chester County farmland educates hikers on water research and land stewardship.

Green Loop Trail meets Red Loop Trail, and both wind to the right, up to a bench, where you can look over the farm fields below. These sloping fields are contour plowed, a water-quality management technique used to minimize soil erosion. The trail bends left and around the outside of a small, private horse farm and along white pines. Just before reaching Lucky Hill Road, it turns right at a map kiosk. At the next T intersection, follow Green Loop Trail to the right. (Red Loop Trail leads left.) The successional-edge habitat here attracts many birds during the spring and summer nesting seasons. At a marked post, follow Green Loop Trail left into the woods. This shady section, just above a hidden stream, winds downhill below a canopy of mature oaks and hickories.

Exit the woods and turn left onto the gravel lane, following it uphill, past wetlands and more farm fields. The fields are planted with hay, corn, and soy—the typical Chester County crop rotation. In planting or harvesting season, you may be fortunate enough to get a close-range view of farmers at work. Near the top of the hill, the gravel lane meets Red Loop Trail; follow Red Loop Trail as it turns right to parallel the road, goes through some woods, and skirts the edge of a field before turning right when the field ends. A bench along the trail offers a view of the hillside where it rises to meet the sky. Just past the bench, turn left to follow Red Loop Trail as it goes briefly uphill and winds into a young woods, crosses a small stream, and follows the woods' edge, climbing gently uphill. On the right, indicated by an interpretive sign, you'll see serpentine barrens: an area underlain by rock deficient in the minerals most plants need to survive. The vegetation on the barrens has adapted to these atypical conditions, and many of the plants grow only on these specific geologic formations. The rock is unusual, but there are several outcrops of it in Chester County.

Just past the barrens, Red Loop Trail crests a hill capped with another bench, offering a beautiful vista of the preserve. The meadow immediately below provides a summer home to nesting grassland birds, including the bobolink, a species whose populations are declining as its habitat disappears. During the nesting season, Red Loop Trail may be detoured along the near edge of the field, but you still may be able to spot the birds from the bench. Look for a dark bird with a prominent white crest and listen for its strange, almost electronic-sounding vocalizations.

Continue on Red Loop Trail as it goes around the edge of the field, turning right at a fence and following the red blazes alongside. Turn right again to follow the wood line until you come to a trail intersection post, at which point you'll turn left to continue on Red Loop Trail, passing a low area where many trees have been planted. On your left, wildflower meadows attract butterflies in summer. When you come to the wetlands, where a bench and interpretive sign await, turn right to leave Red Loop Trail and cross the stream via a footbridge. When you reach the gravel lane, turn left. (If you'd like to shorten the hike, you can follow the lane back to the parking lot.) Once you've passed two intersections with Green Loop Trail, take the gray-blazed connector trail up the hill to your right; you took this downhill near the beginning of the hike. Pass a bench on your left and, when the trail meets the wood line, bear slightly right to continue into the woods. You'll meet Red Loop Trail again; bear left at the intersection to follow Red Loop Trail down the hill. This beautiful wooded hillside above Brandywine Creek is awash with wildflowers in spring. In all seasons, it provides a lovely transition to the last leg of your hike, as the trail emerges from the woods to meet the gravel lane. Turn right and cross the stone bridge. Before returning to your car, consider stopping for a last, lingering look at the creek flowing ever onward below your feet.

MORE INFORMATION

There are no restrooms or portable toilets anywhere in Natural Lands' Stroud Preserve. Horses are permitted on many trails; however, bikes are prohibited. Dogs are permitted on certain trails (see online or onsite map), and must be on a leash at all times. Hunting is permitted in season; check during deer season. The preserve is owned by Natural Lands. For more information, contact Natural Lands' Stroud Preserve, 454 North Creek Road, West Chester, PA 19382; 610-353-5587; natlands.org/stroud-preserve.

16

FRENCH CREEK STATE PARK

Hike in a big woods that feels like a journey back to a time long, long ago.

DIRECTIONS

Take the Pennsylvania Turnpike (I-76) to Exit 312 for PA 100 north toward Downingtown. After 3.9 miles, turn left onto PA 401 (Conestoga Road), continue for 6.4 miles, and turn right onto PA 345 north (Bulltown Road). Stay on PA 345 north for 5.7 miles, watching carefully for signs, as PA 345 follows different roads and makes several turns. You'll pass by a sign reading, "French Creek State Park East Entrance." Turn right onto Shed Road then make the first left into the parking area. There are plenty of spots. *GPS coordinates:* 40° 13.049′ N, 75° 46.545′ W.

TRAIL DESCRIPTION

There's big, and then there's *big*. French Creek State Park anchors Hopewell Big Woods—at more than 73,000 acres, the largest forest in southeastern Pennsylvania. The surrounding woodlands are protected by both public entities and nonprofit organizations.

Once upon a time, trees covered this land as far as the eye could see: a woods so big they named a state after it. (*Sylvania* is a Latin word meaning "forest land." *Penn*, of course, refers to the state's founder, William Penn.) Hiking French Creek State Park lets you travel back in time to an era when big woods were the norm, and when people confronting those woods felt very small.

The park has two distinct sides. West of PA 345, it offers camping, boating, and other recreational activities; trails go through day-use areas near Hopewell Lake and Scotts Run Lake, connecting to the long-distance Horse-Shoe Trail. By contrast, the park's east side—the location of this

LOCATION
Elverson, PA (Berks County)

RATING
Moderate

DISTANCE
6.75 miles

ELEVATION GAIN
1,100 feet

ESTIMATED TIME
3 hours

MAPS
USGS Elverson, USGS Pottstown; trail map available onsite; dcnr .pa.gov/StateParks/ FindAPark/ FrenchCreekStatePark/ Pages/Maps.aspx

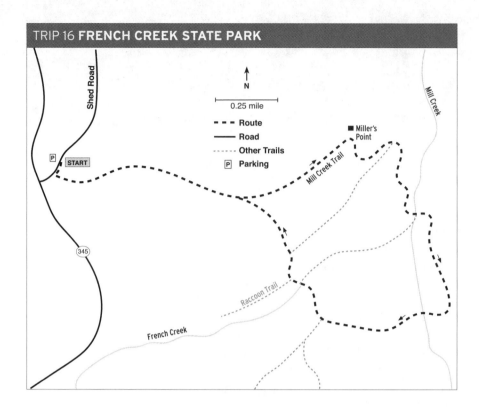

hike—comprises only woods and small streams. Here, people find a natural haven and much of the park's wildlife.

From the parking lot, cross Shed Road (watch for traffic) and go around the metal gate. Take the short connector path to reach the combined Mill Creek and Lenape trails, marked by red-and-white and green blazes, respectively. (Trail intersections are also marked by posts with numbers indicated on the park map.) Turn left and follow this wide gravel trail. After 0.35 mile, bear left at the fork to follow the red-and-white blazes of Mill Creek Trail. Do not follow the green-blazed Lenape Trail as it splits to the right.

Tall oaks, hickories, and maples surround the trail here, but you'll see occasional signs of the area's less forested history. As with most of the hardwood forests in southeastern Pennsylvania, the trees here were cleared in the nineteenth century to provide charcoal fuel for the iron industry. Since then, the woods have grown back, which is why they're referred to as second-growth forests. Bordering the trail on the right are the second-growth forests of Hopewell Furnace National Historic Site, which features a re-created iron-making village. (The entrance is a half-mile south on PA 345, and it's well worth a visit.)

After another 0.75 mile, turn left at a sign: "Miller's Point 1 mile." After the promised mile, you'll see a dark rock outcrop looming ahead. Follow the unmarked spur trail to climb the rock. (Be wary of rampant poison ivy in this

Modern-day visitors to French Creek may feel they've stepped back in time.

area, especially in warm seasons.) Miller's Point, this blocky crag of volcanic diabase, overlooks a steep escarpment. (See "Black Rock, Green Forests," page 77.) The view across the Schuylkill River Valley is somewhat obscured by the forest, but when the leaves have fallen from the trees, the sheer drop is hard to miss. This is an exclamation point punctuating the geological story line: Long ago, a sheet of molten magma burst through the layers of sedimentary rock and hardened into rock itself, called diabase. After the softer sandstone and conglomerate weathered away, the diabase lived—only to die another day, done in by water. The liquid seeped into cracks and, upon freezing, expanded and fractured the rock into the huge boulders that litter the slopes below.

Return to the main trail, turning left to follow it downhill. Descending, you'll enjoy extensive views of the valley while passing large boulders that tumbled from the ridge above. At the bottom of the hill the trail flattens out. Below a canopy of tulip, beech, and birch trees, a swath of running cedar (ground pine) provides a feathery green bottom frame.

Cross a footbridge of rocks and boards over the stream and continue across the valley. Just after the 3-mile mark, you'll rock-hop across Mill Creek. The abundant large, flat rocks in this area are the perfect place to take a lunch break and enjoy the sounds of the forest. Listen for the pileated woodpecker, a bird of mature woodlands with a raucous call and flaming red crest.

The trail continues through a field of boulders and shortly passes the turnoff to Raccoon Trail on the right. (To shorten your hike, take Raccoon Trail to its terminus with Mill Creek Trail; see below.) Bear left, continuing to follow Mill Creek Trail, and use the rocks to cross another wide stream. You'll pass through a stand of mountain laurel and, at about 3.5 miles, reach a T intersection. Turn right to continue on Mill Creek Trail. The red-and-white-blazed footpath eventually begins to climb uphill, following a wide, rocky path. Pass an unblazed shortcut path to the right. At about the 4-mile mark, the trail bends sharply right at a sign with an arrow. You'll soon meet the other end of the shortcut on your right.

Mill Creek Trail now begins to climb back uphill. For the next mile, you'll see a large number of blackened tree trunks, standing dead trees, and plenty of young tulip tree saplings and raspberry bushes. This area was the site of two recent wildfires, one in 2012 and another in 2016. Volunteers leapt into action, containing the fire by quickly digging trenches. The trail itself also served as a firebreak in spots. What remains, though, is a stunning demonstration of the natural "disturbance regime" that ruled forests before humans introduced their strange new ideas about suppressing it. Fire opens the canopy, drives away invasive plants, and generally creates ideal conditions for regenerating forests.

After about 5 miles, Buzzard Trail goes off to the left. This 3-mile loop can be used to extend your hike. About 0.25 mile later, Raccoon Trail comes in from the right. Continuing to follow the red-and-white blazes of Mill Creek Trail, you'll make your way uphill, passing the Miller's Point turnoff at about 6 miles. Continue for another mile, where you'll see the trail to the parking area on your right.

MORE INFORMATION

Restrooms are located at the park office; follow Park Road from the east entrance. Dogs must be leashed. Hunting is permitted in designated areas in season; see map. Hikers may explore other areas in Hopewell Big Woods: Hopewell Furnace National Historic Site, Natural Lands' Crow's Nest Preserve, Birdsboro Waters, Coventry Woods, Warwick County Park, and Woody's Woods. The long-distance Horse-Shoe Trail connects French Creek State Park with several nearby preserves. In 2016, the first 2 miles of the planned 12-mile Big Woods Trail opened, connecting French Creek State Park to Schuylkill River Trail (see Trips 1 and 7). For more information, contact French Creek State Park, 843 Park Rd, Elverson, PA 19520; 610-582-9680; dcnr.pa.gov/StateParks/FindAPark/FrenchCreekStatePark/Pages/default.aspx or visit hopewellbigwoods.org.

BLACK ROCK, GREEN FORESTS

A ring of cold fire stretches from Adams County all the way to Bucks County, Pennsylvania, and on into Mercer and Hunterdon counties in central New Jersey. About 200 million years ago, molten volcanic rock, or magma, spewed from volcanoes deep under the area's sedimentary shale and sandstone bedrock into cracks and crevices in the layers above. In the horizontal space between layers, it spread out like melted chocolate in a s'more; in the vertical space, it oozed up like caulk from a tube. Heat from the intrusive magma baked the surrounding rock and recrystallized it. The magma then cooled and hardened to become an igneous rock called diabase.

Because diabase is dense and hard, it resists erosion. Over time, as the softer rock around them weathered away, sheets and spikes of dark, fine-grained diabase were left standing alone, forming long ridges and rounded hills. Diabase outcrops are visible in the forested ridges of French Creek State Park (Trip 16), Green Lane Park (Trip 17), Nockamixon State Park (Trip 20), Clarence Schock Memorial Park (Trip 21), Baldpate Mountain (Trip 30), and Nolde Forest (Trip 40).

It's no coincidence that diabase is found in some of the Philadelphia region's largest and richest natural areas. Because the rock is so dense, the soil above it drains slowly, creating swampy areas unsuitable for development. Additionally, the rocky soil is not conducive to farming; as a result, many of the places where diabase is prevalent have been sparsely settled. With fewer people around, plants and wildlife have room to thrive. What's more, the diversity of wildflowers and other plants tends to be greater in areas with diabase soil than in the surrounding areas of acidic sedimentary rock.

Ridges of diabase typically have talus slopes: mountainsides covered with rock debris that are formed when water seeps into cracks at the top of the ridge, freezes, and breaks the rocks apart, sending blocks and boulders tumbling down. These large, blocky boulders look like stone steps for giants, which is why a local name for diabase in Pennsylvania is traprock, from the German *Treppen*, meaning "stairs."

Rocks were fundamental in the development of civilization. They underlie the soil in which everything grows, and they form the physical and chemical basis for the community of living things that inhabits a place. Appalachian Trail hikers encountering what seemed an endless path of fragments of sedimentary rock (quartzite, conglomerate, and sandstone) that form the Kittatinny Ridge gave it the moniker "Rocksylvania" (see AT hikes 44, 45, 46, and 49). But the less well-known igneous (volcanic) rock, diabase, underlies many of the Delaware Valley's most beautiful hiking destinations.

17

GREEN LANE PARK

Hike through a diverse landscape of woods, meadows, and deep ravines around a forested lake in upper Montgomery County.

DIRECTIONS

Take the Pennsylvania Turnpike Northeast Extension (I-476) north to Exit 31 for PA 63 (Lansdale) (31A for E-ZPass only; 31B for cash or E-ZPass). Follow PA 63 west 10.0 miles to Green Lane Borough and turn left onto PA 29. After 1.7 miles, turn right on Deep Creek Road, continue another 0.8 mile, and turn right onto Snyder Road. Stay on Snyder Road a short distance until you reach the main office parking lot, where there is ample parking. *GPS coordinates:* 40° 19.937′ N, 75° 28.987′ W.

TRAIL DESCRIPTION

Green Lane Park sneaks up on you. Just when you think it's about the water, and you're admiring the herons and egrets fishing in the shallows, the hilltop meadows astound you with their shimmering beauty. And just when you think it's about the dramatic rock-bottomed creek ravines, the reservoir surprises you with its tree-lined shores reflected in green water.

With water covering 870 of its 3,400 acres, the park, owned jointly by Montgomery County and the Philadelphia Suburban Water Company, attracts large fishing birds of prey, including ospreys and bald eagles, as well as birds that dabble along the shorelines. There are also 2,300 acres of forest—a quarter of which is interior, or deep, forest—hosting a huge diversity of bird species, both migrants and breeding birds.

About that water: Green Lane Reservoir impounds Perkiomen Creek and numerous streams within a shallow but steep valley; the smaller Deep Creek Lake and Knight

LOCATION
Green Lane, PA
(Montgomery County)

RATING
Moderate

DISTANCE
9 miles

ELEVATION GAIN
1,250 feet

ESTIMATED TIME
4 hours

MAPS
USGS Perkiomenville, USGS Sassamansville, USGS East Greenville, USGS Milford Square; trail maps available onsite; montcopa.org/871/ Green-Lane-Park

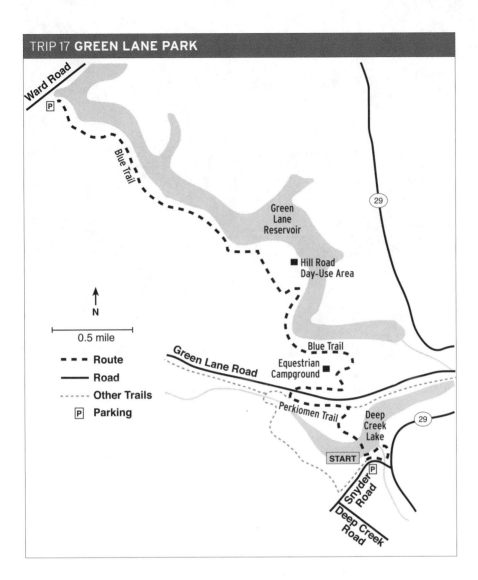

Green
Lane
Reservoir

■ Hill Road
Day-Use Area

29

↑
N

0.5 mile

- - - Route
—— Road
----- Other Trails
P Parking

Blue Trail

Green Lane Road

Blue Trail

Equestrian
Campground ■

Perkiomen Trail

Deep
Creek
Lake

29

START

P

Snyder Road

Deep Creek Road

Ward Road

P

Blue Trail

Lake are adjacent. The water is completely surrounded by parkland, much of it forested. The terrain is hilly, occasionally rocky, and features ravines and rushing creeks.

This is an out-and-back hike, so it easily can be shortened to fit your schedule. The hike begins at the parking lot for the main office on Snyder Road adjacent to Deep Creek Lake. Cross Snyder Road and bear right to take the pedestrian bridge over the Deep Creek Lake dam. (Snyder Road ends at an iron bridge over Perkiomen Creek built in 1903, below Knight Lake; the brief detour affords delightful views, if you have time.) Continue following the paved path to the parking lot and across the meadow, toward Green Lane Road. Don't cross the road; instead, bear left at the gravel path that parallels the road.

A hilltop meadow in Green Lane Park overlooks the Upper Perkiomen Creek Valley.

This is Perkiomen Trail, a 20-mile multiuse trail that begins about 1 mile east, at PA 29. It follows the course of Perkiomen Creek along an old railway, ending at Valley Forge, where the trail joins Schuylkill River Trail. That said, you're on Perkiomen Trail for only a small portion of this hike.

As you approach Deep Creek on your left, you'll see wildflowers, grasses, trees, and shrubs that have been planted to reduce erosion and pollution in this riparian, or streamside, area. Just before the bridge over Deep Creek, turn right to cross Green Lane Road at a sign that reads, "To Blue Trail." Blue Trail begins across the road. The trail is clearly marked by posts painted blue or, in the woods, blue blazes painted on trees. Blue Trail begins as a gravel trail that goes diagonally uphill to the edge of the woods; you'll have nice views of the park and hills beyond. The trail then turns left and goes up through the woods to a lovely meadow covered with grass and wildflowers overlooking the reservoir; a perfectly placed bench at the front edge of the meadow offers views south across the valley.

Follow the trail to the woods, skirting the Marino Equestrian Campground. Blue Trail, a natural footpath, is open to horses (as well as bikes), so watch your step. Shortly after entering the woods, the trail crosses Hill Road and becomes rockier as it continues into an oak-hickory forest with many ferns and wildflowers.

The trail goes up and down along the sloping hills that border Green Lane Reservoir. Through the trees, you'll catch glimpses of the reservoir to the right, and the trail winds down to the shore now and then. You'll cross occasional rocky streams. Much of the park sits atop volcanic diabase; this gray-black rock is characterized by a blocky appearance and deep fractures and crevices. (See "Black Rock, Green Forests," page 77) As Blue Trail proceeds west, the rocks shift to flatter, softer red and gray shales; stream crossings become less dramatic and more peaceful.

This thick forest is characteristic of southeastern Pennsylvania. Oak, hickory, and tulip tree dominate, with dogwood, hornbeam, witch hazel, slippery elm, and black cherry in the understory, and a proliferation of wildflowers and ferns on the ground. In the fall, you'll also notice the many sugar maples, as their leaves turn from green to orange. Rock outcrops along the way provide scenic rest stops. Swimming in the reservoir is prohibited, and very limited boating is permitted on these waters, which means human intrusion on the natural scenery is minimal. The unbroken, forested hills surrounding the reservoir are reminiscent of parts of New England.

At several points, yellow signs warn of difficult trail sections; these areas are steeper than other sections but otherwise should not faze most hikers. Occasionally, Blue Trail forks around these difficult sections; either side will return you to the main trail. The blue markings are well placed and easy to follow; a few unmarked trails intersect the marked trail, some of which are remnants of older versions of Blue Trail.

Blue Trail bends north as it enters the final stretch, ending at the Ward Road parking lot. Here the trail connects to Red Trail, which extends into the north side of the reservoir. For a longer hike, you can continue onto Red Trail, taking it to Hemlock Point Trail, Green Lane Connector Trail, and the Perkiomen Trail. Otherwise, turn around here and retrace your steps to follow Blue Trail back to the Marino Equestrian Campground and downhill to Green Lane Road, where you'll pick up the Perkiomen Trail on the other side, turn left, and cross the day-use area to the dam. From here, return to the parking area.

MORE INFORMATION

Restrooms are located at the main office parking lot. Trails are open from dawn to dusk. At press time, the maps available online and at the park office had not been updated to match revised trail alignments. Hunting is prohibited. Dogs must be on a leash no longer than 6 feet. For more information, contact Green Lane Park, 2144 Snyder Road, Green Lane, PA 18054; 215-234-4528; montcopa .org/871/Green-Lane-Park.

18

PEACE VALLEY NATURE CENTER

This hike offers a number of options for a pleasant walking tour through diverse habitats typical of rural Bucks County: fields, streams, and wooded hillsides.

DIRECTIONS

Take the Pennsylvania Turnpike (I-276) to Exit 343 for PA 611 north. Go 12.2 miles and take the exit for PA 313 (Dublin). At the end of the off-ramp, turn left onto Swamp Road, drive 2.1 miles, and turn left onto New Galena Road. In 0.7 mile, turn left onto North Chapman Road and continue another 0.3 mile until you reach the parking lot on the left. *GPS coordinates*: 40° 20.432′ N, 75° 10.285′ W.

TRAIL DESCRIPTION

When the late educator Carolyn "Corey" Jarin founded Peace Valley Nature Center in 1975, she took as its motto: "Who learns will love and not destroy the creature's life, the flower's joy." This sentiment adorns an outbuilding on the former estate of the nineteenth-century Doylestown iconoclast Henry Chapman Mercer. Like Mercer's three handcrafted tile-and-concrete buildings (now Fonthill Castle, Moravian Pottery and Tile Works, and Mercer Museum), Peace Valley began as an expression of a personal vision and became a Bucks County cultural resource. Jarin's vision was to create an outdoor living museum to teach children about nature.

Peace Valley is a Bucks County park created out of farmland as a flood control/water supply project, with the damming of North Branch Neshaminy Creek to produce the 2-mile-long Lake Galena. A paved multiuse trail circumnavigates the lake. The 750-acre nature center, with its 14 miles of trails, occupies the northeastern portion of the park. Due to its diverse habitats—some natural, some designed—it hosts a wide variety of birds.

LOCATION
New Britain, PA
(Bucks County)

RATING
Easy to moderate

DISTANCE
7 miles

ELEVATION GAIN
150 feet

ESTIMATED TIME
3 hours

MAPS
USGS Doylestown;
trail map available onsite;
peacevalleynaturecenter.org
pdf/map.pdf

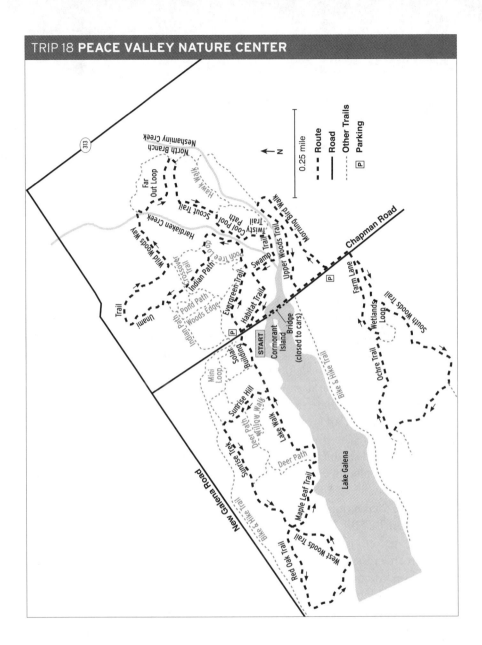

Peace Valley's trail system falls into four rough quadrants around the main parking lot. The trails are designed to accommodate busloads of schoolchildren and other large groups; visitors can start at the entrance, tour a single quadrant covering multiple habitats, and return. (Note that some trails not used for education are minimally maintained, including West Woods Trail, Red Oak Trail, South Woods Trail, and Ochre Trail.) The hike described here passes through all four quadrants but easily can be shortened or completed in a different order. Trails are inconsistently blazed, but most are marked with signs.

WHO LEARNS WILL LOVE
AND NOT DESTROY
THE CREATURES LIFE
THE FLOWERS JOY

The guiding ethic behind Peace Valley Nature Center.

Northwest quadrant (2.5 miles): Begin at the nature center's Solar Building across Chapman Road from the parking area. Lake Walk begins opposite the birdseed shop. Turn right at Sunrise Hill Trail, heading uphill. Like many of the trails, this one is a natural surface worn into the earth and is almost always wet, muddy, swampy, or puddled. The rock underlying the park (and much of Bucks County) is red shale and sandstone, which erodes to form clay, yielding slow-draining soil. Where the red rock is close to the surface, the high water table creates the wetlands, seeps, pools, and muck typically found throughout the nature center. The woods are dominated by oak, ash, and hickory trees, as well as by spicebush and arrowwood shrubs. Wildflowers, such as spring beauties, toothwort, bloodroot, and trout lilies, are common in spring in the moister parts of the woods.

At the top of the ridge, turn left. You'll find good views of the lake along this section. Sunrise Hill Trail crosses a dry streambed and enters the woods after 0.25 mile, becoming the white-blazed West Woods Trail. There are numerous small stream crossings; the trail becomes a stream as it descends, and you'll have to rock-hop. After another 0.25 mile, turn right onto the yellow-blazed Red Oak Trail, which climbs uphill gradually before bending sharply downhill.

Throughout this woods, the understory is almost entirely composed of spicebush or invasive multiflora rose, and there are few young trees. Ubiquitous deer have devoured the park's young trees and shrubs, with the exception of species they dislike. This relative paucity of understory vegetation contributes to erosion of the hillsides, exacerbating the trails' swampiness.

Follow the trail as it descends into one of these swampy areas, turns left, and then ascends again along West Woods Trail until it comes to a T intersection. Turn right onto Maple Leaf Trail, hiking downhill and meeting Lake Trail at the bottom. Turn left; the nature center office is 0.25 mile away.

Southeast quadrant (0.5 mile): From the Solar Building, continue to Chapman Road and turn right. Cross the bridge over the North Branch Neshaminy where it empties into Lake Galena, a natural place to pause and watch the ever present cormorants as they fly, dive, or just sit and dry their wings. Great blue herons fish here in the shallows; painted turtles bask on logs; and water snakes sun themselves on the rocks. Because the lake is a water supply reservoir, its level may change over the year. At times, it is drawn down enough to create mudflats, which attract great varieties of shorebirds, such as sandpipers.

Continue up Chapman Road and make a left onto Morning Bird Walk. This trail skirts the edge of a meadow, in summer a sea of goldenrod and aster. After 0.25 mile, the trail turns left into the woods and meets Upper Woods Trail. Turn left and follow Upper Woods Trail to Chapman Road.

Southwest quadrant (1.25 miles): From the intersection of Upper Woods Trail and Chapman Road, go left and uphill past the parking lot and a meadow. Turn right at the gated former farm lane and, after 50 feet, enter the woods via South Woods Trail. On this trail, you'll see several remnants of the farm buildings that were here before the park. The trail passes a springhouse, which was used to keep food cold before mechanical refrigeration. Spring water still flows through its base. This is a wetlands loop, a quiet open area with small, flowing streams that is an ideal spot for viewing dragonflies in summer.

Instead of making the loop, turn uphill onto South Woods Trail. This part of the hike follows a well-trodden, though not well-marked, trail. It ascends into a woods of mature hickories, oaks, and maples. Spring wildflowers may be found in abundance in the moist, open woods. The trail turns right after 0.25 mile, heading downhill, where it meets a field. Continue downhill along the edge of the field, and, shortly, duck into the woods when you see a trail leading off to the left (note: this trail is not on the official map). Continue downhill to a T intersection. Turn right onto the unmarked Ochre Trail, which passes old ochre, or iron oxide, pits. (Alternatively, if you prefer lake views, turn left at the T intersection to follow the unmarked trail to Limekiln Road; turn right and right again to return via the paved hiking trail/bike path back to Chapman Road.) After ascending to a hedgerow between two fields, continue via this hedgerow to Wetlands Loop and bear left onto it. As you head back through the wetlands, pass several decaying outbuildings of the former farm and a wolf tree—an oak that grew large when this was a clearing and now seems out of proportion to the surrounding young trees. Return via the farm lane to Chapman Road, turn left, and cross the bridge.

Northeast quadrant (2.75 miles): After crossing the bridge, you'll see a trail entrance to the right just before you reach the parking lot. This quadrant of the trail system is complicated but offers an enormous variety of habitats in a small area, and trail intersections are generally well marked. You'll pass through evergreen stands, deciduous woods, streams, swamps, scrub-shrub fields, and meadows. Take Evergreen Trail past small Persimmon Pond and turn right onto Pooh Tree Loop. The highlight of this trail along Hardiaken Creek is the eponymous giant hollow sycamore that begs children of all ages to stand in it. Having had your Winnie the Pooh moment, continue on to Indian Path, then to a T intersection. Go straight onto Unami Trail, which skirts a field in a 0.25-mile hairpin loop; note the deer exclusion/native planting area. Go left into the woods via Wild Woods Way. When Wild Woods Way meets Far Out Loop, bear right, then go right again onto Scout Trail. Bear right onto Cool Pool Path, left onto Twisty Trail (don't cross the stream), right onto Swamp Trail, and left onto Habitat Trail (where there is another deer exclusion/native planting area), and continue to the road. Turn right to reach the parking lot.

MORE INFORMATION

Peace Valley Nature Center's office in the Solar Building is open Tuesday through Sunday from 9 A.M. to 5 P.M. Trails are open daily from dawn to dusk. Restrooms are located at the nature center office. Dogs are not permitted except on the multiuse trail. Boots are advised for hikes here due to the consistently wet trails. The Solar Bulding offers exhibits relating to wildlife, including two spectacular murals by Taylor Oughton. In the park section of Lake Galena (not the nature center), fishing and boating but not swimming are permitted, and boats may be rented on an hourly basis. Trails are maintained by the Friends of Peace Valley Nature Center. For more information, contact Peace Valley Nature Center, 170 Chapman Road, Doylestown, PA 18901; 215-345-7860; peacevalleynaturecenter.org.

HERE TODAY, GONE TOMORROW

Spring comes to deciduous woodlands from the ground up. Even before the vernal equinox, small flowers appear on the forest floor. Hepatica, with bright blue or white blooms; spring beauties, with delicate pink-lined, white flowers; nodding yellow trout lilies; bloodroot; trailing arbutus; wild ginger; Dutchman's breeches; bluebells; toothwort: All these and dozens more have charmed woods-walkers as long as there have been woods to walk in.

These wildflowers take advantage of the sunlight that reaches through the forest canopy before tree leaves appear. Some, such as spring beauties, bloom for a month or more; others, such as bloodroot, last only a day. Spotting these spring ephemerals is one of the joys of an early spring hike. Once you get to know where they grow, you can go back to greet them every year.

The plants time their blossoming to ensure that the sun has warmed the air enough for pollinators (flies, gnats, and bees) to emerge and forage. Ephemerals also need sunlight to photosynthesize and grow, in addition to producing flowers, pollen, and seeds. They've evolved differing strategies to meet the challenge of gathering enough energy to both survive and reproduce. The grasslike leaves of spring beauties appear first, collecting energy and then fading as the blooms appear. Hepatica doesn't bother growing leaves until after its flowers wither, but its round, liver-colored leaves persist over the winter, collecting energy over a long time and storing it for spring.

Spring wildflowers bloom reliably year after year. But the timing of flowering, in general, has been advancing with climate change. If flowers continue to blossom earlier and earlier, plant-animal interactions could be affected. For example, if the timing of pollinator activity doesn't change at the same rate, insects won't be able to gather nectar; flowers won't go to seed; and the birds that rely on insects during the nesting season could find their food source depleted.

Phenology is the study of periodic biological phenomena—for example, bird migration or plant flowering—and their relation to climate. Local data can benefit phenologists, and volunteer members of the public, or citizen scientists, can help by recording their observations of flowering times. Many conservation organizations have programs to collect and analyze such data, including the Appalachian Mountain Club (outdoors.org/conservation), with the goal of understanding how climate change affects natural cycles. The National Phenology Network (usanpn.org) lists scores of additional opportunities. Whether for science or beauty, observing spring ephemerals is one of the timeless pleasures of a woodland spring.

19

RALPH STOVER STATE PARK AND TOHICKON VALLEY PARK

On this hike in the Tohickon Gorge, from the bottom to the top and back again, you can view rushing waters, rocky wooded hills, and—most marvelous of all—the spectacular High Rocks overlooks.

DIRECTIONS

Take the Pennsylvania Turnpike (I-276) to Exit 343 for PA 611 north. Follow it 17.6 miles and turn right onto Stump Road. Follow Stump Road to its end (4.3 miles) and turn left onto State Park Road. The parking lot is just ahead, at the end of the road. *GPS coordinates:* 40° 26.130' N, 75° 06.027' W.

TRAIL DESCRIPTION

Although Bucks County is known for gently rolling hills and a bucolic landscape, it is also home to one of the most dramatic and beautiful gorges in eastern Pennsylvania. Easily accessible, Tohickon Gorge in Ralph Stover State Park and Tohickon Valley Park centers on a 200-foot-tall cliff called High Rocks. Adding to the beauty is Tohickon Creek, which begins in northern Bucks County near Nockamixon State Park (Trip 20). The creek is impounded by the Lake Nockamixon dam and flows southeast out of the lake for 11.5 miles to the Delaware River at Point Pleasant. The creek's course to the river is over gray sandstone, gray argillite, and red shale. As the creek wore through the rock, it carved a meandering course amid sheer vertical cliffs.

This hike starts in Ralph Stover State Park. At the turn of the nineteenth century, the Stover family established gristmills and sawmills along Tohickon Creek. Stover-Myers Mill, just north of the state park, is the only one of these structures that has been preserved; it operated continuously

LOCATION
Point Pleasant, PA
(Bucks County)

RATING
Moderate

DISTANCE
8 miles

ELEVATION GAIN
225 feet

ESTIMATED TIME
4 hours

MAPS
USGS Lumberville; trail map for a portion of this hike available onsite; dcnr.pa.gov/StateParks/FindAPark/RalphStoverStatePark/Pages/Maps.aspx

buckscounty.org/government/parksandrecreation/parks/Tohickon

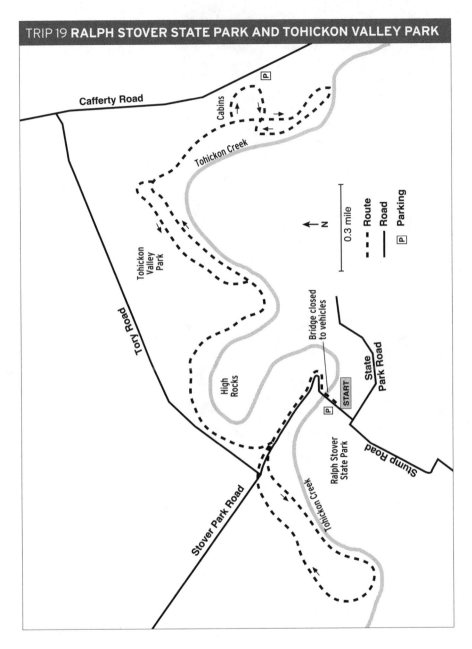

from 1800 to 1956. On the site of the state park was a gristmill, but the only remains of it now are the millrace, which channeled water from the creek to the mill, and the stub ends of a former dam. The dam was removed in 2007 to improve the habitat for aquatic wildlife in the creek.

Walk down to the creek from the parking area to see the remains of the dam. Then continue along the creek (the trail parallels the millrace on the right for

Seen from High Rocks, the Tohickon Creek winds through the gorge it continues to create.

about 1,000 feet) to a footbridge that crosses the creek. On the other side, continue up Stover Park Road (infrequently used by cars) past several private residences.

About 0.25 mile from the bridge, enter an opening in the woods on your right, marked with yellow blazes. You are now in Tohickon Valley Park. The trail travels across a finger of land that forms one of two portions of the great S-bend in the Tohickon, which sweeps southeast from Ralph Stover State Park, northwest toward High Rocks, and southeast again. (This portion of the park was donated by the author James A. Michener.)

The park and the woods are well traveled, and this trail is crisscrossed by bike trails and "social trails," or paths cut into the brush by visitors for whom the official routes are apparently inadequate. Proceed straight over a dry stream crossing, continuing about 1,500 feet until you reach a series of fenced overlooks named Argillite, Balcony, and Cedar.

No written description, or even a photograph, can do justice to the magnificent views of the gorge from the 200-foot-tall High Rocks. There is something about the combination of the sheerness of the drop, the red rock cliffs, and the sinuous curve of the creek that sets off this vista as one of the wonders of the Delaware Valley.

Eventually you must move on, so continue along the trail as it parallels the cliffs. Again, there are many crisscrossing trails. The one you want to follow has white blazes with a red dot; these are old county blazes that are not well maintained. The yellow-blazed trail is above you and eventually intersects with the white-and-red-blazed trail. Bear right at the Y intersection and all subsequent Y intersections you encounter on this hike.

The woods become more rugged (chestnut oak, beech, hickory, hemlock, ash, and cinnamon fern), and rocks jut out above you. The narrow, rocky trail crosses several even rockier streams that plunge down the hills; these streams may become impassable after rainstorms. After about 1.5 miles, bear right at a Y intersection where the white-and-red trail goes uphill to the left. This lower trail comes out close to a paved road, bends right, and continues descending along the side of the hill for another 0.25 mile before darting behind a cabin to meet a paved road. Follow the road down to the right and you'll encounter Tohickon Creek as it emerges from the gorge. You may want to rest on the flat rocks listening to the rushing water as you watch it flow. Now return to the road and follow it all the way uphill until you reach an opening in the tree line with a sign reading, "Trail," opposite the main parking lot. Enter here; when you reach the second clearing, follow the tree line around to the left, to another "Trail" sign. (There is a sign directly across the clearing for a different trail.)

From here, follow the white-and-red trail all the way back to High Rocks. where you'll pick up the yellow trail and follow it to Stover Park Road, retracing your steps along a portion of the hike. Cross to the other side of the paved but lightly traveled road and turn right. After 200 feet, take the unmarked trail on your left heading down the hill. This trail, on county property, heads gradually downhill through pleasant woods and meets the creek after about 1,500 feet. Follow the trail another 1,500 feet along the creek; this quiet, flat portion with steep cliffs opposite contrasts with the earlier dramatic, creekside experience.

The trail then heads steeply uphill to a stone wall. Follow the wall to the right; the trail then goes along a meadow and returns to the woods, proceeds along the ridge, and reenters Stover Park Road. Turn right to follow the road downhill, crossing the bridge and returning via the millrace path to the parking lot.

MORE INFORMATION

The state park office is open when a park ranger is available. Restrooms are located at the trailhead. Trails are open daily from sunrise to sunset. As in other Pennsylvania state parks, pets must be on a leash. Rock climbers use the cliffs. The High Rocks vistas are fenced for safety, but they are extremely dangerous; children must be supervised. Twice a year, usually at the end of March and the end of October/beginning of November, the state park releases the Tohickon Dam at Nockamixon State Park, creating whitewater conditions in the gorge; spectators gather on the banks of the Tohickon to watch kayakers hurtle down the creek. Stover-Myers Mill is now a Bucks County-owned historic site open for public tours. For more information, contact Ralph Stover State Park, c/o Delaware Canal State Park, Upper Black Eddy, PA 18972; 610-982-5560; dcnr.state.pa.us/stateparks/findapark/ralphstover.

20

NOCKAMIXON STATE PARK

Enjoy an ever changing perspective along Lake Nockamixon's wooded shoreline.

DIRECTIONS

Take PA 611 north to Ottsville and turn left onto South Park Road, just past the post office. After 0.3 mile, turn right onto Fink Drive and drive 1 mile until you reach Tower Road. There is a large, unpaved parking lot to the left with plenty of spots. *GPS coordinates:* 40° 29.011′ N, 75° 11.009′ W.

TRAIL DESCRIPTION

Although it was formed by humans, Lake Nockamixon feels natural. Located at the base of Haycock Mountain in Bucks County, this sky-filled expanse of forest-hugged water looks as though it belongs here. The lake is a 5-mile-long impoundment of several streams, primarily Three Mile Run, Haycock Run, and Tohickon Creek (see Trip 19). Once upon a time, the valley below Haycock Mountain—the tallest mountain wholly within Bucks County—was chock-full of small dams that enabled water-powered mills to flourish. Nowadays, the lake, which was created for flood control in the early 1970s, serves as a recreational destination for boaters, anglers, equestrians, bikers, hikers, and general relaxers.

Nockamixon State Park and the adjacent state game lands contain lots of hiking trails. Many of the them, however, are relatively short, and the longer trails are not consistently well-maintained. The hike described here uses a very popular network of trails on the east side of the lake in fine shape. These trails were designed by and for mountain bikers but are open to all. This is an enjoyable hike, the only caveat being that, on nice weekends, you will regularly dodge bikers.

LOCATION

Quakertown, PA
(Bucks County)

RATING

Moderate

DISTANCE

6 miles

ELEVATION GAIN

450 feet

ESTIMATED TIME

3 hours

MAPS

USGS Bedminster, USGS Quakertown; dcnr.pa.gov/StateParks/FindAPark/NockamixonStatePark/Pages/Maps.aspx

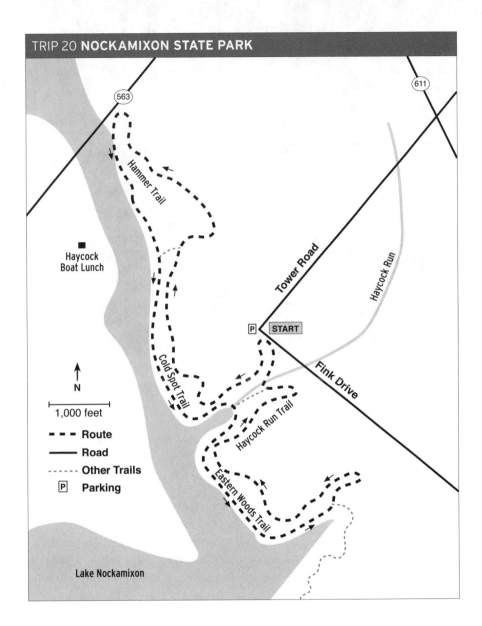

Haycock
Boat Lunch

Tower Road

Fink Drive

Haycock Run

Hammer Trail

Cold Spot Trail

Haycock Run Trail

Eastern Woods Trail

START

Lake Nockamixon

N

1,000 feet

- - - Route
——— Road
----- Other Trails
P Parking

The hike uses a series of loops along the lake: Cold Spot and Hammer trails to the north, and Haycock Run and Eastern Woods trails to the south. To shorten the hike, you can omit one or more of the outer loops. The trails are well marked at intersections; the paths themselves are not blazed but are easy to follow.

Begin the hike at the trailhead kiosk. Walk east on the trail, parallel to Fink Road and heading slightly downhill into the woods. At the post indicating "Cold Spot," bear right at the Y intersection, through a stand of cedar. The lake appears through the trees as the trail winds into oak woods. Haycock Mountain is visible

Designed for mountain bikers who flock on weekends, these trails are quieter for weekday hikes.

to the left. As the trail bends back and forth, the lake disappears and reappears. At about 1 mile, you'll pass a directional post for Tower Road. Continue straight toward Cold Spot. After another 0.1 mile, turn right at a two-way directional post for Hammer Trail, moving away from the lake and into an oak-hickory woods. There are a few moguls for cyclists, but the trail is otherwise flat and rock-free. Light and shadow play tag on the level expanse of open woods.

The peaceful mood shifts markedly after another 0.5 mile. Here, a 0.3-mile-long series of engineered obstacles designed for bikers—including a balance beam, a bump, and a bridge, all made from logs—also makes the trail interesting for those on foot. The trail shortly bends through two stone architectural features then turns back to the lake in advance of the PA 563 trailhead. Turn left at a signpost here to continue on Hammer Trail.

The trail heads south along the lakeshore. After about 0.3 mile, across from the Haycock Boat Launch, a very short path leads down to the shoreline and a nice place to sit and enjoy a view of the lake. Return to the trail, which continues along the lakeshore. At the next intersection, continue straight along the lakeshore to proceed on Cold Spot Trail; the trail is mostly level, with a few brief ups and downs. The trail heads left to follow the banks of Haycock Run where it enters the lake, then crosses the stream; bear right at the Y to follow the shore-line. At a two-way directional post, turn right onto Haycock Run Trail to head toward the lake.

After approximately 0.25 mile, turn right onto Eastern Woods Trail at a sign and follow the trail along the lake. Pass through a stand of cedar and cherry. Eventually the lake will disappear, leaving you in the thick of the woods. At a post indicating Eastern Woods to the left and Jay Walk to the right, make a left. This is a young woods, out of sight of the lake. Without those lake views, trail designers decided to add interesting elements, and here you'll encounter 0.25 mile of engineered features, including log corduroys for texture.

After passing through an area of scrubby woods, you'll again come into view of the lake, on the left. At the two-way directional post for Haycock Run Trail turn right. The trail follows Haycock Run, on your left. Here again are more engineered trail features, including a serpentine, a series of moguls, and a steep-banked curve. This section of woods also features a beautiful display of wild-flowers year-round, providing some natural interest to complement the engi-neered elements.

Briefly pass through a cedar stand then into an oak-beech-hickory woods. At a Y intersection with a post, make a sharp right onto Cold Spot Trail to cross the stream. You'll soon come to a T intersection with a directional post pointing toward Tower Road lot. Turn right and follow this path to return to the parking area.

MORE INFORMATION

There is a portable toilet at the parking area. The closest restroom is at the Hay-cock Boat Launch. The park is open from sunrise to sunset. All dogs must be leashed. Boating is permitted on Lake Nockamixon, and boats are available for rent. Cabins and camping facilities are also available. The trails are maintained by Valley Mountain Bikers for Friends of Nockamixon State Park (ridenox .com); visit this website for trail maps and condition updates. For more informa-tion on the state park, including other trails, visit dcnr.state.pa.us/stateparks/parks/nockamixon.aspx.

21

CLARENCE SCHOCK MEMORIAL PARK AT GOVERNOR DICK ENVIRONMENTAL CENTE

Clarence Schock Memorial Park is one of the largest woods in southeastern Pennsylvania. This forested loop hike leads to an observation tower with a 360-degree view.

DIRECTIONS

Take the Pennsylvania Turnpike (I-76) west to Exit 266. Merge onto Lebanon Road/Route 72 South toward Lancaster for 1.4 miles. Turn right onto Cider Press Road; go 0.4 mile and turn right onto Pinch Road. The entrance to the park's environmental education center is on the right after 1.7 miles. The parking lot accommodates twenty cars. *GPS coordinates:* 40° 14.223′ N, 76° 27.640′ W.

TRAIL DESCRIPTION

The 1,105-acre Clarence Schock Memorial Park is one of the largest contiguous woodlands in southeastern Pennsylvania. Due to their size and lack of fragmentation, the woods are an important habitat for a wide variety of wildlife, including resident amphibians and migrating songbirds. These are second-growth woods that grew up in the twentieth century, after the hills were logged to provide charcoal for iron forges, particularly the Cornwall Iron Furnace. Flattened, circular areas of blackened soil ("charcoal circles") are visible artifacts of this historically important industry.

The wooded hill on which the park is located is named for "Governor" Dick, a former slave who gained renown among locals as a woodsman and collier, or charcoal maker, in the late 1700s. Clarence Schock, an industrialist and philanthropist, acquired the tract in 1934. Schock had a passion for building towers, which he indulged on this site. His wooden towers have since been dismantled, but a concrete observation tower attracts crowds on nice days.

LOCATION
Mount Gretna, PA
(Lebanon County)

RATING
Moderate

DISTANCE
7 miles

ELEVATION GAIN
400 feet

ESTIMATED TIME
3.25 hours

MAPS
USGS Manheim; park maps available onsite; parkatgovernordick.org

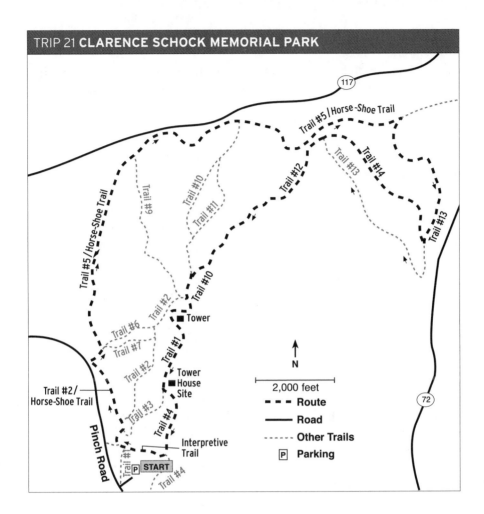

In 1953, Schock deeded the land in perpetuity to a local school district. Most of the park, managed by a co-trusteeship of the Clarence Schock Foundation and Lebanon County, feels like a quiet, remote wilderness.

From the parking lot, head west away from the environmental center and toward the trailhead marked by a sign reading, "To the Tower." (This hike takes a roundabout route to the tower.) Most trails in the park are numbered and blazed with distinct colors and shapes; there are also markers at intersections. The rocky soil is wet in places; bikes and horses that use the trails can create some muddy patches along the way, but the paths are easily traversed for the most part.

Turn left at the next T intersection, marked, "To 1." Then turn right onto a footpath with yellow rectangular blazes, indicating that this section of the park's trail system coincides with the long-distance Horse-Shoe Trail (H-ST). You'll follow the easy-to-spot H-ST blazes for the next 2.7 miles. Turn right onto Trail 1, a crushed-stone fire road; at the intersection with Trails 2 and 3, turn left onto Trail 3.

Here and in several other locations along the hike, you'll pass large, fenced-in sections of forest. These are reforestation areas. Park staff and volunteers have planted thousands of tree seedlings with the aim of improving forest diversity and regeneration. These so-called exclosure fences prevent deer from eating or damaging the young trees. (See "Bambi, Keep Out," page 100).

Follow the H-ST as it bears right, away from the road, at a parking area, after 0.6 mile. Oak, birch, white pine, and tulip trees predominate here, with an understory including hophornbeam, dogwood, and redbud. The trail merges with Trail 5 (white rectangles), a rocky, narrow footpath; this trail becomes a gravel road that passes through a residential area before turning back into the forest onto an old woods road. These deep woods are quiet, save for the music of wind and birdsong.

Continue on Trail 5/H-ST past Trail 9. The trail bears right at a yellow gate, away from PA 117, and follows a narrow, rocky footpath uphill, leveling off at the remnants of a charcoal circle. Pass another parking area and an intersection with Trail 10. Trail 5/H-ST becomes a woods road. Go through an area scattered with many large boulders. Governor Dick Hill is a diabase ridge (see "Black Rock, Green Forests," page 77); the rocks have broken off and toppled from above.

Pass the connector trail to Trails 12, 13, and 14. Take in a brief view of the hills through an opening in a residential area before the forest closes in again. At about 3 miles from the beginning of the hike, leave Trail 5/H-ST and turn right onto Trail 13, a narrow footpath marked by green diamonds. Pass Trail 14A on the right and, after another 0.25 mile, pass an access trail to old PA 72 and Trail 14 on the left. Road noise from new PA 72 briefly intrudes, and the trail bends away. This area has many boulders; above are the high, dramatic outcrops from which the rocks fell. It is so quiet you can almost hear the rocks slowly fissuring at their geologic pace.

Turn right at a T intersection onto Trail 14, which heads steeply uphill. Pass Trail 14A on the right. Follow Trail 14 up and over the ridge then back down the

The park is home to one of the largest areas of contiguous woodlands in southeastern Pennsylvania.

hill. At a T intersection, continue straight onto Trail 13; not long after, you'll turn left at the intersection with Trail 12 (blue diamonds). This often muddy trail runs through the saddle between two steep hills and includes several boardwalks. Pass through an extensive patch of pawpaws, a large-leaved understory tree occasionally found in moist, rich woods.

At an unmarked T intersection, turn right, continuing on Trail 12. At the T intersection with Trail 10 (marked with red-and-white rectangles), turn left. As the trail (once a road to a now-defunct radar installation) crests the hill, you will see the observation tower. After another 0.1 mile, turn left onto Trail 2 then pass Trail 8 before reaching the tower at the summit of the 1,148-foot-high ridge. The 66-foot-high, 15-foot-wide tower was built in 1954. A series of ladders leads to a circular platform, from which you can see the park's extensive, contiguous woodlands and, on a clear day, Lebanon, Dauphin, York, Lancaster, and Berks counties. (If you're averse to confined spaces, don't plan on climbing the tower.)

Continue around the tower, picking up Trail 1 (a wide gravel road) at the edge of the clearing. Turn left onto the red-diamond-blazed Trail 4, passing the foundations of the wooden Schock "Tower House" on the left. The trail winds steeply downhill through numerous boulders. Continue until you reach a turnoff on the right marked, "Interpretive Trail." (This is a loop trail; brochures available at the education center.) Take this trail, then bear left at the first Y intersection and follow the trail back to the environmental center, where you started.

Around the environmental center, trails meander through meadows planted with wildflowers. In summer, these attract butterflies, bees, moths, bee flies, and hummingbirds; in spring and fall, look for American goldfinches, common yellowthroats, sparrows, and other birds of open fields.

MORE INFORMATION

Trail maps and a portable toilet are located outside the environmental center. Trails are open dawn to dusk. Trails may occasionally be open until 9 P.M. in winter; check the website. The environmental center is open April through November, Wednesday through Saturday from 10 A.M. to 4 P.M. and Sunday from 1 to 5 P.M. In March, the center is open Saturdays from 10 A.M. to 4 P.M. and Sundays from 1 to 5 P.M. Hours change for special events. Bicycles and horses are allowed on multiuse trails. Dogs are allowed but must be leashed. For more information, contact Clarence Schock Memorial Park at Governor Dick, 3283 Pinch Road, Mount Gretna, PA 17064; 717-964-3808; parkatgovernordick.org.

BAMBI, KEEP OUT!

The white-tailed deer is both an emblem of the woods and a threat to it. This gentle, graceful animal—a vegetarian whose only crime is eating twigs—inspires enmity from Delaware Valley conservationists.

A century ago, deer had virtually disappeared from Pennsylvania, New Jersey, and Delaware. Unregulated hunting had devastated the population, and forest clearing had eliminated their habitat. Game managers in Pennsylvania and New Jersey worked to reintroduce deer, to establish management regimes, and to support restoration and protection of deer habitats.

The results of those good intentions have been either successful or disastrous, depending on one's perspective. Deer populations have rebounded to historical levels—and beyond. Today it is not deer but forests that are disappearing, as they are eaten to death. If left unchecked, deer will eat nearly all of the plants they can get. Unfortunately, humans eradicated deer's natural predators—wolves and mountain lions—long ago; the only animals that regularly kill deer nowadays are people.

As development has spread into deer-inhabited woods, deer have begun feasting on suburban gardens and landscaping. This extra food supports a higher population than could subsist on forest vegetation alone. In urban and suburban areas, hunting is limited or prohibited. As a result, deer population density in certain areas has increased far beyond the forest's capacity to regenerate. There are an average of 30 deer per square mile in Pennsylvania, compared with an estimated 8 to 10 per square mile prior to European settlement. Deer eat seedlings faster than trees, shrubs, and wildflowers can regnerate. Deer dislike multiflora rose, beech trees, spicebush, honeysuckle, and most ferns; in some woods, these are now the only plants that remain.

The contrast between a deer-browsed woods and a healthy forest is startling. A good rule of thumb is that a healthy forest is one you can't see through. At summer's height, a green curtain extends from the canopy to the floor: mature trees, young trees, shrubs, wildflowers, ground cover. A deer-browsed woods has no young trees, a sparse or absent shrub layer, bare ground, and an overall open look.

If left alone, deer-ravaged forests will die. Mature trees will expire, with no young ones to replace them. Wildlife that depends on the woods will die off too. As the acreage of healthy forests in Pennsylvania and New Jersey has decreased, so, too, has the number of forest birds in the region.

There are no easy answers. Managed hunting can't address the influx from surrounding areas. Deer exclosures, or fenced-in sites, support forest regeneration but are impractical for large areas. In the end, something has to give. Whether it is the deer, the forest, or our expectation of what a forest is, only time will tell.

22

MONEY ROCKS COUNTY PARK

This multiloop hike includes an overlook of Lancaster County farmland, impressive rock outcrops, and the wooded hills of the Welsh Mountains.

DIRECTIONS

From the Pennsylvania Turnpike (I-76), take Exit 298 for I-176 and PA 10. Take PA 10 south 0.9 mile to PA 23. Turn right and take PA 23 west 7.8 miles to PA 897 (Springville Road). Turn left and go south 0.6 mile until you reach US 322. Turn left to take US 322 for 2.9 miles then turn right onto Narvon Road. In 1.2 miles, you'll reach the park entrance on the right, across from Alexander Drive. The parking lot accommodates twenty cars. *GPS coordinates: 40° 05.734′ N, 75° 58.906′ W.*

TRAIL DESCRIPTION

The name Money Rocks comes from a local legend, in which Pequea Valley farmers supposedly hid cash among the boulders during the Civil War. You may not find any money cached around the dramatically situated rocks, but you will discover plenty of green: Lichens, mosses, and ferns abound here. So, too, does the evergreen mountain laurel.

From the parking lot facing Narvon Road, you'll see a kiosk to your left, where Overlook Trail enters the woods. Pass to the left of the kiosk and follow Overlook Trail. The park trails are well marked; this one has white blazes and a rocky, natural surface. At an intersection with Cockscomb Trail, step over a wooden beam and continue straight on Overlook Trail for 0.2 mile. Here the trail comes to a T intersection marked with white double blazes indicating a turn; go left.

LOCATION
Narvon, PA
(Lancaster County)

RATING
Easy to moderate

DISTANCE
3 miles

ELEVATION GAIN
275 feet

ESTIMATED TIME
1.5 hours

MAPS
USGS Honey Brook;
co.lancaster.pa.us/
DocumentCenter/View/514

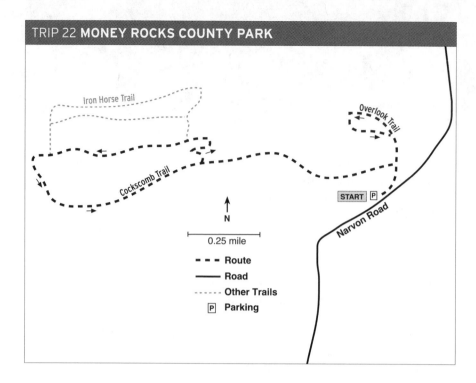

In less than 15 feet, you'll come to the beginning of the Overlook Trail loop. Turn right, following the white blazes downhill; you'll begin to see rock outcroppings to the left of the trail. At the bottom of the hill, you'll see the Narvon Clay Mine below the trail and the base of the impressively high rock outcrops above and to the left. Keep an eye out along the trail for skolithos, or long straight tubes up to 12 inches long. These are the fossilized burrows of ancient worms that lived on a sand beach; over time, the sand recrystallized into quartzite, trapping the fossils within. To reach the top of these rock outcrops, continue on the white-blazed trail as it follows the hillside's outer perimeter. "No Trespassing" signs indicate the park's boundary with the Narvon Clay Mine. About 150 feet after these signs, Overlook Trail turns left and heads toward the outcrops over three steps. The trail then turns right, over a wooden beam, and continues uphill 30 feet over a series of six wooden steps. Mountain laurel, Pennsylvania's state flower, is abundant as an understory plant; its pink-and-white flowers bloom in late May and June. After the sixth step, the trail turns left to go over the highlight of the park, Money Rocks. The 1,000-foot-high rocks afford views of Lancaster County's farmland, towns, and distant wooded hills. The dominant tree species growing on and among the rocks is black birch.

Carefully climb across the top of the rocky spine. Scrambling is not required, but balance and patience are. Be on the lookout for graffiti reportedly dating from the 1860s. Immediately after passing a black metal railing at the end of the

Despite local legend, the prominent spine of boulders in Money Rocks Park does not hide any cash, but the park is rich in natural beauty for the hiker to discover.

outcrop, bear right. Descend 150 feet to the beginning of Overlook Trail loop. After 15 feet, turn right and head downhill to the red-blazed Cockscomb Trail.

Turn right onto the wide, rocky Cockscomb Trail, which leads into the remainder of the park's 300 acres of woods. After 0.5 mile, you'll come to a four-way intersection with a wooden beam. Turn right to stay on Cockscomb Trail and continue to follow the red blazes. In 0.15 mile more, Cockscomb Trail intersects with another trail to the right; continue straight to stay on Cockscomb Trail. On your left for the next 200 feet are the spiky rock outcrops from which Cockscomb Trail gets its name. About 0.3 mile from the wooden beam intersection, look closely on the right for double red blazes and an obscure opening. Turn right at the double red blazes and follow the rocky trail downhill. This is the beginning of Cockscomb Trail loop. (Should you miss this turn, no worries; simply follow the loop in reverse.)

Follow the red blazes downhill, taking care to avoid loose rocks. After approximately 30 feet, Cockscomb Trail turns to the left, indicated by double red blazes. Continue winding downhill, passing a large hole to the right. This is a test pit, which former owners used to explore for clay. The trail bottoms out at a T intersection; turn left at this old woods road. The trail becomes flat and wide but remains rocky. An old wellhead by the trail provides another artifact of clay mine exploration. At 0.5 mile from the T intersection, you'll see a large tree with double red blazes in the middle of the trail. Bear to the left of the tree and continue for 50 feet, crossing a small stream. Turn left and climb slightly uphill.

Turn left again at the double red blazes. Shortly thereafter, you'll cross a stream before heading 20 feet uphill. Turn left at the double red blazes then right almost immediately to begin a steep uphill climb via a series of wooden beam steps.

At the top of the hill, Cockscomb Trail turns left then continues straight, at which point you've reached the beginning of the loop. Backtrack, following the red blazes to the four-way intersection with the wooden beam. Turn left and continue 0.5 mile to the intersection with the white-blazed Overlook Trail. Turn right onto Overlook Trail to return to the parking lot.

MORE INFORMATION

Money Rocks County Park features 3.5 miles of scenic multiuse trails for hiking, mountain biking, horseback riding, and cross-country skiing. Dogs are permitted but must be leashed. Hunting is permitted in many parts of the park in season. Trails are open from sunrise to sunset. The park is managed by the Lancaster County Department of Parks and Recreation. For more information, contact Money Rocks County Park, 936 Narvon Road, Narvon, PA 17555; 717-299-8000; co.lancaster.pa.us/288/Money-Rocks-County-Park.

23

KELLY'S RUN-PINNACLE OVERLOOK PRESERVE

On this challenging but extremely rewarding hike, you'll explore a rugged, wild gorge sheltered by cascading rhododendrons and an old-growth forest, and take in sweeping views of the lower Susquehanna River.

DIRECTIONS

Take US 1 south to PA 472 north, toward Quarryville. In 12.1 miles, turn left onto PA 372. Continue another 9.3 miles and turn right onto Hilldale Road. Take the first left onto Old Holtwood Road; in 0.7 mile, bear right onto Street Road. The parking lot for Holtwood Recreation Area will be just ahead on your right, where you will find ample parking. *GPS coordinates:* 39° 50.438′ N, 76° 18.991′ W.

TRAIL DESCRIPTION

One of the region's most beautiful and challenging day hikes explores the Kelly's Run–Pinnacle Overlook Preserve along the lower Susquehanna River. This scenic trek combines the sublime beauty of a deep ravine with the serenity of a high riverside promontory. Flowing water here encounters resistant rock, creating tumbling waterfalls, sheer cliffs, and sculpted landforms. The natural areas surrounding Kelly's Run comprise a lush valley of wildflowers, mosses, ferns, and cliff-hugging trees and shrubs that harbor abundant wildlife.

Kelly's Run and Pinnacle Overlook Preserve, owned by the Lancaster County Conservancy, together make up most of the former Holtwood Preserve, onetime property of the utility that operates the hydroelectric Holtwood Dam on the Susquehanna River. Lake Aldred is the stretch of the Susquehanna impounded by the dam.

On this hike, trekking poles are advisable—and almost essential—for traversing the slippery rocks along the

LOCATION
Holtwood, PA
(Lancaster County)

RATING
Difficult

DISTANCE
7 miles

ELEVATION GAIN
1,200 feet

ESTIMATED TIME
3.5 hours

MAPS
USGS Holtwood;
lancasterconservancy.org/
wp-content/uploads/2013/07/
Kellys-Run-Pinnacle-1.pdf

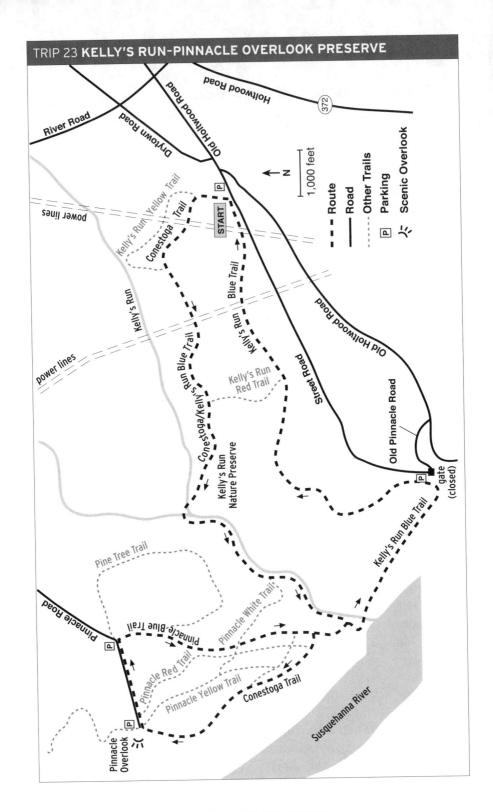

Holtwood Road

River Road

Drytown Road

Old Holtwood Road

372

1,000 feet

N

Route
Road
Other Trails
P Parking
Scenic Overlook

power lines

Kelly's Run Yellow Trail

Conestoga Trail

P

START

Kelly's Run Blue Trail

power lines

Kelly's Run

Conestoga/Kelly's Run Blue Trail

Kelly's Run Red Trail

Kelly's Run Nature Preserve

Street Road

Old Holtwood Road

Old Pinnacle Road

P gate (closed)

Kelly's Run Blue Trail

Pine Tree Trail

Pinnacle Road

P

Pinnacle Blue Trail

Pinnacle Red Trail

Pinnacle White Trail

Pinnacle Yellow Trail

Conestoga Trail

Susquehanna River

P

Pinnacle Overlook

stream, as well as for crossing the stream itself. Begin the hike by taking the orange-blazed Conestoga Trail from the parking lot. The Conestoga Trail runs north–south through Lancaster County for 63 miles, from the Horse-Shoe Trail to the Mason-Dixon Trail in York County (see Trip 24).

Continue a short distance to the woods' edge, behind the comfort station. The preserve trails are identified by painted blazes on trees; with few exceptions, intersections are clearly marked. Enter the woods and turn left at the first T intersection. The trail now follows orange and blue blazes: the Conestoga Trail and Kelly's Run Blue Trail, respectively. You'll enter a moist bottomland woods of yellow birch and silver maple, shortly finding yourself in an extensive pawpaw patch. This large-leafed understory tree bears fragrant purple flowers and green fruit directly from its branches. The fruit, which tastes similar to a combination of banana and mango, is ripe when it falls off the tree, usually in early autumn. Until then, it is mouth-puckeringly tart.

In 0.29 miles from the trail merge, you'll go under a power line and pass Kelly's Run Yellow Trail on the right. Continue under another power line. Here the vast woods host a great many species of forest-interior birds, and a sprinkling of rhododendrons provides a foretaste of the splendor to come in the gorge. The trail passes Kelly's Run Red Trail to the left, turns right, and heads downhill via steep, slippery, rocky footing beneath a canopy of rhododendrons. After about 1 mile, you'll reach the bottom and enter the gorge.

The stream has cut into bedrock over time, carving a 350-foot-wide gash and leaving vertical cliffs standing like sentinels overhead. Wide boulders that have fractured and fallen off the bluffs now line the sides and bottom of the creekbed, their corners rounded by the force of rushing water. Rhododendrons amass on the slopes and along the banks; fern fronds wave in the breeze from the rushing creek; hemlocks hold on to precarious landings; and very tall, old tulip trees and sycamores found a foothold long ago. The deep, V-shaped ravine doesn't allow moisture to evaporate easily, so the cliffs and boulders are covered with moss. On certain days, mist fogs the valley, rendering the scenery in sublime soft focus.

All that moisture makes clambering over the roots and rocks slippery in typical conditions and quite treacherous in rain or snow. You'll cross the stream four times via stones, which may be partially submerged. In spring, the banks are crowded with an amazing display of delicate wildflowers, contrasting the dramatic encounter between rock and water. Shortly after the fourth stream crossing, the blue-blazed trail continues along the creek, but you'll want to turn right to take the orange-blazed Conestoga Trail up the steep hill via stone steps and rock outcrops.

Follow Conestoga Trail to a three-way intersection. This spot can be confusing; the steep trail directly ahead is an unofficial shortcut uphill while the trail to the left is closed. Turn right to follow Pinnacle Blue Trail, an old woods road, a very short distance then take a sharp left at the orange blaze for Conestoga Trail. Go uphill; at a Y intersection with Pinnacle Red Trail, bear left to follow

Conestoga Trail. The path winds around to the river side of the ridge, where it traverses prominent sidehill rock outcrops. These require occasional careful footwork but no scrambling, and you'll enjoy outstanding river vistas. Along with chestnut oak and pitch pine, blueberries are common on these slopes.

Near the hill's crest you'll come to another old woods road; turn left to continue steadily uphill on Conestoga Trail, which runs concurrently here with Pinnacle Yellow Trail. In summer and fall, you'll see blackberry bushes and grapevines lining the trail.

At the end of the climb, you'll come to a picnic area and parking lot. This is Pinnacle Overlook, the top of an anticline (a fold of rock with the oldest rock layers in the middle) of metamorphic phyllite rock that is folded like a blanket. Take in majestic views of the river from both the official overlook and from a rock outcrop about 900 feet farther along Conestoga Trail. Invisible far below are 2-mile-long, 125-foot-deep trenches of unknown origin in the riverbed.

From this point, you can complete the hike by retracing your steps or you can complete it as a loop covering the same distance. The loop is not recommended for high-summer hiking, as there is excessive sun exposure, and the river views are obscured by foliage. In other seasons, though, the return loop offers a variety of terrain complementary to that of the outbound route.

To complete the loop, exit the overlook parking lot and walk along the drive to the Pinnacle Road parking area, passing Pinnacle Red Trail on your right. You will see Pinnacle Blue Trail, also on your right, after the yellow gate. Follow this trail; it is a grassy lane that descends gradually into the woods, passing an unmarked intersection to the right. Pinnacle Blue Trail narrows and becomes quite wet then crosses Pinnacle White Trail and narrows further. Views of the river appear ahead. Pass the turnoff for Conestoga Trail; you should recognize this as the way you went up the hill along Conestoga Trail. When its orange blazes veer left, follow them back down the rock outcrops and stone steps to meet Kelly's Run Blue Trail. Turn right. (If you've changed your mind and want to retrace your steps, this is your chance; turn left here instead.) Kelly's Run Blue Trail descends to an old fire road and a disused bridge over Kelly's Run. Do not cross the bridge. Follow the blue blazes to the left of the bridge and cross the stream via the stones.

On the other side of the stream, follow Kelly's Run Blue Trail uphill and to the right; soon it meets an old road. The road becomes macadam and climbs the hill. As you ascend, enjoy views of the river and Holtwood Dam to your right and of wildflowers and spring-flowering trees covering the rocky cliffs to your left. The old road ends at a yellow gate marking a paved road. Just past the gate, take a

Rhododendrons grow on the slopes in Kelly's Run and form tunnels along the trail.

sharp left turn into the woods, following the blue blazes. Continue climbing uphill on a wide, grassy path through pleasant successional woods. The climb is long but relieved by occasional benches. At the top, you'll enter a farm field; follow blue-blazed poles around the edge and then down the middle of the field before reentering the woods. Pass Kelly's Run Red Trail on the left, walk under two power lines, and come out at the parking lot.

MORE INFORMATION

There is a portable toilet in the parking lot. (Note: Holtwood Park/Holtwood Recreation Area is proposed to be reopened, but facilities remained closed at press time.) The preserve is open from sunrise to sunset. Parts of the preserve are open to hunting; wear orange in season except on Sundays. Dogs are permitted on leash. Kelly's Run–Pinnacle Nature Preserve is managed by the Lancaster County Conservancy. For more information: 117 South West End Avenue, Lancaster, PA 17603; 717-392-7891; lancasterconservancy.org/preserve/kellys-run-pinnacle.

24

MASON-DIXON TRAIL: HOLTWOOD DAM

Hike up steep bluffs to take in sweeping views of the Susquehanna River; trek through gorgeous, rugged ravines; and amble through a bucolic landscape surrounded by farmland vistas. You're almost guaranteed to see bald eagles and, in breeding season, their nests.

LOCATION
Slab, PA (York County)

RATING
Moderate to difficult

DISTANCE
7 miles

DIRECTIONS

This is a shuttle hike, meaning you'll want to leave one car at the hike's beginning and one at its end. To park at the endpoint, take US-1 south to PA 272 North to Buck; at Buck, turn left onto PA 372 West. Go 9 miles. Turn right onto Slab Road. In 0.5 mile, turn right onto PA 74 North. In 3 miles, turn right onto PA 425 North. In 3.9 miles, turn right onto Indian Steps Road. The parking area will be 0.7 mile ahead, at the York Furnace boat ramp.

To proceed to the beginning point, return to PA 372; turn left to head south. Go 3.9 miles. Turn left onto PA 74 South. Go 3.4 miles and turn left onto PA 372 East. Go 2.3 miles. The Lock 12 parking lot will be on your left. Park in the lower parking lot. (In winter, when the lot is closed, park in the upper lot.) *GPS coordinates: 39° 51.680′ N, 76° 22.450′ W.*

ELEVATION GAIN
700 feet

ESTIMATED TIME
3.5 hours

MAPS
USGS Airville, USGS Holtwood; trail maps available (for a fee) at mason-dixontrail.org/maps_membership.html

TRAIL DESCRIPTION

The rugged cliffs and gorges that line the lower Susquehanna River contain some of the most beautiful scenery and most challenging hikes in Pennsylvania. These rocky landforms are hidden in plain sight between the rolling hills of the rural countryside and the slow curve of the river sweeping toward the Chesapeake Bay; it's only where land meets water that one can fully experience the drama

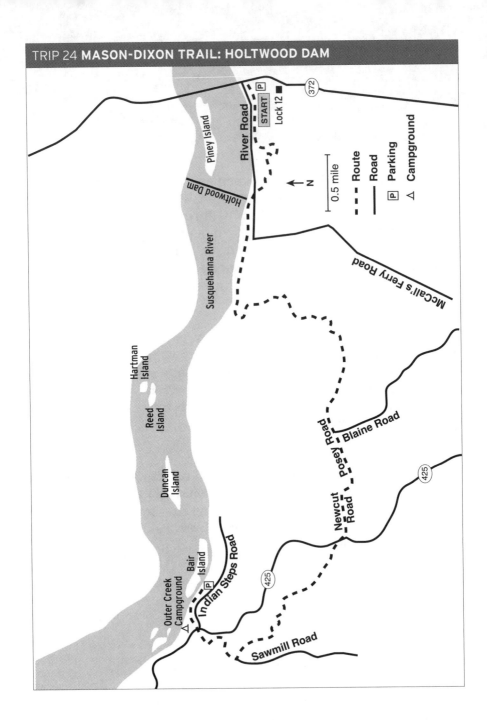

Bald eagles, once endangered, have made a strong comeback after the banning of the pesticide DDT, and now nest in substantial numbers along the Susquehanna River.
Photo by PPL Corporation.

of plunging ravines and soaring promontories, as well as the gentle beauty of rhododendron-covered hillsides and mist-haloed streams.

This hike traverses the York County (or west) side of the Susquehanna River along the Mason-Dixon Trail (M-DT). The 199-mile-long M-DT connects Brandywine Trail in Chester County, Pennsylvania, with the Appalachian Trail in Cumberland County, Pennsylvania. Spectacular rock bluffs along the river's western bank overlook Lake Aldred, the impounded part of the river above Holtwood Dam. (The east side of the river is equally terrific for hiking; see Kelly's Run–Pinnacle Overlook Preserve, Trip 23.)

Begin the hike on the north side of the parking lot, near the river; note the signpost for the M-DT. The M-DT is exceptionally well-marked. You'll become familiar with its blue blazes. The trail goes downhill, crossing the remains of Lock 12 of the defunct Susquehanna and Tidewater Canal, a 43-mile waterway between Wrightsville, Pennsylvania, and Havre de Grace, Maryland, in use from the 1830s to the 1890s. The trail follows the old canal's flat, wide towpath for 1 mile and turns uphill toward River Road, passing the foundations of a sawmill, a millrace, and a cannery. Cross the road and turn right to go over a bridge then immediately turn left to climb the steep ravine via a narrow footpath. Follow the right bank of Mill Run as it bounds over boulders and slips into mossy pools. Rhododendrons cover the hills, making for a spectacular display in late spring.

Turning sharply right, the M-DT climbs very steeply up the rocky hillside. It is tempting to hold on to trees as you climb; first make sure they're well anchored in the thin soil. Follow the ridge crest to the edge of the sheer bluffs, where several outcrops offer panoramic views of the river, Lake Aldred, and Holtwood Dam. Looking south past the dam, you can see some of the Conowingo islands, an unusual landform consisting of vertical chunks of very hard schist bedrock, eroded into knobs by the Susquehanna River over eons.

Descend the ridge to River Road, passing beneath power lines and alongside the foundation of a former hotel. Just above the road, you will pass a "whispering" rock outcrop that amplifies sounds from below.

At River Road, turn left and cross the road toward the dam overlook. While enjoying the spray and thunder of the waterfall, imagine what it's like to be a fish trying to swim upriver to spawn. Near the overlook is a fish ladder, installed in 1910 to assist migrating shad, herring, and other species. Prior to the construction of the Holtwood, Conowingo (downstream), and Safe Harbor (upstream) dams on the Susquehanna, huge schools of fish journeyed annually from the ocean to spawning grounds in the upper watershed. The Holtwood fish ladder is defunct. A modern fish elevator across the river is marginally more effective, but today millions of shad and herring are transported annually by truck and released above the dams. At the base of the old fish ladder is a whitewater playboat area, activated at scheduled dam releases.

Follow the road for 0.29 miles then bear right into the woods; the trail passes through residential yards, joins a dirt road, and bears left up a bank at a sign for a cable crossing before bearing right into the woods. Descend along the river, which laps at the low shore, upstream from where McCall's Ferry once crossed.

Notwithstanding the barriers that the Susquehanna presents to migrating fish, the river's piscine population is robust enough to support a burgeoning community of bald eagles. Lake Aldred is a prime location to observe eagles year-round, and you can often spot eagle nests from this section of the trail. From March through May, look for large nests made of stout sticks high in trees or even on power line towers. Do not disturb! (The trail may be temporarily rerouted to bypass nests.)

Turn left to climb up a beautiful ravine along Oakland Run as it plunges down to the river. Rhododendrons crowd the gorge, creating narrow passageways as the trail threads through them, up and along the side of the ridge. Cross the stream and enter rich woods; you're now in Pennsylvania state game lands. Walk along a woods road, tending uphill. After a long, straight climb, you will pass a gate. The next section of the hike (almost 2.5 miles) takes you down picturesque roads with great views of the surrounding countryside. Turn left on Posey Road and right onto Newcut Road, then cross PA 425 and head straight across a farm field. Turn right onto Bare Road and walk about 100 feet, then turn left to follow a power line maintenance road 0.5 mile. (Note: From October 1 through December 31, this road is closed for hunting season. Instead, take a detour at Newcut Road by making a right onto PA 425, turning left onto Indian Steps Road, and continuing to the endpoint of this hike.) Watch the blue blazes carefully to make a sharp right turn and then a left into the woods, returning to the game lands. You'll cross several streams, including Furnace Run, which seems to change direction while you're not looking. Follow Furnace Run to

Sawmill Run. Turn right onto the dirt Sawmill Run Road and follow it for 1 mile. Turn right onto PA 425, turn right again, and walk 0.25 mile to Indian Steps Road. From there, bear left and follow it 1 mile to the parking lot.

MORE INFORMATION
Restrooms are located below the Lock 12 parking lot. The Mason-Dixon Trail is maintained by the Mason-Dixon Trail System (masondixontrail.org), which provides trail maps, and York Hiking Club (yorkhikingclub.com). Indian Steps Museum, at the end of the hike, features an extensive collection of American Indian artifacts (indiansteps.org).

CENTRAL AND SOUTHERN NEW JERSEY

New Jersey can be divided into three parts: high ground, or the mountains of the northwest; middle, or the Piedmont of central New Jersey; and low, or the coastal plain of South Jersey, which roughly follows a northeast–southwest line along US 1.

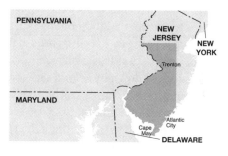

South Jersey is all coastal plain, the dominant characteristic of which is its soil: flat, sandy, fast-draining, low in nutrients and organic matter, and high in iron. While the soil is dry, South Jersey does have access to productive groundwater aquifers fed by rainfall farther north. Many South Jersey rivers—including the Mullica, Maurice, Batsto, and Wading—are aquifer-fed rather than dependent on runoff, as most Piedmont streams are. As a result, these coastal plain rivers are cool year-round and colored brown from the iron and the cedar trees common in this region. Depending on the availability of water close to the surface, the dominant habitat type varies from pine forest to mixed pine-hardwood forest to cedar swamp.

The Pinelands National Reserve is a 1.1-million-acre federal and state reserve—and a unique cultural, historic, and natural area. As the Pinelands Preservation Alliance notes, "It is the largest surviving open space on the eastern seaboard between the northern forests of Maine and the Everglades of Florida." This area was historically known as the "Pine Barrens," and is still commonly referred to as such, although the newer term continues to gain adherents. Almost half of the Pinelands is publicly owned, including the Wharton and

Brendan T. Byrne State Forest in New Jersey's Pine Barrens represents a mix of forested woodlands, wetlands, lakes, and ponds. This varied ecosystem makes for a diverse array of plant and animal life. Photo by Richard Lewis/AMC Photo Contest.

Brendan T. Byrne state forests. Pinelands hikes include Mullica River Trail (Trip 27), Batona Trail (Trip 28) and Pakim Pond (Trip 29).

On the coastal plain but not in the Pinelands is Cape May (Trip 25); straddling the Pinelands and the coastal plain is Parvin State Park (Trip 26). The coastal plain extends into central New Jersey, with its northern edge, or fall line, roughly corresponding to US 1.

Hiking in the coastal plain is, as one would expect, typically a trek across flat, sandy soils, whether through pine forests, upland woods, or along an ocean beach. Although the coastal plain is flat, it is never monotonous. Hikers can observe subtle changes and details, from the varying sounds of the wind in the trees to the texture of lichens on tree trunks. Coastal plain hikes are often best in fall, winter, or early spring, before the insect population becomes intolerable and the sunscreen ineffective.

Central New Jersey north of US 1 is part of the Piedmont, or foothills, of the mountains to the north. Piedmont terrain is much more varied than that of the coastal plain, ranging from rolling hills to flat valleys and also including diabase mountains and ridges. It is composed primarily of sedimentary rock formed from deposits laid down by inland seas long ago. Having weathered over time, this sedimentary rock varies considerably in shape, so the landforms vary as well. The hike at Bull's Island, Delaware Canal, and D&R Canal (Trip 32) traverses the flat floodplain valley along the river, while the hike in the Musconetcong Gorge Preserve (Trip 34) follows a ravine.

Diabase ridges are part of a visually but not geologically continuous band of forested ridges that extend from Pennsylvania into New Jersey. Because these ridges are rocky, with thin soil and little access to groundwater, they did not develop as quickly as the surrounding area. As a result, they are richer in habitat, with diverse woods and wildlife. Diabase ridge hikes in central New Jersey include Ted Stiles Preserve at Baldpate Mountain (Trip 30) and Sourland Mountain Preserve (Trip 31).

25

CAPE MAY

Cape May is an internationally renowned birding site with a popular, long-established hawk watch. This hike passes through varied habitats: dunes, meadows, ponds, and freshwater and saltwater marshes.

DIRECTIONS

To reach The Nature Conservancy's South Cape May Meadows, take the Garden State Parkway to its southern terminus. Continue straight on NJ 109. The road becomes Lafayette Street; at its end, turn right onto Jackson Street. Continue on this road (its name will change to West Perry Street and then to Sunset Boulevard) for 1.2 miles; the refuge will be on your left. *GPS coordinates:* 38° 56.277′ N, 74° 56.686′ W.

TRAIL DESCRIPTION

Cape May, a Victorian-era Jersey Shore community two hours from Philadelphia, has long attracted vacationers. Its recognition as a natural area is more recent. Refuges, sanctuaries, and nature centers have proliferated, preserving much of the peninsula's irreplaceable habitat for wildlife as diverse as birds, butterflies, and horseshoe crabs. Cape May's hawk watch sets the standard for migration research. Given Cape May's unique location, this is the only hike in this book for which the recommended footwear is (in season) sandals, flip-flops, or no footwear at all. Optional equipment includes binoculars and a beach-combing bucket.

Begin at The Nature Conservancy's 218-acre South Cape May Meadows refuge (commonly known as the Meadows) on Sunset Boulevard. In the fall, southbound songbirds rest and feed in Cape May's woods and meadows—full of berries, nuts, and seeds—before the long Delaware Bay crossing. In spring, they stop on their way

LOCATION
West Cape May, NJ
(Cape May County)

RATING
Easy

DISTANCE
5 miles

ELEVATION GAIN
Minimal

ESTIMATED TIME
2.5 hours

MAPS
USGS Cape May; trail maps available onsite

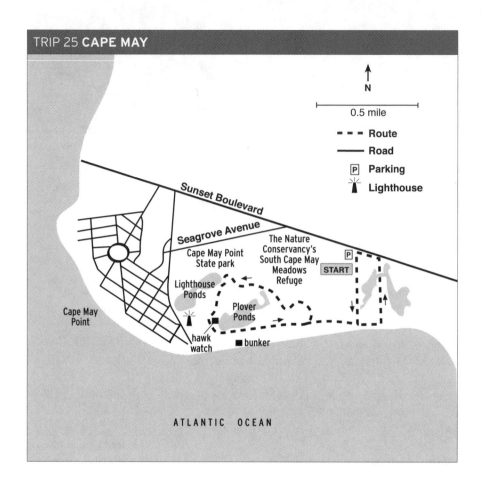

back. Raptors are attracted to the abundance of prey. From spring through fall, shorebirds and waterfowl congregate in and around meadows, marshes, ponds, and beaches—a conservation haven for migrating and nesting birds.

From the entrance, follow the wide, flat, pebbly Main Trail as it passes through extensive wetland meadows. Trails in the refuge trace the tops of levees, which enable refuge managers to control water levels in the freshwater wetlands. The levees' elevation provides excellent angles for viewing ducks, egrets, herons, and other birds in the ponds and marshes. The trail rises to go over a recently restored mile-long sand dune that protects the inland marshes from wind and is a unique habitat in itself. Look for the burrows of sand fiddler crabs, 1-inch-wide holes excavated in the sand; you may even spot the white crabs. Follow the trail over the dune to the beach. From March 15 to August 31, large portions of the beach are fenced off to protect endangered piping plovers, whose nests on the ground are vulnerable to disturbance. Refuge rules require beach visitors to keep moving during those times.

The sea, the lighthouse, and the beach: essential components of a walk around Cape May.

Turn right, take off your shoes if you feel like it, and head down the beach toward the Cape May Point lighthouse, walking as close to the ocean as you want. The view south is unobstructed, as the shore here is undeveloped. Sanderlings run back and forth with the surf, feeding on small invertebrates; gulls and terns wheel overhead. Depending on the season, you'll see all kinds of birds flying, resting, and feeding along the shore.

Not quite 1 mile down the beach is "the bunker," a World War II-era concrete structure that was part of a coastal defense system. When built, it was 900 feet inland. Coastal erosion, exacerbated by storms and by the numerous jetties and beach protection structures to the north, has robbed Cape May of a great deal of sand.

Turn right at the bunker, put your shoes back on, and head up the beach to enter Cape May Point State Park, with the parking lot on your left. The large wooden platform to the right is a hawk watch. In prime raptor migration season, it is packed with birders and spectators scanning the sky for hawks, eagles, and vultures. Feel free to join the crowd; it's a great place to learn the art of spotting and identifying raptors.

Continue along the sidewalk and enter the Cape May Point State Park trails to your right. The trails, many of them boardwalks, wind through wetlands, around ponds, and among dune forests. Bear left and follow the blazes for Blue Trail, passing through cool, low woods of black gum, bayberry, holly, cedar, pine, and oak trees and pausing at small ponds. Blue Trail loops back to the hawk watch along the beach, with Plover Ponds 1 and 2 to your right. At the hawk watch, return to the beach and walk back past the bunker to the Meadows. As you near The Nature Conservancy refuge, look for the large interpretive sign next to the dune; otherwise, it may be difficult to pick out the trailhead from the continuous dune line. (During nesting season, watch for the end of the plover fencing.) Ascend the dune, turning right at the top and following the trail along the dune. Turn left to cross the wetlands via East Trail, which features a viewing platform. Turn left again on a trail paralleling Sunset Boulevard, completing the circuit at the parking lot.

MORE INFORMATION

There is a portable toilet at South Cape May Meadows from April through October. A map of that portion of the refuge is available at the information kiosk and at nature.org.

Restrooms are located at the visitor center for Cape May Point State Park. A trail map is available at the park office. The lighthouse is worth a visit; pay the fee and climb the stairs to the open-air observation deck for a 360-degree view of the Point. For more information on South Cape May Meadows: 692 Sunset Boulevard, Cape May, NJ 08204; 908-879-7262; nature.org. For more information on Cape May Point State Park: P.O. Box 107, Lighthouse Avenue, Cape May Point, NJ 08212; 609-884-2159; state.nj.us/dep/parksandforests/parks/capemay.html.

OUT OF THE BLUE, INTO THE WHITE

Down from the Arctic circle, along Greenland's coast, and across the Labrador Sea to eastern North America come millions of birds every fall during the migration from northern to southern latitudes. Some birds winter in the southern United States; others continue on to Central and South America. Birds reverse direction from south to north in springtime to breed. Along the way, the migrants need to stop, rest, and eat. Some land on the forested ridges of the Delaware and Lehigh valleys and in the tidal wetlands of Delaware and South Jersey during these stopovers.

Because most songbirds migrate at night, even those who know that birds appear and disappear seasonally may not notice this great movement. Scientists use radar to track their flight, though, so we know what birds are doing under the cover of night. For example, researchers have learned that the weather influences flight. The northwest winds of an autumn cold front push birds forward. But when weather conditions are adverse—for example, when a tropical storm blows in—birds literally drop from the sky, exhausted, particularly if a long water crossing lies ahead or behind.

Unlike the smaller songbirds, raptors (hawks, vultures, eagles) migrate during the daytime, riding the thermals, or columns of warming air, and updrafts that form along a ridge. They can be observed kettling in groups: spiraling up and up and up the wind elevator. Birds ride the airstream up and then glide along wind pathways that follow ridgelines. Atop ridges throughout the Appalachian and Highlands regions, hawk-watchers gather to count raptors in the fall. The cry of a hawk-watcher, binoculars focused on an infinitesmal spot high in the sky moving through the scattered clouds, arrests the attention of any nearby hiker, who must strain to see a hint of a dot overhead: "There! In the blue, heading to the white!"

Hawk Mountain on Kittatinny Ridge is the most popular hawk watch in Pennsylvania. Perhaps more famous among Delaware Valley hawk-watchers, though, is Cape May, New Jersey. Not a ridge but a peninsula between the Atlantic Ocean and Delaware Bay, Cape May is a natural funnel for migrants heading south along both shorelines to cross the bay. Tired songbirds collect in the scrubby forests, preparing for the long overwater trip. Raptors, too, are tired and hungry, and those songbirds make a nice lunch. Cape May is a birder's heaven—and a raptor's cafeteria.

26

PARVIN STATE PARK

This easy, level hike winds through a variety of pine and hardwood forests at the southwestern fringes of the New Jersey Pine Barrens.

DIRECTIONS

Take I-76 East into New Jersey; continue onto NJ 42 South. After 1.5 miles take Exit 13 for NJ 55 south toward Glassboro and Vineland. Travel approximately 25 miles; then take Exit 35B for Garden Road toward Brotmanville and drive 2 miles. Turn left on Alvine Road (CR 655) and drive 2 miles then turn right onto Almond Road (CR 540). Continue 1.3 miles until you reach the entrance to the park, on the right. *GPS coordinates:* 39° 30.679′ N, 75° 07.935′ W.

TRAIL DESCRIPTION

The word "ecotones" sounds like it means nature's music, and in a way, it does. Ecotones are transition zones created by the meeting of different ecosystems, such as pine forests and hardwood swamps. Just as different notes combine to create diverse harmonies and melodies, ecosystems converge to create diverse, distinct plant and animal communities.

Parvin State Park in southwestern New Jersey lies on the margins of the Pine Barrens, where the dry, sandy soil that underlies pinelands meets slow-draining, claylike, peaty uplands. Within this 1,137-acre park are upland pine-oak forests, hardwood swamps, pitch pine lowlands, and Atlantic white cedar swamps, as well as ecotones in between. Enjoy Parvin's continually shifting "music" as you hike from one kind of habitat to another.

The hike begins at the state park's main office. This white-painted brick building, along with other structures in the park, was constructed by the Civilian Conservation Corps

LOCATION
Pittsgrove, NJ
(Salem County)

RATING
Easy

DISTANCE
5 miles

ELEVATION GAIN
Minimal

ESTIMATED TIME
2.5 hours

MAPS
USGS Elmer; trail maps available onsite; state.nj.us/dep/parksandforests/parks/maps/ParvinFinalDraft2_reduced_Area_broc.pdf

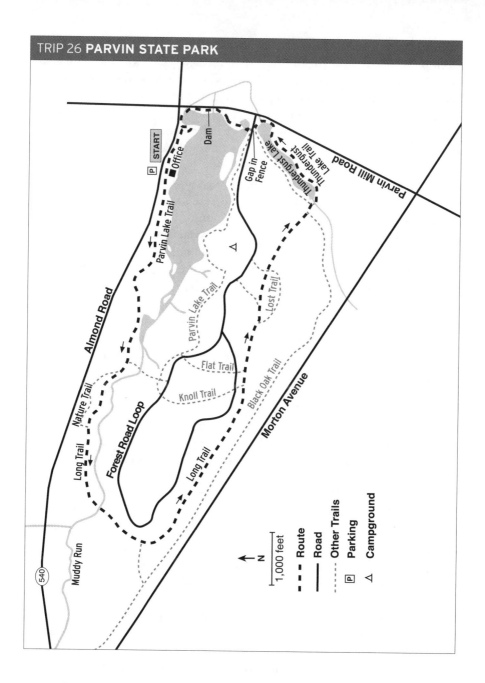

(CCC) in the 1930s. The office and associated buildings sit by Parvin Lake Beach, popular for swimming. Parvin was a private recreational facility long before the state purchased it in 1929. Only a small portion of the lakefront is cleared; otherwise, the shoreline seems carved out of deep forest.

Turn left from the office and head northeast to pick up the packed-gravel, green-blazed Parvin Lake Trail. The trail immediately enters a sandy floodplain forest beneath a canopy of swamp white oak, red maple, and sweetgum trees. The understory consists of dogwood, holly, mountain laurel, blueberry, arrow-wood shrubs, and a forest floor of ferns. This changes gradually into a dry, sandy pitch pine forest with ground cover that includes Canada mayflower, teaberry, and bracken fern and a dense understory that includes sweet pepperbush. In spring and summer, the woods are alive with singing birds. The trail passes to the left of an old CCC camp, where the workers stayed while constructing the state park buildings; on the other side of the trail is a view of a small marsh.

The trails are blazed with colors at intersections, although not all intersections are on the map. Follow Parvin Lake Trail's occasional green blazes until the trail intersects the red-blazed Long Trail, at about 0.8 mile. This is the dividing line for the park's official 400-acre natural area; bikes are not permitted here, and the trails seem slightly quieter and more remote than those on the eastern side.

The narrow Long Trail parallels the course of Muddy Run, the creek that was dammed to create Parvin Lake. The creek's name seems to refer to its dark brown color, which comes from tannins in the Atlantic white cedars that thrive in Pinelands bogs. Where the trail crosses these bogs, look for bright green sphagnum carpeting the peaty forest floor. The trail crosses Muddy Run after 0.5 mile; pass a connector trail going left to continue on Long Trail, which soon meets a clear stream, notable for its contrast with the cedar-brown streams. The trail passes through a low, moist area thick with hollies and enters a pine forest, which becomes a pine woods. Long Trail becomes sandy as it continues into an open pine-oak forest with tall trees, sparse understory, and a floor of lowbush blueberry.

As you continue, note the continual changes in the heights of trees, the thickness (or openness) of the understory, the terrain underlying the footpath, and the dryness or swampiness of the surrounding soil. This is the "music" of the ecotones.

About 1 mile from its start, Long Trail crosses a connector trail; continue straight (south) and follow the Long Trail as it bends eastward. About 0.5 mile later, the trail reaches intersections with the orange-blazed Knoll Trail on the left and, shortly thereafter, an unblazed trail on the right. You'll soon come to another intersection, this one with the pink-blazed Flat Trail; an unmarked trail leads to the right about 800 feet later, and an intersection with the yellow-blazed Lost Trail follows about 50 feet after that. This area can be confusing; when in doubt, keep heading straight (east) and follow red blazes if you see them.

Long Trail intersects with Black Oak Trail, going off to the right 2.75 miles from Long Trail's start, then almost immediately ends. Go straight onto the yellow-blazed Thundergust Lake Trail, cross Thundergust Break (a small, quiet,

Trails in Parvin State Park wind through mixed pine and hardwood forests.

clear-running stream), and continue straight. Thundergust Lake appears on the left. This is a small fishing lake with a bare shoreline. Walk halfway around the lake. Where the trail approaches the road, it passes over the lake's outlet. Take the next right, cross the paved drive, and walk about 50 feet to a gap in the fence and head straight, taking the bridge over Parvin Lake. You are now back on the green-blazed Parvin Lake Trail.

The trail goes around the edge of Parvin Lake, traversing a concave dam from which you can watch the acrobatics of barn swallows as they rocket from their roosts under the footbridge to twist and turn over the lake, catching insects on the fly. Cross the lovely CCC footbridge; the trail ends at the park office, where it began.

MORE INFORMATION

Hiking is free, although there is a seasonal fee ($2) to use beach facilities. Restrooms are located at the park's main office. For more information, contact Parvin State Park, 701 Almond Road, Pittsgrove, NJ 08318; 856-358-8616; state.nj.us/dep/parksandforests/parks/parvin.html.

27

MULLICA RIVER TRAIL

Walk on soft, needle-covered sand trails through shady pine forests and cedar bogs, and along the beautiful red-brown Mullica River.

DIRECTIONS

This is a shuttle hike, meaning you'll want to leave one car at the hike's beginning (Atsion) and one at its end (Batsto), although there is a loop option.

To Batsto: To drive from the hike start in Atsion to Batsto, drive 4.4 miles south on US 206 and turn left onto CR 613. In 1.3 miles, turn left onto South Myrtle Street and left again onto Airport Road (CR 693). In 2.7 miles turn left onto Nesco Road, continuing on as it becomes Hammonton Road (CR 542), and go 4 miles until you reach Batsto Lake Road. Turn left, and a parking area with enough room for six cars is just ahead on the right, identified by the sign: "Canoe Launch." If the area is full, or you prefer to park in a monitored location, use the main Batsto Village office lot (about .25 mile farther east on CR 542), where parking is ample. *GPS coordinates:* 39° 38.551′ N, 74° 39.295′ W.

To Atsion: From I-295 South, take Exit 29 for US 30 and turn left onto Copley Road at the end of the off-ramp. In about 0.25 mile, turn left onto US 30 east. From I-295 north, take Exit 29A for US 30 east. Take US 30 east for 8.8 miles and turn left onto Jackson Road. Drive 8.7 miles until you reach Atsion Road and turn right. In 4.6 miles, turn left onto US 206. The parking lot will be just ahead on your right. *GPS coordinates:* 39° 44.534′ N, 74° 43.553′ W.

TRAIL DESCRIPTION

The Mullica River is one of the great little rivers of the Pine Barrens. Along with the Batsto, Oswego, and Wading

LOCATION
Atsion and Batsto, NJ
(Wharton State Forest)

RATING
Moderate

DISTANCE
9 miles

ELEVATION GAIN
25 feet

ESTIMATED TIME
4 hours

MAPS
USGS Atsion; state.nj.us/
dep/parksandforests/parks/
maps/WhartonAreaMapFinal_
reduced.pdf

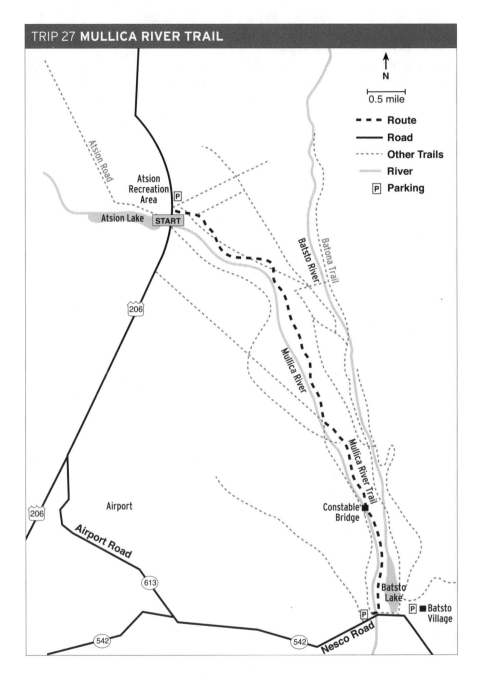

rivers, it flows southeast into New Jersey's Great Bay, north of Atlantic City. This watershed is the largest in the Pine Barrens and the only one wholly within it. The Mullica is pure Pine Barrens.

The Mullica's swift current, broad curves, swimming holes, consistently cool temperatures, shaded banks, and sandy beach landings make it a paddler's paradise. A hike along its banks lets you experience its beauty, serenity, and dynamism without having to get wet.

You can hike between Atsion and Batsto, spotting a car at each end or arranging a pickup from a local outfitter, or you can hike to the Mullica Wilderness Camp and back via a loop trail. The very ambitious can hike out and back for a daylong (but level) excursion. There are connector trails to the Batona Trail as well, enabling a 12-mile loop from Batsto via Wilderness Camp Connector and a 14-mile loop via Beaver Pond–Quaker Bridge Trail.

As described here, the hike goes on the Mullica River Trail between Atsion and Batsto, allowing the hiker to experience a continuous section of the Mullica as it widens and narrows, rushes and rests. The beginning and end points are reminders of the historical human presence along the river. Both towns were vibrant ironworks settlements in the nineteenth century. Batsto has been restored to demonstrate what it was like as a living community, while Atsion exists only in the form of scattered structures.

The Mullica River Trail begins behind the Wharton State Forest office at Atsion, just across from Atsion Lake, which dams the Mullica on the other side of US 206. The trail is blazed with yellow markers on trees. Trailheads, intersections, and road crossings are marked by posts, which may be obscured by vegetation. There are also mileage markers about every 0.5 mile.

From the office, walk left (east) onto Quaker Bridge Road, a sand road, passing by the Atsion church and cemetery, remnants of Atsion Village. The road's name comes from the long-vanished Quaker settlement that stood where the road-crosses the Batsto River.

About 450 feet after Atsion Village, across from an old red, wooden building, the trail turns left into the woods along a narrow, sandy footpath pillowed with pine needles. Ubiquitous pitch pines and various oaks provide the canopy, with an understory of blackjack oak and mountain laurel, bracken fern, greenbrier, sheep laurel, huckleberry, and blueberry. Teaberry (wintergreen) and bearberry form the ground cover, along with false reindeer lichen. All of these plants, and others typical of the upland Pine Barrens, thrive in dry, sandy soil, for that is what you are walking on: sand. There is little else, such as clay or organic matter, mixed in with the finely ground quartzite particles, so the soil doesn't hold rainwater. For the plants here, life is a perpetual drought. Without clay or organic matter, the soil is also nearly devoid of nutrients but very high in iron; it is highly acidic as well. The plants that do grow here are tough—tough but beautiful.

This walk, typical of the Pine Barrens, is shaded year-round by the long green needles of the pines, through which the breeze seems to whisper as it rises and falls. Sunlight is filtered downward through green needles and reflected upward from reddish-brown dried ones, meeting at eye level to form a unique piney light. Hopping from tree to tree, pine warblers sing their trilling song throughout spring and summer.

Pine Barrens cedar swamps have pure, clean, tea-brown waters.

The trail winds through this upland woods with occasional glimpses of the river and small streams. In the lowland swampy areas, you'll find cedars, with their reddish, shreddy bark and flat, scale-like evergreen leaves. Atlantic white cedar has long been a commercially valuable tree for its resistance to decay—a useful characteristic in a tree that makes its home in swamps. Cedars are to the Pine Barrens what sycamores are to the Piedmont woods: They indicate the presence of water. If you see a stand of cedars, you'll be almost certain to find flowing or standing water. Cedars, along with bog iron in the soil, are the source of the tea color of Pine Barrens waterways. In cedar swamps and along the river, look for red maple and black gum trees, sphagnum moss mats, sweet pepperbush, sweetbay, inkberry, and golden spike. The endangered swamp pink is also found in cedar swamps.

Around the 0.5-mile mark, you'll cross a railroad track; 0.25 mile later, you'll cross an old road and veer around a small, pretty pond. Because the Pine Barrens is so uniformly level, almost all ponds and lakes are the products of human engineering, many dating from the days of mills and forges. Beavers were common in the Pine Barrens until 1850, by which time they had been virtually extirpated by trapping; as a result of reintroduction and protection programs, they're making a comeback. Indeed, at about the 3-mile mark, you'll come upon the aptly named Beaver Pond–Quaker Bridge Trail (connecting to the Batona Trail), which intersects Mullica River Trail at a large cedar swamp with active beaver colonies.

The shoreline offers several fine viewing spots. Return to the Beaver Pond Trail intersection; continue to follow the yellow-blazed Mullica River Trail along a sand road, veering left after about 20 feet as it becomes a narrow footpath that closely follows the river. Wilderness Camps Connector Trail (to Beaver Pond–Quaker Bridge Trail) intersects at about the 4-mile mark. (For a loop hike, take this 0.75-mile trail to Beaver Pond–Quaker Bridge Trail and return to Mullica River Trail by going north about 1.8 miles.)

The trail turns onto a sand road and continues as such for about 2.5 miles. You'll quickly realize the benefits of walking on soft, needle-covered sand trails under a pine canopy. Roads of fine ("sugar") sand cause your feet to sink with every step; the sunny, open road feels harsher on the eyes and ears as even the wind seems to whine instead of whisper.

At around the 4.5-mile mark, you'll pass the Mullica Wilderness campsite beside the river. After another 2 miles, the trail returns to the pine woods. Here is a large patch of pyxie, a tiny evergreen shrub that creeps along the ground; in spring, it bears little white flowers.

About 1.5 miles from the end of the hike, you'll reach Constable Bridge, which spans the Mullica River. This is a popular canoe and kayak launch and impromptu swimming pool. Mullica River Trail used to cross the bridge, but a washout farther on necessitated a long-term detour that now takes the trail away from the river and onto Batsto Lake Road. This flat sand road becomes scenic once the lake comes into view on your left. The 9-mile trail ends at the edge of Batsto Village. If you parked here, you're done. If you parked at the main office, simply pass on through the gate and continue another 0.5 mile through the restored village and past Batsto Lake to the parking area.

MORE INFORMATION

There are restrooms at Batsto but none at Atsion, although there are restrooms at Atsion Lake, across US 206. There's no fee at Atsion; Batsto Village charges an entrance fee per vehicle from Memorial Day weekend through Labor Day. For information on local transportation, contact Wharton State Forest, 31 Batsto Road, Hammonton, NJ 08037. For the Batsto office, contact 609-561-0024; for the Atsion office, contact 609-268-0444; state.nj.us/dep/parksandforests/parks/wharton.html.

28

BATONA TRAIL: CARRANZA MEMORIAL TO APPLE PIE HILL

This is a level walk past cedar swamps and through pine woods to one of the highest points in the Pine Barrens, with spectacular views possible from the fire tower.

DIRECTIONS

From I-295, take Exit 34A for NJ 70 east. In 13.4 miles, at the traffic circle, merge onto US 206 south, and continue on US 206 for 5.1 miles then turn left onto Tuckerton Road. Go another 5.2 miles and turn left onto Carranza Road for 1.4 miles. There is ample parking for the Carranza Memorial on your right, hidden slightly behind the pine trees. *GPS coordinates*: 39° 46.668′ N, 74° 37.984′ W.

TRAIL DESCRIPTION

Emilio Carranza was a celebrated Mexican aviator, a contemporary of Charles Lindbergh. In June 1928, when he was just 23 years old, he flew from Mexico City to New York, a flight that mirrored Lindbergh's New York–Mexico run. On the July 13 return trip, Carranza encountered a thunderstorm over the Pine Barrens, and his plane crashed; he did not survive. The Carranza Memorial, a stone marker located at the start of this hike, was carved in Mexico and commemorates his flight and tragic death. From the memorial, turn right onto the sand road. In about 300 feet, you will see the pink blazes of Batona Trail as it crosses the road.

Batona Trail is a 50-mile linear trail through the Pine Barrens. Created in 1961, it was designed—and is still maintained—by the decades-old Batona Hiking Club of Philadelphia, whose name is a portmanteau formed from the saying "Back to nature," reflecting the club's original objective of encouraging city dwellers to get outside.

LOCATION
Tabernacle, NJ
(Burlington County)

RATING
Moderate

DISTANCE
9 miles

ELEVATION GAIN
110 feet

ESTIMATED TIME
4 hours

MAPS
USGS Indian Mills; state.nj.us/dep/parksandforests/parks/docs/batona14web.pdf

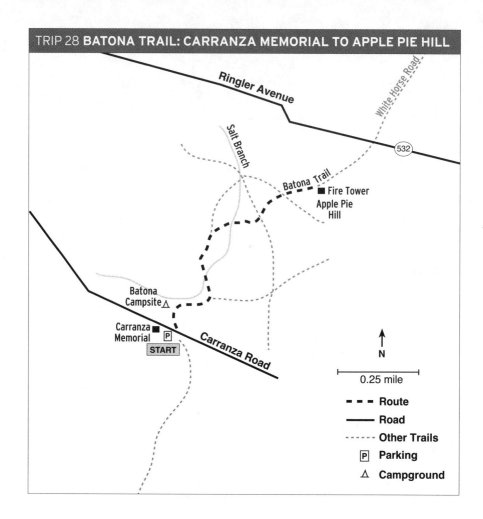

Ringler Avenue

White Horse Road

Salt Branch

Batona Trail

■ Fire Tower

Apple Pie Hill

532

Batona Campsite △

Carranza Memorial ■
P

START

Carranza Road

N

0.25 mile

– – – Route

——— Road

- - - - Other Trails

P Parking

△ Campground

Turn left to follow the trail into Batona Campground, one of several primitive campsites along the trail. This section of Batona Trail is representative of its best characteristics: a quiet, easy trek through one of the great overlooked wilderness areas of the Delaware Valley. Like all other Pine Barrens trails, it is best hiked in late fall, winter, or early spring, before the mosquitoes, ticks, and chiggers become unbearable.

The trail winds hither and thither through the campground; the pink blazes are easy to spot in full sunlight but occasionally hidden by shadows. Just past a pit toilet, the trail ducks into the woods. Follow the trail, which parallels (and at several points joins) a sand road as it weaves in and out of shrubby highbush blueberry and mountain laurel under pitch pine and blackjack oak. The trail skirts a wide cedar swamp, the Skit Branch of the Batsto River. After 0.75 mile, Batona Trail hits the road again and bends left onto a footbridge over a bubbling brown creek.

A stone obelisk commemorates the Mexican aviator Emilio Carranza's 1928 solo flight and tragic crash in the Pine Barrens.

Tea-colored waterways are characteristic of the Pine Barrens. The color comes from the Atlantic white cedar that thrives in the acidic bogs surrounding creeks and rivers; the nut-brown tannins of the cedar bark, leaves, and cones seep into the water. These tannins, along with the high iron content of the boggy soil, give the area's streams and ponds their distinctive coloring.

Once over the bridge, the trail turns right into the woods. The soft sand, covered with long pine needles, makes for easy footing as the narrow, level trail undulates gently over the occasional tree root. All is quiet except for the wind in the pines and, in spring and fall, the trill of the pine warbler: a cheery yellow bird that, true to its name, favors pine forests. Greenbrier brambles may catch your clothes as you pass. Mounds of light green false reindeer lichen spread along the forest floor. Touch one gently: A natural hygrometer, it will be soft after rain and crusty if the weather has been dry. Splotches of shield lichen also splatter the tree trunks.

The trail crosses several small cedar swamps over low wooden bridges. Sphagnum moss forms dense green mats on the peaty soil. The land is so low, flat, and sandy that the swamps and creeks seem to have been carved from the bottom up, and indeed they have—these waterways are fed by underground aquifers.

At the 3-mile mark, the trail abruptly ascends about 20 feet onto a 10-foot-wide gravel ridge. Marked on older maps as Tea Time Hill, a sign reading "Mount Korbar" has been posted at this ridge in honor of Walter Korszniak and Morris Bardock, members of Batona Hiking Club who created the Batona Trail.

Descend the "mountain" and continue on the trail, which crosses several sand roads. After about 0.5 mile, the trail crosses a long firebreak, a ditch dug to mark the edge of a controlled burn area. The New Jersey Forest Fire Service regularly sets controlled fires in the Pine Barrens, preventing fires from spreading by trenching the margins of a targeted burn area. Controlled burns reduce needles, duff, and other dry tinder—fuel that could ignite from a spark or lightning strike and cause a wildfire. Controlled, or prescribed, burns are intended to contribute positively to the regeneration of the pine-dominated forest, because pitch pine seeds are more likely to take root in fire-burned soil than are the acorns of the blackjack oak. Indeed, pitch pines are the dominant pine along this trail; identify this species easily by noticing long, bright green needles that sprout directly from its trunk.

After another 0.5 mile (about 4.25 miles from the start), the trail crosses a road and suddenly, rising before you, is Apple Pie Hill. Both Apple Pie Hill and Mount Korbar are composed of Beacon Hill gravel, an ancient marine deposit of the Pliocene era, some 2 million to 6 million years ago. These deposits are the remnants of an ancient waterway that, like the creeks and streams of our era, left gravel and sediment as it changed course.

This mound of sand atop gravel climbs 100 feet to one of the highest points in the Pine Barrens—208 feet above sea level—and is crowned with a 60-foot-high working fire tower. Unfortunately, the public's long-enjoyed open access to the tower has been restricted since 2016 due to ongoing theft and vandalism. If fire observer staff is present (typically in summer), take the opportunity to climb the tower and, from its intermediate platforms, enjoy spectacular panoramic views of the Pinelands, with glimpses of Atlantic City and even Philadelphia possible on clear days.

Return the way you came to reach the parking lot.

MORE INFORMATION

Batona Hiking Club (batona.wildapricot.org) maintains the trail along with Outdoor Club of South Jersey (ocsj.org). There are primitive restrooms at Batona Campground. Camping at Batona Campground requires an advance reservation; the nightly fee is $3 per person for residents and $5 per person for nonresidents. For more information, contact Wharton State Forest, 31 Batsto Road, Hammonton, NJ 08037; Batsto office: 609-561-0024; Atsion office: 609-268-0444; state.nj.us/dep/parksandforests/parks/wharton.html. Call ahead to find out whether the Apple Pie Hill fire tower will be staffed: New Jersey Forest Fire Service Division B Headquarters, 8 A.M. to 4:30 P.M., 609-726-9010.

BROWN IS NOT DIRTY

Close your eyes for a moment and picture a clean river. What do you see in your mind's eye? Is the water in the river crystal clear? Or is it perhaps a glacial blue?

Your imaginary clean river surely isn't the rusty brown of a sewer pipe. Not unless you've been to the New Jersey Pine Barrens, an hour's drive from Philadelphia, where brown is clean, and the purest water runs russet out of the swamps. Two unique features of the Pine Barrens, swamp cedars and bog iron, are responsible for tinting the waters brown.

Waterways in the Pine Barrens—including the Batsto, Wading, Mullica, and Maurice rivers, and Rancocas Creek—are primarily fed by the Kirkwood-Cohansey Aquifer, a natural underground storage area that holds 17 trillion gallons of water, replenished as rain filters through the fast-draining, sandy soils. Because the Pine Barrens is largely uninhabited, its rivers are cleaner than those in developed areas fed by surface runoff, which carries pollutants. Supplied by underground sources, Pine Barrens rivers are also refreshingly cool—a year-round 55 degrees Fahrenheit.

When water from the aquifers reaches the surface, it feeds into swamps, where the water table is high. Dominating the Pine Barrens swamps is the Atlantic white cedar, commonly known as the swamp cedar or bog cedar. Reaching 50 to 80 feet in height, this tall, straight tree with scale-like dark green leaves grows in dense stands in seeps, springs, and ponds, and along riverbanks.

Despite its name, the white cedar has reddish bark. The red color is indicative of the tree's high tannin content, one of the two main contributors to the color of Pine Barrens river water. Cedar bogs are also high in iron content. Water percolating down through peaty soil composed of decayed cedar is highly acidic. The acidic water reacts with minerals in the sand below the organic layer, precipitating iron out of the water. The iron rises to the surface, where it reacts with air and turns red, then sinks to the bottom of slowly moving rivers that have been fed with the bog water. Mining these deposits of bog iron from the rivers, then forging and casting them into ironware, was a major Pine Barrens industry in the eighteenth and nineteenth centuries. No longer a commercially viable product, bog iron today is simply the other source of the distinctive brown color of the clean Pine Barrens rivers.

29

PAKIM POND

Quiet paths lead through subtly changing pine forests to a Pine Barrens pond featuring beaver dams and pitcher plants.

LOCATION
Woodland Township, NJ

RATING
Easy to moderate

DISTANCE
7 miles

ELEVATION GAIN
240 feet

ESTIMATED TIME
3.25 hours

MAPS
USGS Browns Mills; state.nj.us/dep/ parksandforests/parks/ maps/BrendanByrneAreaMap FinalDraft.pdf

DIRECTIONS

From I-295 in New Jersey, take exit 34A for NJ 70 east, toward Marlton. Follow it for approximately 21 miles until you reach a traffic circle at the junction with NJ 72. Take NJ 72 east about 1 mile until you see a sign on the right for the entrance to Brendan T. Byrne State Forest. Follow the entrance road to the state forest office for plenty of parking. *GPS coordinates:* 39° 53.692′ N, 74° 34.509′ W.

TRAIL DESCRIPTION

For hikers accustomed to Philly-area hikes on rocky, up-and-down trails, Pine Barrens trails can be a liberating experience. A wide, flat, rock-free trail lets you look up and enjoy your surroundings without worrying about where your next step is going to land. In this hike through the Pine Barrens you'll experience subtly changing light and colors, sounds and shapes, and flora and fauna while walking through different types of woods to a pretty pond.

The hike starts at the sign for Cranberry Trail, next to the park office. This trail was designed to be ADA-accessible, so it is wide and level, with fine gravel laid over a natural surface. Red blazes on posts mark the trail. You'll cross the road then continue into the woods.

The surrounding forest is composed of white and pitch pines, as well as oaks. Lowbush blueberry covers the ground under the light canopy. Mountain laurel appears along the way, its twisty forms graced in May by beautiful hexagonal blossoms of white and pink. You can identify bracken fern, common in dry areas, by its tripartite structure of flattened fronds.

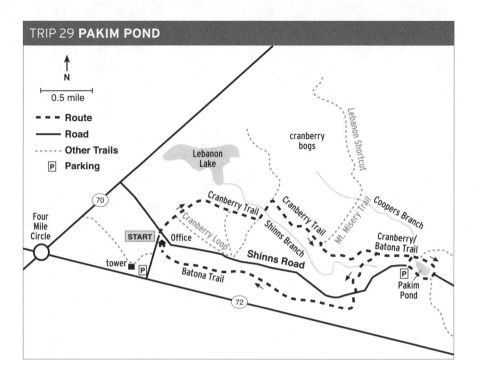

After about 0.3 mile, you'll pass a turnoff for Cranberry Loop Trail. (This nonaccessible natural footpath meets up again with Cranberry Trail in another mile. Taking it, should you opt to do so, adds about 0.5 mile to this hike.) Continue on Cranberry Trail, making a sharp right after another 0.4 mile. You'll now begin seeing highbush blueberry. After passing the other end of Cranberry Loop Trail, turn right, following the arrow on the gravel trail.

The forest becomes noticeably more dense after this turn, with more maples and hollies, as well as sweet pepperbush in the understory—all indicators of moist, well-drained, acidic soil. As you continue through these woods, it's worth marveling at nature's resilience. The landscape as we know it today is much different than it was in the mid-nineteenth century, when the Lebanon glass factory was operating at full capacity, devouring the woods to feed its appetite for fire. Eventually the forest was cleared. In 1867, the glass works had to shut down for want of firewood. The forest surrounding you grew up since that time. Today, Brendan T. Byrne State Forest (originally named Lebanon State Forest and renamed in 2004 to honor the governor who signed the Pinelands Protection Act in 1979) covers 36,000 acres within the Pine Barrens.

After about 1.5 miles from the start of the hike, turn left as Cranberry Trail reaches a T intersection to go alongside a sand road; follow the red posts behind the guide rail. The forest is now very dense, full of cedars. Cross Shinns Branch, a typical cedar-brown Pine Barrens stream, over a wooden bridge. You're

Look for dams—a sign of an active beaver population—around Pakim Pond.

passing through a cedar swamp, a peat bog topped with a carpet of bright green sphagnum moss. Shortly the trail turns to cross the road; continue, following it past a picnic table, through a gate, and past a boulder marking the Cedar Swamp Natural Area. The trail bends left and passes the turnoff for Mount Misery Trail on your left. Soon you'll pass through a large area of white pines, planted in the 1930s by the Civilian Conservation Corps.

Cranberry Trail makes a sharp right as it merges temporarily with the pink-blazed Batona Trail. Follow the combined pink- and red-blazed trail. Shortly you will come to a gate where the path forms a T intersection at a road. Although signs here indicate the "end" of "Red Trail," the combined trail crosses the road. Once across the road, as Batona Trail bears left, follow Cranberry Trail's red blazes to the right, toward a picnic area. The view opens up to encompass the shoreline of Pakim Pond, with its dark brown water reflecting the wide sky above, ringed by green trees.

This name of this small pond is the Lenape word for "cranberry." The native wild cranberry plant thrives alongside peaty Pine Barrens streams, ponds, and bogs. In autumn, it bears bright red berries above elliptical leaves on trailing stems, similar to those borne by cultivated cranberries.

Having taken in the pond view, return to the pink-blazed Batona Trail, which leads across a bridge over the pond; follow Batona Trail to the right, around the pond. Along the shore look for abundant pitcher plants: carnivorous plants that collect water in their purple-veined, vase-shaped leaves to drown tiny, unsuspecting insects. In spring, pitcher plants are marked by hanging, dark red flowers. At the far end of the pond, Batona Trail passes over (and may ford) high water dammed by beavers. Their engineering projects are in full view of the path.

When Batona Trail meets and crosses the paved park road, turn right to follow the road about 800 feet. There, leave the blazed trail and turn right to follow the park road, passing some cabins, back to the picnic area. From the "Cranberry Trail" sign, follow the red and pink blazes to retrace your steps back to the road, past the gate, and into the woods. At a T intersection where the trail splits, follow the pink blazes of Batona Trail to the left.

The pink-blazed Batona Trail is narrower than the accessible Cranberry Trail, and although it is still mostly level, it features some gradual rises and descents. With a natural sand-and-pebble surface, the footpath winds through the progression of forest types that you encountered along Cranberry Trail. You'll also cross a number of firebreaks, or long trenches dug into the sand to contain fires, some of which may have been set by state forest managers to help renew the pine forests and control outbreaks of dangerous wildfires.

Approximately 1.75 miles after leaving Cranberry Trail, you'll cross a sand road. About 0.75 mile later, you'll cross a second sand road and, in another 0.75 mile, you will see a blue trail going to the right, with a sign reading: "Office 0.1 mile." Turn here to return to the parking lot, passing by the trailhead marker for Batona Trail. (Note: If you miss the turnoff, you'll soon reach the Lebanon Fire Tower, where you can take in the view and turn around.)

MORE INFORMATION

There are restrooms at the Brendan T. Byrne State Forest office (open during office hours) and at Pakim Pond, as well composting toilets along the way. Cranberry Trail is open from sunrise to sunset. The park office is open from 8:30 A.M. to 4 P.M. daily. Camping and cabins are available. Dogs are permitted on a leash no more than 6 feet in length. For more information, contact Brendan T. Byrne State Forest, Mile Marker 1, Highway Route 72 East, Woodland Township, NJ 08088; 609-726-1191; state.nj.us/dep/parksandforests/parks/byrne.html. Trail map at state.nj.us/dep/parksandforests/parks/docs/batona14web.pdf.

30

TED STILES PRESERVE AT BALDPATE MOUNTAIN

A mere hill compared with the peaks in the Appalachian Range farther north, Baldpate Mountain has features that belie its size. The highest point in Mercer County, it is a mountain in miniature, boasting deep forests, rushing streams, and ridge-top meadow views—making for a surprisingly wild and seemingly remote hike.

LOCATION
Titusville, NJ (Mercer County)

RATING
Moderate

DISTANCE
5.5 miles (shuttle hike) or 8.25 miles (loop)

ELEVATION GAIN
500 feet

ESTIMATED TIME
3 hours (shuttle hike) or 4.25 hours (loop)

MAPS
USGS Lambertville; trail map available onsite; njtrails.org/wp-content/uploads/2013/01/Ted-Stiles-at-Baldpate-Mountain.pdf

DIRECTIONS

This can either be a shuttle hike, with cars left at its beginning and end, or a loop hike. For a loop hike, park at Fiddlers Creek. For a shuttle hike, park one car at Fiddlers Creek and the other at Church Road, starting the hike at Fiddlers Creek.

To get to Fiddlers Creek from I-95, take Exit 1 for NJ 29 north, drive 4.7 miles, and turn right onto Fiddlers Creek Road. The parking area is 0.3 mile ahead on the left. *GPS coordinates:* 40° 19.102′ N, 74° 53.429′ W.

To reach the Church Road parking area, continue on Fiddlers Creek Road 1.3 miles to an intersection with Church Road. Turn left then immediately right onto the gravel-surfaced Brick Yard Road. You'll see a parking area for six cars just ahead. *GPS coordinates:* 40° 19.111′ N, 74° 51.966′ W.

TRAIL DESCRIPTION

Admit it: You're skeptical. A mountain? In central New Jersey? Only 10 miles from Trenton?

Yes, there is a mountain. And this mountain along the Delaware River—the highest peak in Mercer County at 479 feet—boasts not only a view of Philadelphia's skyline from its crest but also rocky forested slopes, rushing streams, historic ruins, old logging roads, rugged trails,

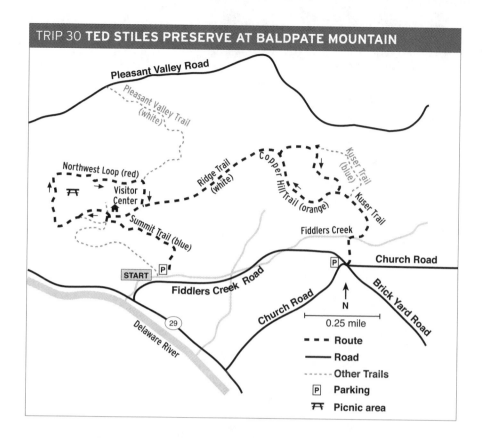

and wildflower meadows. Within its deep woods breed diverse species of forest-dwelling birds, such as scarlet tanagers and veeries. Such features are the norm for the "real" New Jersey mountains in Warren County up north, where another peak called Baldpate Mountain reaches 1,165 feet. The Mercer County Baldpate Mountain, however, has outsize hiking value for its modest height.

Edmund "Ted" Stiles, for whom the 1,800-acre preserve was named in 2007, had a similarly outsize role in the region. A Rutgers biology professor, avid birder, and tireless conservationist, Stiles was a powerful force in central New Jersey land preservation.

The Sourlands region of diabase ridges, of which Baldpate is a part, extends from Mercer to Hunterdon and Somerset counties. Like its geologic Pennsylvania kin, the region's hard volcanic bedrock (traprock) discouraged dense settlement, resulting in extensive areas of continuous, relatively undisturbed forest. The eastern section of the mountain was the site of a late-nineteenth- and early-twentieth-century African American community called Honey Hollow; remnants of some buildings and roads can be glimpsed in the woods along the trails. This hike explores the forest and the ridgeline crest, which was the site of the Kuser family estate before the preserve was purchased by Mercer County in 1998.

Turkey tail mushrooms tend to colonize dead wood.

The hike is a loop, but if you have two cars, you can shorten it and add a trail to explore a wooded stream valley. The color-blazed trails are generally well marked.

Begin at the Fiddlers Creek parking area. The blue-blazed Summit Trail, a level path through a woods of oak, hickory, and tulip trees, begins just beyond the map kiosk. After 0.5 mile, it ascends a remarkable staircase built by volunteers from on-site sandstone boulders then continues steeply uphill through rich woods, leveling off as it crosses the paved road.

Continue on Summit Trail as it enters an old orchard and wends around small groves to a meadow. Here, picnic tables provide an expansive view and a perfect rest stop. Look southwest, taking in the long-range vista over the Delaware River. On clear days, Philadelphia skyscrapers can be seen just above the horizon; binoculars help.

Below the meadow is a cluster of buildings that made up the Kuser estate, now the Ted Stiles Preserve visitor center, where you'll find restrooms and a plaque in honor of Ted Stiles.

At the western edge of the meadow, enter the woods via the red-blazed Northwest Loop Trail. On this side of the ridge, sounds of the quarry below occasionally echo through the woods, and ominous signs indicating blasting in progress are posted on trees. The trail descends steeply then becomes an old, occasionally muddy road with a flat grade for about 0.5 mile. Northwest Loop Trail then turns right and climbs back up the ridge very steeply, joining the white-blazed Ridge Trail after less than 0.25 mile.

The combined trail now follows the crest of the mountain along a gentle, flat, rock-surfaced footpath. After about 0.75 mile from the trail merge you will pass an old farmstead and a pond. In another 1.25 miles, you'll come to a large parking area at the Pleasant Valley trailhead. Just past the trailhead kiosk, bear right into the woods to enter the orange-blazed Copper Hill Trail, marked by a sign with the letter "C." Copper Hill Trail begins as a level path through a young woods along flat red sandstone. Begin a descent down the east side of the mountain. Pass a T intersection with the red-blazed Kuser Trail after 0.4 mile. (For the shuttle hike, descend the mountain on Kuser Trail through a moist beech-maple-ash woods to a pretty stream, Kuser Run, and wetlands. Cross Fiddlers Creek on stones and ascend a short hill then cross Fiddlers Creek Road and continue to the Church Road parking lot.) Copper Hill Trail descends, passing a ruin with a chimney, and bends right to climb a long, steep slope. This part of the mountain is great for observing birds in the spring and summer.

Copper Hill Trail ends at Ridge Trail. Turn left onto Ridge Trail and continue about 1.75 miles to Summit Trail, on the left. Follow the blue blazes of Summit Trail downhill to the Fiddlers Creek Road trailhead.

MORE INFORMATION

There are restrooms at the Ted Stiles Preserve visitor center. Horses are permitted on trails, and bikes on some trails. Dogs must be leashed. Trails are open daily from sunrise to sunset; hunting is permitted by arrangement in season (except on Sundays from mid-November to mid-February), and trails may be closed; contact Mercer County Parks for exact dates (mercercountyparks.org/parks/baldpate-mountain). Trails are maintained by Mercer County Parks, with the assistance of New Jersey Trails (njtrails.org). Across from Baldpate Mountain is Fiddlers Creek Preserve, which features more hiking trails. For more information, contact Mercer County Park Commission, 8 Fiddlers Creek Road Titusville, NJ 08560, (609) 303-0700.

31

SOURLAND MOUNTAIN PRESERVE

Hike up and down a rugged ridge through a rich, rocky woods, highlighted by an "amusement park" of ridge-top boulders featuring rock outcrops, crevices, overpasses, and underpasses.

DIRECTIONS

Take I-95 to Exit 7B for US 206 north, toward Lawrenceville and Princeton. Stay on US 206 for 14.7 miles and turn left onto CR 601 (Trent Avenue, becoming Blawenberg Belle Mead Road). In 1.1 miles, turn right onto East Mountain Road. In another 1.1 miles, the entrance to the preserve will be on your left. *GPS coordinates:* 40° 28.431′ N, 74° 41.655′ W.

TRAIL DESCRIPTION

The Sourlands is a discontinuous, 20-mile-long region in central New Jersey defined by a unifying geology. Looming over flat valleys of sedimentary rock are vertical ridges of volcanic diabase, including Baldpate Mountain in the southwest corner of the region (see Trip 30) and Sourland Mountain in the northeast corner. Diabase splits into blocks and boulders that tumble off the ridges and down the sheer slopes. The name "Sourlands" may derive from the nature of the soil; the stone slopes yield thin soil and hold little water, making for "sour" farmland. It may also derive from the word "sorrel," as the reddish color of the surrounding soil recalls that of the flowering sorrel. Because the soil was not ideal for farming, the ridges were largely undeveloped (although extensively quarried) and thus remained a rich wildlife habitat and an important resource for protecting water quality.

On the south- and east-facing slopes of Sourland Mountain lies Somerset County's 4,000-acre Sourland Mountain Preserve, where trails access the rocky hills and provide

LOCATION
Hillsborough Township, NJ
(Somerset County)

RATING
Easy to moderate

DISTANCE
5 miles

ELEVATION GAIN
400 feet

ESTIMATED TIME
2.25 hours

MAPS
USGS Rocky Hill; trail maps available at trailhead; somersetcountyparks.org/genInfo/maps/SourlandsMap.pdf

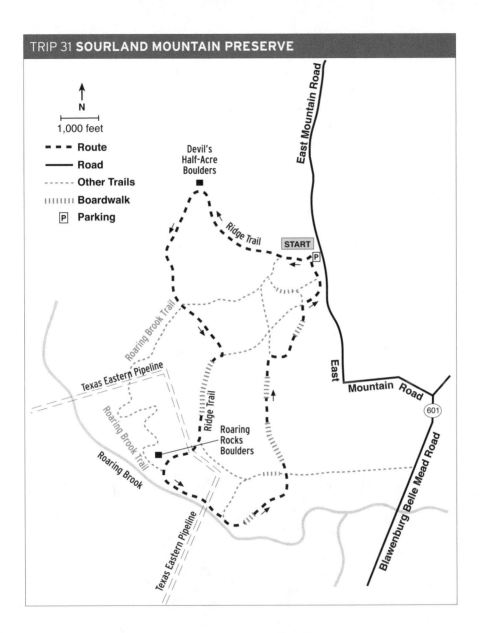

glimpses of the valley. This hike focuses on Ridge Trail, a 5-mile circuit that makes its way up to a boulder field near the crest and meanders through streams and quiet woods on its way there and back.

The hike starts behind the information kiosk near the main trailhead, at the edge of the woods. It begins as a wide gravel path with a few rocks in and around it. Numbered trailside posts correspond to numbers on the preserve map, available onsite, making it easy to discern trail connections, assess elapsed distance, and—important in an essentially homogenous landscape—be reassured that you're not going astray. Trails are marked with distinct shapes. For Ridge Trail, these are squares.

At marker 1, continue straight; do not cross the bridge. The trail, now a narrow, rocky footpath, climbs steeply up and across the ridge. Maple, tulip, oak, and beech trees predominate; as the trail ascends, hickory, birch (gray and black), and basswood trees begin to appear. (Basswood, typically a bottomland tree, indicates where the woods are wet.) The whistle of the eastern pewee, a forest-dwelling bird seen in spring and summer, is a sign that the woods are deep and healthy.

The trail passes by large boulders, first a few, then more and more, until finally, near the top of the ridge, the trail begins reeling crazily around the field of boulders that pepper the ground, as if the trail designer became giddy with delight. You'll have to squeeze through, climb over, or brush by boulder after boulder. Just when you think you're past them, the trail enjoys a close encounter with yet another grouping. The tumbled, jumbled quality of these huge rocks shows the immense power of water to break off pieces from the parent mountain and toss them around and down the slope.

Ridge Trail eventually settles into a southwesterly direction downhill. At marker 4 it meets a connector trail that leads back to the trailhead. Shortly thereafter, Roaring Brook Trail, blazed with red circles, goes to the left. (A worthwhile detour down this trail leads to the extensive Roaring Rocks field of

Boardwalks carry Ridge Trail through wet areas in the diabase woods of Sourland Mountain.

massive boulders, where you may be able to hear the eponymous roar, if the creek flowing beneath them is full; continue the hike by rejoining Ridge Trail after marker 7.) Continue straight and downhill through the woods. At marker 5, after a small stream, you'll reach a wide clearing: a gas pipeline crossing. This is the best view on the trail, so be sure to pause and take it in. The trail then turns slightly to the right (uphill and away from the view) then quickly turns left to reenter the woods. Boardwalks carry Ridge Trail over a particularly muddy section, of which there are many in this woods. The rocks don't drain water easily, so it sits on the surface. At marker 6, another short connector trail leads to the Roaring Rocks boulder field.

At marker 7, Ridge Trail begins a gradual descent, and after marker 8, it goes over a boardwalk, crossing a connector trail at marker 9. More boardwalks take the trail over swampy areas. Turn right at marker 10 and descend toward marker 11. Cross the lower end of the pipeline clearing, reenter the woods, turn right at marker 12 and left at marker 13, and emerge from the woods at the trailhead.

MORE INFORMATION

A portable toilet is located at the parking lot. The park is open from dawn to dusk. Bikes are permitted on the trails. The Sourland Planning Council (sourland.org) has a wealth of information on the history and natural resources of the region, as well as on conservation initiatives. Somerset County owns and manages the Sourland Mountain Preserve. For more information, contact Somerset County Parks, 421 East Mountain Road, Hillsborough Township, NJ 08844; 908-722-1200; somersetcountyparks.org/parksfacilities/sourland/sourlandmtpreserve.html.

32

BULL'S ISLAND, DELAWARE CANAL, AND D&R CANAL

Walk through an old-growth floodplain forest at Bull's Island then continue along the canals and along both sides of the Delaware River, where mules once towed barges and locomotives pulled trains.

DIRECTIONS

From Exit 1 on I-95 in New Jersey, take NJ 29 north. Follow it about 16.5 miles to Bull's Island Recreation Area. The entrance is on the left; you will find ample parking. *GPS coordinates:* 40° 24.650′ N, 75° 02.029′ W.

TRAIL DESCRIPTION

This portion of the Delaware River, 12 miles upstream from its industrialized tidal segment, is a miracle. In a region that has been growing and developing for centuries, here is a wild, undeveloped riverscape that hasn't changed appreciably since William Penn sailed upstream to his country estate north of present-day Philadelphia. The river here runs swiftly, just as it has for centuries, beneath ragged red cliffs, past tree-clad hills dotted with picturesque villages, and around islands populated only by turtles.

Ironically, the best way to experience the untamed river—other than by paddling or tubing with its current—is to walk the vestiges of riverside industry that line its banks. Because the Delaware wasn't navigable above Trenton and Morrisville, canals were built early in the nineteenth century. In Pennsylvania, the Delaware Canal ran between Easton and Bristol, and in New Jersey, the Delaware & Raritan (D&R) Canal stretched from Trenton to New Brunswick, fed in part by a smaller canal from Bull's Island to Trenton. Although water continues to run through them, the canals today are used only for recreation. The towpath

LOCATION
Lumberville, PA; Bull's Island and Raven Rock, NJ

RATING
Moderate

DISTANCE
9 miles

ELEVATION GAIN
Minimal

ESTIMATED TIME
4 hours

MAPS
USGS Lumberville, USGS Stockton

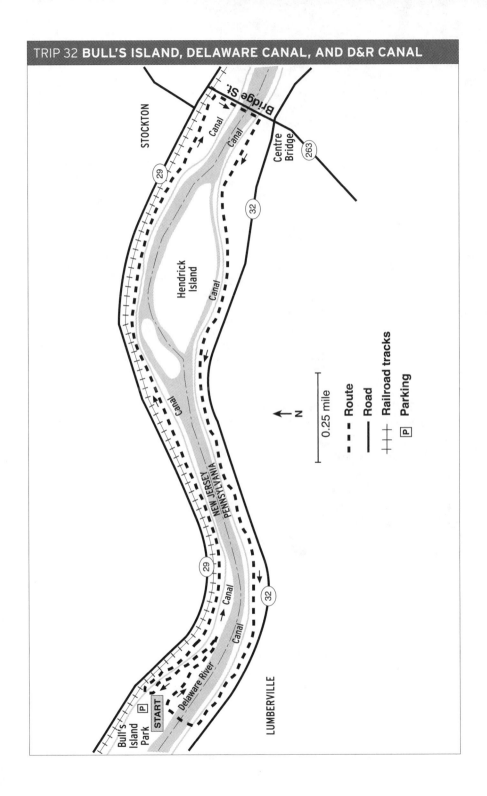

The D&R Canal parallels the Delaware River in New Jersey, as does its counterpart in Pennsylvania, the Delaware Canal.

(from which mules once pulled boats) and a railroad track along the feeder canal have been converted into trails.

The hike begins at Bull's Island, with a 1-mile loop to the tip of the island and back. The feeder canal, dug in the early 1830s, enlarged a creek between the island and the mainland. The downstream portion of the island contains a large and unusual old-growth floodplain forest. You'll find the trailhead for Nature Trail opposite the park office mailboxes. Enormous trees—such as sycamore, silver maple, tulip, and river birch—wrapped with giant vines soar over a lush, green, primitive bottomland choked with 5-foot-tall ferns. The trees predate the canal's construction.

Follow the narrow dirt footpath along the canal to the left, with the forest on the right. Watch out for the stems of stinging nettles crowding the trail; although it is harmless and smarts for only a few minutes, the sting is painful. Nature Trail runs to the endpoint of the island then stops abruptly at the top of the low dam, with the canal on one side and the river on the other. Don't fall! Turn around here then bear left into the woods after 0.1 mile. Exceptionally large, old-growth trees envelop the trail in green and brown.

Nature Trail parallels the river for 1 mile and emerges onto a paved path just after the canoe landing. Follow this path to the parking area, turn right, head over the canal bridge to D&R Canal Trail, and turn right again. This wide, flat gravel path extends 3 miles, paralleling NJ 29 on the left and the canal and floodplain forest on the right, with the river playing peek-a-boo through the thick trees. The last 0.5 mile threads past the historic Prallsville Mills, passes over the mill dam bridge, and travels through the backyards of Stockton.

In Stockton, cross Bridge Street, turn right, and cross the river via the bridge, entering the town of Centre Bridge, Pennsylvania. The bridge itself, with its open-grate steel truss, replaced a covered wooden bridge whose dramatic destruction in a 1923 fire was depicted by the Pennsylvania impressionist Edward Redfield in a celebrated painting titled *The Burning of Center Bridge*.

To get to the Delaware Canal towpath, descend the stairs just below the bridge and turn right. To the left is the canal, which is narrower and shallower than the one on the New Jersey side. To the right is the river, which is much closer to the path than it is on the New Jersey side; sometimes it will be just a few feet away and rarely more than 10 feet.

The Delaware Canal towpath is a flat, stabilized turf surface. This section, along with most of the rest of the path, has been reconstructed on more than one occasion after suffering flood damage. Unlike the canal on the New Jersey side of the river, Pennsylvania's Delaware Canal runs along steep, rocky slopes for much of its length. The natural floodplain for the Delaware River includes both the towpath and the canal. When the river floods, the water washes away the towpath. Some say the path is not worth reconstructing because the river will take back what belongs to it, but the community has continued to support this beloved amenity.

The towpath continues 3.5 miles, providing an intimate experience of the river and its islands, as well as the canal and the red rock cliffs above, covered with unusual ferns and wildflowers. The last mile passes in the shadow of Lumberville, located on the banks above. Go under the bridge and climb the stairs to cross the river to Bull's Island. This historic, pedestrian-only footbridge—one of two on the river—was built in 1947 on an 1856 masonry substructure by John A. Roebling's Sons, of Brooklyn Bridge fame. Follow the paved path back to the parking lot.

MORE INFORMATION

Restrooms are located at Bull's Island Recreation Area and at Virginia Forrest Recreation Area on the Pennsylvania side of the Delaware River. Bikes are permitted on the canal paths. The Bull's Island Recreation Area and the Virginia Forrest Recreation Area are open from sunrise to sunset. For more information on Bull's Island Recreation Area: 2185 Daniel Bray Highway, Stockton, NJ 08559; 609-397-2949; state.nj.us/dep/parksandforests/parks/bull.html. For more information on Delaware Canal State Park: 11 Lodi Hill Road, Upper Black Eddy, PA 18972; 610-982-5560; dcnr.state.pa.us/stateparks/findapark/delawarecanal.

HOW GREEN IS MY VALLEY?

Residents of the region surrounding Philadelphia—including the suburbs and exurbs of southeastern Pennsylvania, central and southern New Jersey, and northern Delaware—refer to the area as the "Delaware Valley." This may surprise those residents of upstate New York who use the same name for their region. But the river is wide enough and long enough to accommodate any number of people who claim it as a geographical frame of reference.

The Delaware basin extends north to the Catskill Mountains of New York, where its west and east branches arise. After passing through reservoirs that supply water for New York City, the branches meet at Hancock, New York, where the main stem of the Delaware River begins its journey south. For the next 331 miles, it flows free to the sea, emptying into Delaware Bay; it is the longest undammed river east of the Mississippi. Two major rivers empty into the Delaware River—the Lehigh at Easton, Pennsylvania, and the Schuylkill at Philadelphia—and 214 other creeks and rivers feed into it. All told, the Delaware River drains a four-state watershed of 13,539 square miles.

The Delaware is tidal up to the fall line between Morrisville, Pennsylvania, and Trenton, New Jersey, where the sandy Atlantic coastal plain meets the rocky Piedmont province. The line is marked by a mass of large boulders in the river; these inhibited the path of big ships upriver, so major industry is concentrated below the line. Because it is free-flowing and largely undeveloped, the river has been designated a national Wild and Scenic River for most of its length.

In the mental geography of the region's residents, the Delaware Valley extends up to the confluence of the Lehigh River and Delaware River at Easton, the eastern edge of the Lehigh Valley. The Delaware River divides Pennsylvania from New Jersey, but it also unites the two states, for it is the two sides that make a whole valley.

Much of the lower nontidal Delaware River retains the feel of a natural shore. The river flows swiftly between tree-lined hills and alongside high red cliffs; small towns hug the banks; herons fish in the shallows, and ospreys soar overhead. A paddler's delight, this section of the river is also enjoyed by pedestrians—a result, ironically enough, of the remnants of alternative transportation systems. Canals and rail lines built in the nineteenth century have been repurposed to serve as walking paths on both sides. Today's hikers have a 21st-century relationship with the river: appreciative of its gifts, accepting of its pace.

33

ROCKHOPPER TRAIL AND DRY RUN CREEK TRAIL

Two complementary short hikes make for one delightful walk through historic woods near twin river towns.

DIRECTIONS

From I-95 in New Jersey, take Exit 1 for NJ 29 north toward Lambertville. Drive 9.5 miles; when you reach Lambertville, turn right onto CR 518 (Brunswick Pike). After 2.1 miles, turn right into a parking area marked by a sign: "D&R Greenway Natural Area." There is room for six cars. *GPS coordinates: 40° 21.510′ N, 74° 54.507′ W.*

TRAIL DESCRIPTION

Near the twin Delaware River towns of New Hope, Pennsylvania, and Lambertville, New Jersey, is a set of twin hiking trails. As with a visit to the river towns, you can experience one or both; each has its charms, and together they provide contrasts and complements. The trails are separated by a wide road rather than a broad river, but water is never far away on either hike.

Rockhopper Trail (2.3 miles) extends between the outskirts of Lambertville and Brunswick Pike (CR 518), passing through woods surrounding a reservoir. Dry Run Creek Trail (1.2 miles) meanders along a creek valley between Brunswick Pike and the road to the Howell Living History Farm. Hiking routes abound, including out-and-back treks from either end, with the option to continue into Lambertville or Howell Farm. This hike takes the Solomonic approach, starting in the middle. You can choose to hike north or south from the starting point; this description heads north first.

From the parking area, cross CR 518. (Caution: Although the highway is not always busy, cars do go fast.) Rockhopper Trail, marked with prominent blue blazes, begins to the

LOCATION
Lambertville, NJ

RATING
Moderate

DISTANCE
7 miles

ELEVATION GAIN
350 feet

ESTIMATED TIME
3 hours

MAPS
USGS Lambertville; partial map available onsite; njtrails.org/wp-content/uploads/2013/02/Rockhopper2.pdf

njtrails.org/wp-content/uploads/2012/11/DryRunCreek1.pdf

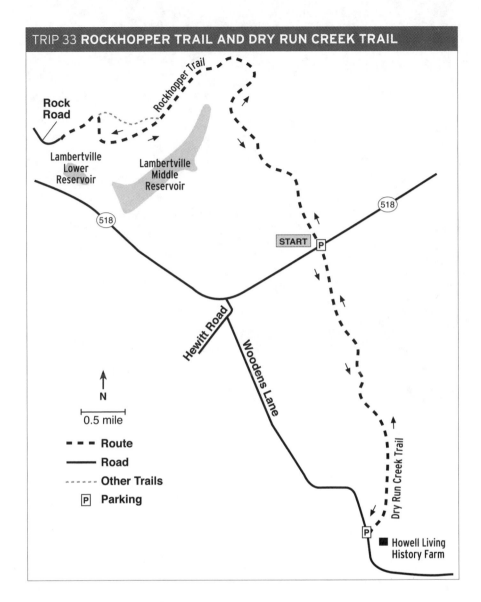

right of the hedgerow. Follow the hedgerow along a grassy area and past a barn then enter the woods. Under a high canopy of towering oak, birch, tulip, hickory, and beech trees, the trail ascends briefly before descending very gradually into an increasingly moist and rocky terrain abundant with ferns. The hill is composed of hard, volcanic diabase. (See "Black Rock, Green Forests," page 77.) Here and there along the trail, you'll pass deep pits, remnants of early-nineteeth-century quarrying. Rocks were split by hand using the "plug and feather" technique, which left behind telltale cylindrical scars on the rocks as wedges and shims were hammered into stone.

A hiker prepares to hop the rocks across a wooded stream.

Rockhopper Trail reaches its zenith of rockiness at a stream crossing augmented by stone steps. You can cross by hopping the rocks, except after heavy rains, when the steps are welcome. Past the stream, everything changes. The trail, now flat, grassy, and rock-free, has crossed onto the remains of Rock Road, built in the 1700s. Until the 1820s, when Brunswick Road was constructed, Rock Road was the main thoroughfare between Lambertville and Hopewell. You're treading the same road that George Washington's troops marched on en route to the Battle of Monmouth. Look for stone walls and relict foundations that date to the eighteenth century. The trail crosses a nineteenth-century stone bridge over a little brook and passes into a wetlands, away from the historic road.

Continue on the blue-blazed Rockhopper Trail as it intersects other trails, some marked with other colors (any of which may be explored), and skirts several fields before returning to woods. Through the curtain of trees to your left is the Lambertville Middle Reservoir. About 2 miles from the trailhead, you will reach a power line clearing. The trail turns right and then, shortly afterward, left to rejoin the old Rock Road along a stream, becoming a grassy lane again at Quarry Road. (Parking is prohibited along Quarry Road, but you can walk about 0.9 mile from here into the heart of Lambertville.) Return to the CR 518 trailhead by retracing your steps.

Cross CR 518 to continue onto Dry Run Creek Trail, past the trailhead kiosk. D&R Greenway Land Trust, a regional conservation nonprofit, has preserved the land surrounding this trail, enabling hikers to enjoy the beautiful creek views afforded by the sloping valley. On this side of CR 518, the rocks are broader and flatter than on the Rockhopper side. The blue-blazed Dry Run Creek Trail descends from the parking area, past the site of a former pond, and behind a long-ago breached earthen dam on the creek. Cross a cedar footbridge made onsite by trail volunteers. Descend, occasionally via wooden steps, to a path that goes along the creek, occasionally crossing rock ledges.

From the creek, Dry Run Creek Trail gradually ascends the valley again before descending. The leisurely ups and downs through open woods of beech and oak bring the creek into view more than once. The trail ascends through a grove of red cedars to its terminus at the parking lot on Woodens Lane. You can continue along this quiet road about 0.25 mile to visit Howell Living History Farm, a nice place to have lunch. Families, in particular, may enjoy learning about the history of local farming at this interactive museum. To return to your starting point, simply retrace your steps back through the valley to the parking area.

MORE INFORMATION

There are no restrooms along this hike, although restrooms are available at Howell Living History Farm during business hours. Trails are maintained by volunteers for D&R Greenway Land Trust; information and trail maps can be found at njtrails.org. Dogs are permitted on leash. For more information, contact Howell Living History Farm, 70 Woodens Lane, Lambertville, NJ 08530; 609-737-3299; howellfarm.org. Both Lambertville and New Hope are eminently walkable towns once you find parking. Full of shops and restaurants, they are popular tourist destinations.

34

MUSCONETCONG GORGE PRESERVE

This hike is short in length but rich in challenges and history. Its rugged terrain encompasses rocky ravines and waterfalls, views of Kittatinny Ridge, and glimpses of the Musconetcong River.

LOCATION
Holland Township, NJ
(Hunterdon County)

RATING
Easy to moderate

DISTANCE
4 miles

ELEVATION GAIN
250 feet

ESTIMATED TIME
3 hours

MAPS
USGS Bloomsbury, USGS Easton; co.hunterdon.nj.us/depts/parks/ParkAreas/MusconetcongGorge/trailmap.pdf

DIRECTIONS

From I-95 in New Jersey, take Exit 1 for NJ 29 north and continue 25.4 miles. In Frenchtown, turn left onto Bridge Street and then take a quick right onto Harrison Street (CR 619). Continue 8 miles; the road becomes NJ 519 after 3.5 miles. When you reach Dennis Road, bear right and continue 0.6 mile to the parking area on the right, with space for seven to eight cars. *GPS coordinates: 40° 37.627′ N, 75° 08.151′ W.*

TRAIL DESCRIPTION

An irony of hiking in the Philadelphia area is that many of the wooded streams and rivers we enjoy for their scenic beauty and recreational value are reclaimed industrial sites. Early settlers discovered a rich resource in the region's forested valleys. Dammed and channeled, swift-running waterways powered mills and forges; cleared and burned forests yielded charcoal. The stripped, smoke-filled hillsides resounded with gears turning and mill-stones grinding. Even after water-powered industries disappeared, rivers continued to be a cheap source of water and places to dispose of waste.

Musconetcong Gorge Preserve is a prime example. Mills and forges operated along the Musconetcong River Gorge for centuries. Hunterdon County obtained the 524-acre preserve, near the river's confluence with the Delaware River, in 1974 from a paper company that had used the

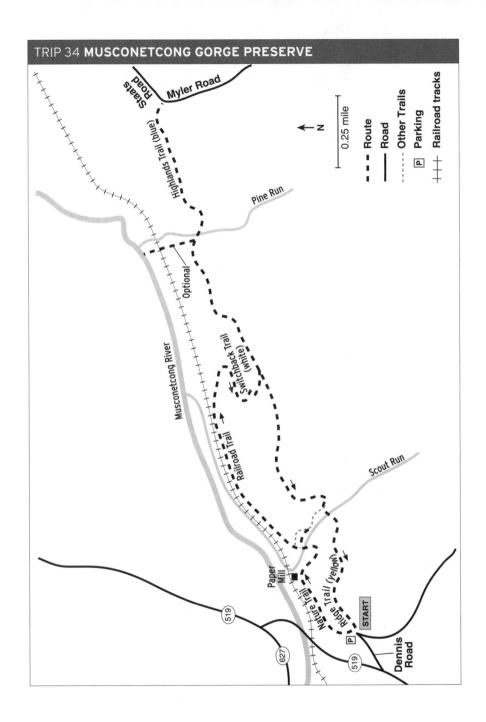

TRIP 34 **MUSCONETCONG GORGE PRESERVE**

river for power and the woods for raw materials. Although they no longer function, the mill and dam still exist, as does a railbed. Today, the preserve is a cool, quiet, forested ravine sloping toward the river. The fresh air is filled with the sounds of birdsong and rushing water, and the hills are so thick with trees that the river is barely visible. Yet reminders of its industrial past form as much a part of the site's fabric as its natural features do.

The hike starts at the blue-blazed Nature Trail on the north side of the parking lot, marked by a large wooden sign about 20 feet down the hill—not the yellow-blazed Ridge Trail starting at the eastern end. (This loop hike can be done in the other direction, taking the more difficult option of descending rather than ascending the long, steep Switchback Trail in the middle.) Descend the hill along a narrow rocky footpath (note occasional numbered posts). The trail levels off, then descends steeply into the Scout Run Valley, crossing the stream twice, once on rocks and then on a bridge via a midstream island. Continue about 100 feet to a gravel road (the blue-blazed Gas Line Trail).

Turn right onto the road; after 20 feet bear right into the woods to go up the steep and rocky red-blazed Waterfall Trail; it returns to the Scout Run and follows it uphill to a multilevel waterfall. Return downhill via the same trail; at the three-way intersection, turn right to follow the orange-blazed Railroad Trail into the woods.

Enter a moist, rich hardwood forest of birch, ash, oak, maple, tulip tree, and dogwood, with abundant shrubs and ferns, and wildflowers in spring. This forest is a haven for songbirds, including the deep-woods residents veery and scarlet tanager. The trail continues along the slope of the hill, paralleling the rail bed near the base of the ridge below. In winter there are decent views of the river and the paper-mill dam. The trail is wet and swampy in some places.

After 0.5 mile, just before the trail reaches the rail bed, it intersects the white-blazed Switchback Trail. Turn right and climb the hill. The half-mile trail is steep and rocky; note the changes in size and type of rock as you ascend. Near the top, stone steps aid in the climb.

Ridge Trail is marked with yellow diamonds. The trail is also marked with blue diamond badges indicating that it is part of the Highlands Trail, a long-distance trail under development that traverses the Highlands region of New Jersey and goes into New York. The Highlands Trail will eventually continue through Pennsylvania.

Turn left and follow the Ridge/Highlands Trail blazes. Descend the ridge after 0.75 mile, down the ravine to the Pine Run. Cross the stream on rocks and continue up the other side, up the slope. The trail climbs steeply up the rocky hill, then levels out, winding past sunny fields and wildflower meadows. The preserve, though not the Highlands Trail, ends at Myler Road. (To continue on the Highlands Trail, turn right and follow the blue diamonds.) Turn around, and return down the Highlands Trail until you meet the Pine Run again. Cross the stream.

A hiker takes time out to enjoy taking time out at Musconetcong Gorge.

For an optional, *strenuous* half-mile detour to gain the only access to the river in the preserve, turn right to head downhill along the creek. The descent along the stream is over rocks, along an old trail (not maintained) that is rocky, steep, and slippery, especially close to the stream, as it descends to the bottom of the ravine. It crosses an abandoned gravel rail bed, which had been a spur line for the paper mill. The preserve includes a very small portion of the rail bed several hundred feet on either side of the stream, and the rest is off-limits to the public. Continue along the stream until it joins the river. Return to the Ridge/Highlands Trail the way you came down.

As it winds downhill, the trail passes several charcoal landings. Look for flattened, cleared circular areas with black soil. The landings are remnants of a long-ago industry. Trees were cut down and burned to make charcoal, which was used as fuel in nearby forges or shipped downriver. Because charcoal is lighter than raw wood, it was economically more efficient to burn it onsite than to ship logs. Charcoal-making devastated huge swaths of forest in Pennsylvania and New Jersey, until anthracite coal replaced charcoal as an economical fuel.

Go by several enormous boulder outcrops, excellent vantage points from which to view Kittatinny Ridge to the northwest or just to contemplate the passage of time. Immediately upon passing these rocks, you will hear the sound of a waterfall.

Descend into a rocky ravine via steep wooden steps to cross the Scout Run, passing an artificial waterfall (note the hardened bags of concrete). Bear right to continue uphill and along the ridge via the Ridge/Highlands Trail for another 0.5 mile to the parking area.

MORE INFORMATION

There are no restrooms. Musconetcong Gorge Preserve is open from sunrise to sunset. Dogs must be leashed. Hunting is permitted throughout the preserve; during hunting season, wear orange or visit only on Sundays, when hunting is prohibited.

The trails are maintained by the Hunterdon Hiking Club. For more information, contact Musconetcong Gorge Preserve, 182 Dennis Road, Bloomsbury, NJ 08804; 908-782-1158; co.hunterdon.nj.us/depts/parks/ParkAreas/MusconetcongGorge/info.htm.

PENNSYLVANIA HIGHLANDS TRAIL NETWORK

In Pennsylvania, a surge of trail-building has occurred in recent years—a response to growing demand from people looking for places to enjoy healthful outdoor exercise, bolstered by increased public support for trail funding. Perhaps the most ambitious trail project in the southeastern part of the state is the Pennsylvania Highlands Trail Network (PHTN), a collaborative initiative led by the Appalachian Mountain Club (AMC).

A forested region stretching from the Delaware River in Bucks County to South Mountain on the Maryland border in Adams County, the Pennsylvania Highlands includes the largest contiguous forest in southeastern Pennsylvania (see Trip 16), as well as rural farmland, suburban hillsides, and urban areas. The Pennsylvania Highlands is home to natural, cultural, and agricultural resources and recreational opportunities that are significant due to their proximity to population-dense regions. From east to west, the Highlands encompasses four major watersheds: those of the Delaware, Lehigh, Schuylkill, and Susquehanna rivers. For centuries, each of these landscapes has shaped and been shaped by the interaction between people and nature. Trails in the region offer hikers opportunities to experience this cultural history while exploring diverse natural features.

The PHTN effort aims to create a cohesive network of trails within the Pennsylvania Highlands by linking hundreds of miles of existing trails. These include parts or all of long-distance trails, such as Delaware & Lehigh, Schuylkill River, Perkiomen, Horse-Shoe, and Mason-Dixon trails. Where there are gaps, crews are constructing new trails, such as the 1.3-mile trail built by AMC connecting Bucks County's popular Ringing Rocks County Park with Delaware & Lehigh Trail in Delaware Canal State Park. The trails in the PHTN are not necessarily limited to foot traffic; many miles can accommodate both pedestrians and cyclists.

In addition to linking natural areas, the PHTN will also connect historic sites, such as mills, canals, and early industrial centers. A theme common to many of these sites is their relationship to the iron industry, which thrived in this region from the colonial era until the late nineteenth century. As noted in many trips in this book, ironmaking altered Pennsylvania's landscape. Its legacy is still felt long after the forges have closed, forests have returned to reclaim the hills, and hikers—rather than colliers—tread paths into the woods.

To learn more about the Pennsylvania Highlands Trail Network, please visit pahighlands.org.

BERKS COUNTY AND LEHIGH VALLEY, PENNSYLVANIA

The Lehigh Valley names a cultural area rather than a geographic one; what is called the Lehigh Valley is a subset of the actual valley of the Lehigh River. The river flows 103 miles south–southeast, from the Lehigh Marshes in the Poconos into the Delaware River at Easton, Pennsylvania. Pennsylvania's Lehigh Valley, however, refers to only the greater Allentown–Bethlehem–Easton metropolitan area, or Lehigh, Northampton, and Carbon counties—three of the seven counties in the river's watershed.

Linking Lehigh Valley and Berks County to the west is the area's most prominent geographic feature: the Kittatinny Ridge, also called Blue Mountain. The easternmost ridge of the Appalachian Range, Kittatinny (1,500 to 1,700 feet high) marks the southern boundary between the ridge-and-valley province and the Piedmont.

The ridge-and-valley province is a series of parallel ridges composed of hard metamorphic rock, primarily quartzite, and valleys of softer sedimentary rock, such as shale, sandstone, and limestone. All of the ridges, including the Kittatinny, tend in a southwest–northeast direction. Finding Blue Mountain in its way as it sought to head south, the Lehigh River decided to make its own path. It excised an opening in the ridge—the Lehigh Gap—and then proceeded south before turning east toward the Delaware.

Glen Onoko Falls is one of eastern Pennsylvania's most dazzling hiking destinations. Featuring waterfalls, a gorge, and riverside forests, it's a challenging hike with ample rewards.

Driving north toward Kittatinny Ridge from Philadelphia never fails to elicit chills of delight. As my car approaches from the south and the long ridge comes into view, stretching across the horizon, I usually exclaim: "There it is! The Appalachian Trail!" That the Appalachian Trail could span more than 2,000 miles between Maine and Georgia is such a tremendous feat of its planners' imagination, its builders' determination, and its contemporary maintainers' devotion that it deserves commemoration every time we see it. Hikes on the Appalachian Trail trace the top of the ridge. (See Trip 44, Appalachian Trail: PA 309 to Bake Oven Knob; Trip 45, Lehigh Gap Nature Center; and Trip 46, Lehigh Gap East.)

To the south of the Kittatinny is the Piedmont section of the Lehigh Valley, a region of varied topography and terrain described more fully in the Southeast Pennsylvania and Delaware section (see page 1). The southern boundary of the Lehigh Valley is marked by South (or Lehigh) Mountain. Hikes in the Lehigh Valley–Piedmont include Trexler Nature Preserve (Trip 36), Jacobsburg Environmental Education Center (Trip 37), Monocacy Way (Trip 38), Lehigh Parkway (Trip 42), and South Mountain Preserve (Trip 43).

Farther north, in the ridge-and-valley region, the rugged terrain and dramatic topography make for qualitatively different hikes. The hikes in this area include Hickory Run State Park (Trip 47) and Glen Onoko Falls and Lehigh Gorge State Park (Trip 48).

35

NATURAL LANDS' MARITON WILDLIFE SANCTUARY

Trails in Natural Lands' Mariton Wildlife Sanctuary wind up and down steep, rocky, forested hills in a dramatic cliffside setting above the Delaware River.

DIRECTIONS

From Exit 343 of the Pennsylvania Turnpike (I-276), take PA 611 north toward Riegelsville. After 33.3 miles, turn left onto Spring Hill Road. Drive 0.6 mile and turn right onto Sunnyside Drive. In 0.5 mile, the entrance to the sanctuary will be on the left; you will find parking for nineteen cars. *GPS coordinates:* 40° 36.450′ N, 75° 12.283′ W.

TRAIL DESCRIPTION

Natural Lands' Mariton Wildlife Sanctuary packs more diversity, history, and scenic beauty into its 200 acres than many natural areas contain in their much larger expanses. In part this is because of the sanctuary's heritage—forest, then farmland, then country residence, then forest again. In part it is because of Mariton's enviable location—on the slopes of Bougher Hill along the Delaware, on the border between two geologic provinces. And in part it is because the sanctuary is so well laid out and well maintained, balanced between the interests of wildlife and humans.

Begin the hike at the nature center, which has exhibits relating to the site's natural history. Take the lower of the two trailheads that begin at the woods' edge, behind the nature center, not Woods Trail (your return route) but Main Trail, which is slightly downhill and past the Manager's Residence. Note the wooden post painted yellow at the top. Each trail is blazed with a different color, noted on the trail map. The posts are well spaced, not obtrusive but frequent enough to reassure you you're on the right trail.

LOCATION
Easton, PA
(Northampton County)

RATING
Easy to moderate

DISTANCE
3.5 miles

ELEVATION GAIN
500 feet

ESTIMATED TIME
2 hours

MAPS
USGS Riegelsville, USGS Easton; available onsite at nature center; natlands.org/wp-content/uploads/2017/05/MaritonBrochInside.pdf

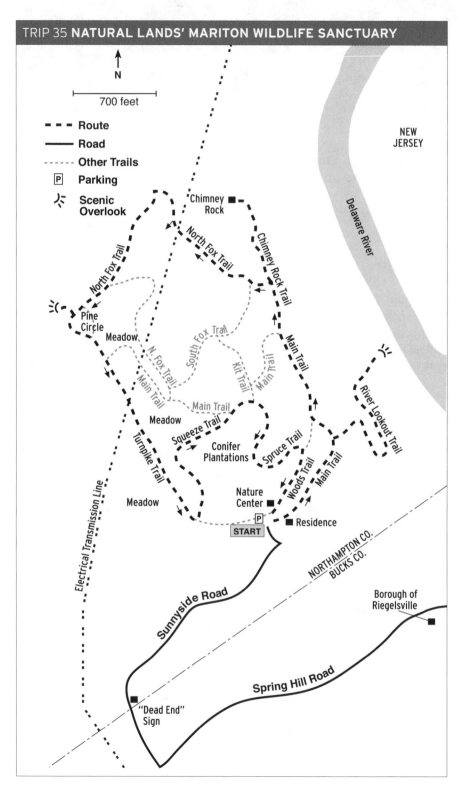

The wide, natural-surface trail heads downhill and into a woods dating back 50 to 75 years, with many tall tulip trees. Natural Lands' Mariton Wildlife Sanctuary is an excellent place to observe the stages of forest succession. Until the mid-1900s, the formerly wooded slopes were mostly cleared for farming, but by the time Mary and Tony Guerrero (the "Mar" and "Ton" of Mariton) acquired the property in 1944, cultivation had ceased. Forests regrew in abandoned fields. The first trees to recolonize this area were sassafras and eastern red cedar, which still continue to grow in the sanctuary; however, they've been overtaken by tulip trees, oak, birch, hickory, maple, and others. Under the tall trees, you can spot sassafras and red cedar skeletons. In younger woods, the sassafras and red cedar are thriving, but in very old woods they have disappeared.

Main Trail passes a bird blind after about 750 feet then goes through a gap in an old wall of local fieldstone. Such walls are remnants of the boundaries between parcels of farmland, which offered up the stones when they were plowed.

About 350 feet later, turn right onto the narrower River Lookout spur trail (dark blue blazes), which heads downhill, levels out, and turns sharply left to traverse the east-facing slope. You can see the Delaware River through the trees, which are older and larger here than the ones above. After about 0.25 mile, a rustic sign warns of sheer cliffs. River Lookout Trail turns right and steeply downhill, becoming increasingly rocky. It passes through a profusion of rhododendrons and, in another 350 feet, abruptly ends at a bluff overlooking the river to the northeast. Edge out onto the outcrop where, in winter, you can take in excellent views.

The knobby, light-pink, black-speckled rocks are granitic gneiss, a rock characteristic of the Reading Prong, which underlies the Highlands region stretching from southeastern Pennsylvania into Connecticut. Much of the exposed gneiss in this area is Precambrian: 1 billion years old, making it some of the oldest rock in North America. The granitic gneiss stands in contrast to the Triassic-era red shales and sandstones, which are much younger (200 million to 250 million years old) and can be seen just south along the Delaware River, below the Monroe border fault at Riegelsville. Look for this spectacularly exposed rock at the Nockamixon Cliffs in Pennsylvania and the Milford Bluffs in New Jersey.

Backtrack to Main Trail, turn right, and continue through the woods, parallel to River Trail below. The deer exclosure, a fenced-in area to the right, is a long-term experiment to assess whether excluding deer affects the diversity of vegetation. You shouldn't see much of a difference between the exclosure and the rest of the woods. Many properties surrounding the sanctuary are hunted, so the deer population has not yet adversely affected the quality of the woods.

Continue slightly uphill on Main Trail, bearing right at the next intersection. At the next junction, bear right onto the black-blazed Chimney Rock Trail, which begins as a continuation of an old road that goes downhill gradually, then more steeply, becoming narrow and rocky. About 0.3 mile from its start, it turns sharply left to Chimney Rock, an eroded remnant of a Precambrian gneiss scarp. The rock formation is easy to climb, affording a 360-degree view of the woods and, in winter, a 90-degree bend in the Delaware.

Backtrack, but before reaching Main Trail, turn right at the red-blazed Fox Trail, then right again after 0.1 mile onto North Fox Trail, a narrow footpath that parallels Chimney Rock Trail below. Head downhill, passing under a power line after 0.25 mile, then continue very steeply down for another 0.15 mile (rocks may be slippery) to a hairpin turn back uphill. At the hilltop, bear right onto the gray-blazed Pine Circle. After 0.1 mile, take the very short spur trail (right) to the Stouts Valley overlook. In winter, the northwest-facing cliff affords a view of the Frya Run Valley toward Elephant Rock (right) and Hexenkopf Rock (or Witch's Head, far left), outstanding formations of extremely old Precambrian gneiss.

Return to Pine Circle (note the private drive to right); bear right as the trail forks. Stay straight at the intersection with Main Trail, continuing uphill. Exit the woods and wander the unmarked mowed paths that crisscross the meadows. The meadows, primarily sassafras saplings and wildflowers, are in the first stages of forest succession—and they'll never get to the next stage. Preserve managers mow these 15 acres annually to prevent them from becoming forest, adding diversity to the sanctuary's habitat to support wildlife, such as butterflies and ground-nesting birds.

Old roads following stone walls indicate these woods were former farm fields.

Return to Pine Circle. At the Y intersection, bear slightly right onto Turnpike Trail (light blue blazes), following the power line for about 100 feet then veering left, downhill, through a grassy area to woods. Turnpike Trail, an old, straight road, follows a stone wall downhill. Contrast the size and density of tree species to the right and left of the trail; the woods to the right is at least 25 years younger. Because many trees were significantly damaged by Hurricane Sandy in 2012, young tulip trees are elbowing their way in to colonize the openings in the canopy.

After about 0.2 mile, bear left at a Y intersection onto the tan-blazed Squeeze Trail, which forges uphill at a steep incline, leveling off as it follows an old road. To the right are conifer plantations of Norway spruce, planted in the 1950s and 1960s as erosion control. These also show some effects of Hurricane Sandy. Bear right at the intersection with Main Trail then make a sharp right onto Spruce Trail (green blazes). The dense, dark green conifers to the right contrast dramatically with the light, open canopy of oak, gray birch, hickory, and other hardwoods to the left. Owls nest in the conifer woods.

The trail winds downhill, ending at Woods Trail (brown blazes). Turn right and continue another 0.2 mile to the nature center, where you began.

MORE INFORMATION

Restrooms are located at the nature center. The preserve is open from sunrise to sunset. Dogs must be leashed. For more information, contact Natural Lands' Mariton Wildlife Sanctuary, 240 Sunnyside Road, Easton, PA 18042; 610-258-6574; natlands.org/mariton-wildlife-sanctuary.

36

TREXLER NATURE PRESERVE

This banana split of a hike comes with a dollop of everything: long-distance views, wildflower meadows, shady woods, lovely creek crossings, chestnut and apple orchards, and to top it off, elk and bison.

DIRECTIONS

From Exit 56 (Lehigh Valley) on I-476, take US 22 east for 0.8 mile then take the exit for PA 309 north toward Tamaqua. Follow it for 4.7 miles then turn left onto Old Packhouse Road. After 0.9 mile, turn right on Orchard Road and follow it 0.35 mile to the park entrance. The lot has plenty of parking. *GPS coordinates: 40° 39.321′ N, 75° 36.876′ W.*

TRAIL DESCRIPTION

If you're craving a hiking feast, Trexler Nature Preserve serves up a splurge. This 1,108-acre Lehigh County park provides the ingredients for more beautiful, enjoyable, and challenging hiking than even the most gluttonous hiker could consume. Like a banana split, this hike packs as much variety into a single jaunt as possible. You'll enjoy long views from plump hilltops; oodles of wildflower meadows; flowing creeks; and deep, dark woods—all topped off by herds of elk and bison.

Harry C. Trexler created the park in the early 1900s as a game preserve to provide a habitat for imported deer, elk, and bison, all of which had been hunted to near extinction. A century later, white-tailed deer populations have rebounded to the point where they are a threat (see "Bambi, Keep Out!" page 100), but elk and bison have never repopulated the greater Philadelphia region. The preserve still protects these large animals, which may be observed if they are nearby, in large fenced-in areas visible

LOCATION
Schnecksville, PA
(Lehigh County)

RATING
Moderate to difficult

DISTANCE
7 miles

ELEVATION GAIN
3,350 feet

ESTIMATED TIME
4 hours

MAPS
USGS Slatedale; trail map available at trailhead; lehighcounty.org/ Departments/ Parks-And-Recreation/ Trails

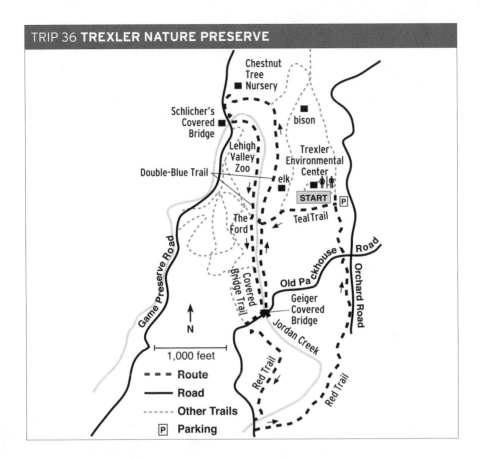

from the trails. Trexler bequeathed the preserve to Lehigh County in 1933. In addition to its exotic wildlife, Trexler Preserve also provides habitats for myriad other species, including songbirds that flock to its woods, bees and butterflies to its meadows, and fish to its waterways.

Start the hike at the Trexler Environmental Center, a short walk uphill from the parking lot via the gravel road. This state-of-the-art, environmentally sustainable building sits atop one of the highest hills in the preserve and provides a lay of the land from the roof's viewing platform, which also offers a showcase of methods for reducing energy and using stormwater runoff. The preserve is bisected by Jordan Creek, which flows to the west of the environmental center.

Walk around the building—noticing the slanted windows, which help prevent birds from crashing into them—and find the signed "Mile 0.0" entrance to Red Trail on the south side of the building, along the gravel road. Follow Red Trail from the grassy meadow to the second right, marked by a teal triangular blaze. Follow this Teal Trail west along the wood edge and downhill into a stream valley. Cross Park Road and continue on the same trail, crossing a small stream on stones, then proceed along the streambank. Just before the ford at Jordan Creek, turn right, passing a kiosk, and take Double Blue Trail steeply uphill, savoring the quickly receding sights and sounds of the Jordan Creek pedestrian bridge below.

As Double Blue Trail starts to crest the hill, you'll see side trails to the right. If elk are out browsing in their grasslands, you can see them from these trails. Follow Blue Triangle Trail along the ridge to the paved road on the hilltop. Behind and below you are great south-facing views, including the Lehigh Valley Zoo, which sits in the middle of the preserve. Turn left to follow Double Blue Trail along the paved road to an information kiosk; turn right and cross the road here.

Continue about 100 feet to view the 4-acre, fenced-in orchard of American chestnuts. These have been bred to resist blight, with the objective of eventually reintroducing this once-dominant species to regional forests (see "The King Is Dead; Long Live the King," page 194). Across the road, opposite the orchard, check to see if the bison herd is hanging out behind the fence. A close encounter with these huge, shaggy animals is dramatic, especially during winter, when they use their horns and shaggy manes to sweep away snow and uncover the grass below.

Return to the kiosk at Double Blue Trail and bear left to follow the trail steeply downhill through woods. At the bottom of the hill, cross the wide Jordan Creek

A bison at Trexler Nature Preserve snacks on an upcycled Christmas tree.

via a pedestrian bridge located beside the Schlicher Covered Bridge (used by vehicles). Continue onto a gravel road that parallels the creek (the trail is unmarked here) and hike past picnic sites. The road becomes paved; watch for cars on busy days. After a short walk, you will come to the main pedestrian bridge over Jordan Creek at the ford. On hot days, this is a popular spot for wading and swimming. It is also entertaining to watch cars fording the creek. Continue to the sign reading, "Covered Bridge Trail," and take this ADA-accessible, red-blazed route along the creek, at the bottom of a steep hemlock ravine. Moss-covered rock outcrops are on your right, the wide creek on your left.

At Geiger Covered Bridge, turn right and walk about 400 feet up the paved road to the junction with Red Trail, on your left. Red Trail is an 8.5-mile loop that starts at the environmental center; mileage from the start is marked on posts every 0.5 mile in a counterclockwise direction, as indicated on the preserve trail map. Follow Red Trail as it winds into the woods, continues up a hill, and then levels out on a path along the edge of a series of meadows.

Red Trail then descends through the woods. At Jordan Road, turn left to cross Jordan Creek via the bridge on Ruheton Hill Road, making sure to follow the arrows. Just past the bridge, turn left on Red Trail to return to the woods. The trail becomes wet as you cross through a marshy area past a shelter then climbs steadily uphill. At the top, there's a nice bench for resting beneath a mulberry tree. Continue on a more level path past some fields, briefly venturing onto an old road before returning to more fields with marvelous views to the west. The trail emerges from the fields, descending after the 8-mile mark. It then crosses Old Packhouse Road and climbs uphill through an old apple orchard. Before you get to the end of Red Trail (around the 8.3-mile mark) there is a turnoff to the right, which you can follow to return to the parking lot. If you miss the turn, take Red Trail to the gravel road and turn right to reach the parking lot.

MORE INFORMATION

There are restrooms on the north side of the Trexler Environmental Center, as well as at the Lehigh Valley Zoo, that are always open, and there are portable toilets at the Jordan Creek ford. Dogs are allowed on leash. Trexler Nature Preserve is owned by Lehigh County, with the Wildlands Conservancy partnering in the preserve's stewardship (wildlandspa.org). For more information, contact Trexler Nature Preserve, 4935 Orchard Road, Schnecksville, PA 18078; 610-871-0281; lehighcounty.org/Community/Trexler-Nature-Preserve.

37

JACOBSBURG ENVIRONMENTAL EDUCATION CENTER

This is a short, easy hike with great scenic variety. It winds through ridge-top meadows to an old-growth forest along a dramatic ravine in an area resonant with history.

DIRECTIONS

From I-78, take Exit 71 for PA 33 north. In 10.4 miles, take the Belfast exit. Bear right onto Henry Road then turn left onto Befast Road. In 0.7 mile, you'll reach a parking lot, on the left, with ample parking. *GPS coordinates:* 40° 46.966′ N, 75° 17.599′ W.

TRAIL DESCRIPTION

The peace and beauty of the Jacobsburg district belie its history. The deep hemlock-studded ravine through which Bushkill Creek flows feels as if it has been wild forever, and the ridge-top fields seem to have been placed exactly where the mountain views are best. Yet it was here that the family of William Henry manufactured guns used in the American Revolution and the Civil War, as well as by the settlers who explored the Western frontier. A century ago, Jacobsburg was an industrial community, and nature was not celebrated but ravaged. Bushkill Creek was dammed for waterpower; the hills were cleared of trees to fuel the furnaces; and the ravine echoed with the sounds of small arms manufacturing.

You can hike through Jacobsburg's 1,168 acres of woods, meadows, and streams without contemplating its historical significance. But knowing the context adds another dimension to the hike. The essential characteristic of this place is not the despoliation of nature but rather its redemption through preservation and conservation. Indeed, it was James Henry, a gunsmith, forester, and

LOCATION
Wind Gap, PA
(Northampton County)

RATING
Easy to moderate

DISTANCE
2.5 miles

ELEVATION GAIN
200 feet

ESTIMATED TIME
1.75 hours

MAPS
USGS Wind Gap; trail map available at trailhead; docs.dcnr.pa.gov/cs/groups/ public/documents/ document/dcnr_004250.pdf

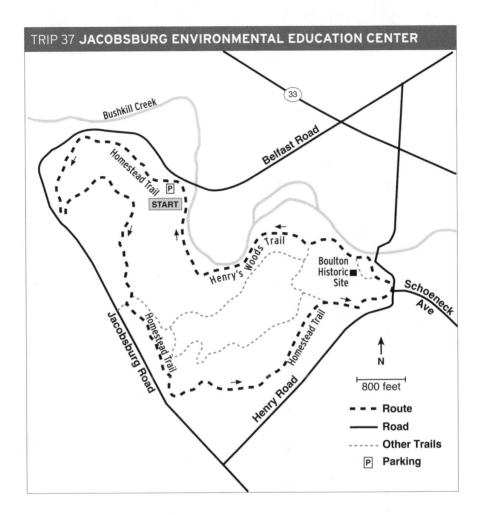

descendant of the Henry family who, in 1883, championed the first Pennsylvania stream-protection regime, promoting reforestation of cleared streambanks.

This hike begins at the main Belfast Road parking lot. Head south (away from the information kiosk) to the trailhead for the blue-blazed Homestead Trail. Trails in this park are generally well signed at intersections and consistently blazed. Homestead Trail is a multiuse trail open to bikes and horses, as well as hikers.

The trail gradually ascends through a meadow then enters young woods of oak, ash, hickory, walnut, and cherry trees. In spring and summer, wildflowers abound on the forest floor, and warblers sing in the treetops. Follow Homestead Trail as it bends away from Belfast Road below, climbing the hill. Bear left when the trail forks, just past a power line crossing. Pass under the power line again and reach a meadow, where the trail forks once again.

Jacobsburg meadow with Wind Gap in the background.

Bear right, following the blue blazes, through a meadow of summer-blooming wildflowers. Pass through a hedgerow to reach another meadow, once farmland. After a cluster of park maintenance structures, Homestead Trail turns right, continuing through meadows where bluebird boxes have been placed. Tree swallows are just as likely to have taken up residence here; both of these blue species dart out from fieldside perches to snag insects.

As the trail passes the Jacobsburg Road entrance (small parking lot), you'll reach another fork. Both paths here are part of Homestead Trail; take the right-hand one (not the spur to the parking lot) to follow the edge of the field. The trail then reaches its high point, a ridge-top meadow with sweeping views of Kittatinny Ridge (Blue Mountain); Wind Gap is directly to the north.

The trail descends past private residences on the right then reaches a T intersection; turn right, heading southeast. The way becomes steeper, reaching the bottom of the hill at the intersection of Henry Road and Schoeneck Avenue. Follow the yellow-blazed trail along Henry Road, continuing left around the bend, paralleling the creek. Homestead Trail passes through the Boulton Historic Site, which preserves public access to some of the buildings from the small arms manufacturing era. Interpretive signs along the trail describe the self-sufficient Boulton community.

Follow the "All Trail Traffic" signs around the site, to the bridge over Bushkill Creek. At this point, the orange-blazed, pedestrian-only Henry's Woods Trail begins. This is a loop that follows the creek from the parking lot, so you can take either side to get to your car. Each has its merits; if you have time, try both. The far, flatter side (0.75 mile) traces the course of the creek through the valley and offers views up the gorge; the near, steeper side (0.5 mile) climbs the ravine and looks down through the dense forest. The steep side is the one described here.

Henry's Woods is an old-growth forest. Spared from logging by the Henrys, its stands of hemlock; yellow and black birch; red, white, and chestnut oak; sugar maple; basswood; and sycamore contain huge trees up to 350 years old. Like all hemlock ravines, this one is dark, shady, moist, mossy, and often misty, its rocky slopes covered with ferns, maple-leaf viburnum, and rhododendron. This ravine, with its giant trees, seems deeper, darker, and mistier than most—a primitive forest that survived to see the modern era.

The narrow, steep trail has slippery roots, but the signs warning of danger seem overly dramatic, perhaps in keeping with the outsize scale of the place itself. The trail ascends steeply to a crest, offering some views to the east, then drops steeply and continues down a set of wooden steps. At the bottom, a path along the creek leads to the parking lot.

MORE INFORMATION

The center office on the corner of Belfast and Jacobsburg roads is open Monday through Friday from 8 A.M. to 4 P.M. The main parking area on Belfast Road is open daily from sunrise to sunset. There are more than 18.5 miles of trails in the park; all are multiuse with the exception of Henry's Woods, which is for hiking only. Restrooms are across the bridge from the parking lot for Homestead Trail. For more information, contact Jacobsburg Environmental Education Center, 835 Jacobsburg Road, Wind Gap, PA 18091; 908-879-1339; dcnr.state.pa.us/stateparks/findapark/jacobsburg.

Monocacy Way parallels the scenic Monocacy Creek while unveiling the past and present city of Bethlehem. The hike is an out-and-back route with flat terrain, traversing wooded areas and the historic downtown.

DIRECTIONS

Take the Pennsylvania Turnpike Northeast Extension (I-476) north to Exit 56 (US 22 east toward Allentown). Take the exit for Center Street/PA 512. Turn left at Bath Pike/Center Street/PA 512 and drive 1.7 miles. Turn right onto Illick's Mill Road. At the bottom of the hill, take the first left after Monocacy Creek Road to enter the parking lot across from Illick's Mill. There is space for 40 cars. *GPS coordinates:* 40° 38.464′ N, 75° 22.788′ W.

TRAIL DESCRIPTION

Monocacy Way parallels the last 3 miles of the 20-mile-long Monocacy Creek, a small but high-quality waterway, as it winds through historic Bethlehem. The creek harbors a rich aquatic wildlife population and attracts many species of migratory birds. The hike traverses a history in miniature of Pennsylvania industry, ranging from grain mills to steel mills. The turnaround at the Lehigh River follows the creek as it flows from rural, open woods to Sand Island, which connects to the Lehigh Canal Towpath—a section of the 165-mile D&L Trail between Wilkes-Barre and Philadelphia that celebrates the coal and iron mining heritage of the region. Monocacy Way also provides opportunities to explore the heart of Bethlehem's historic district.

The Appalachian Mountain Club's Mid-Atlantic regional office is located in the historic Illick's Mill, which was an operational water-powered gristmill from 1856

LOCATION
Bethlehem, PA
(Northampton County)

RATING
Moderate

DISTANCE
6 miles

ELEVATION GAIN
Minimal

ESTIMATED TIME
3 hours

MAPS
USGS Catasauqua;
illicksmill.com/getoutside/

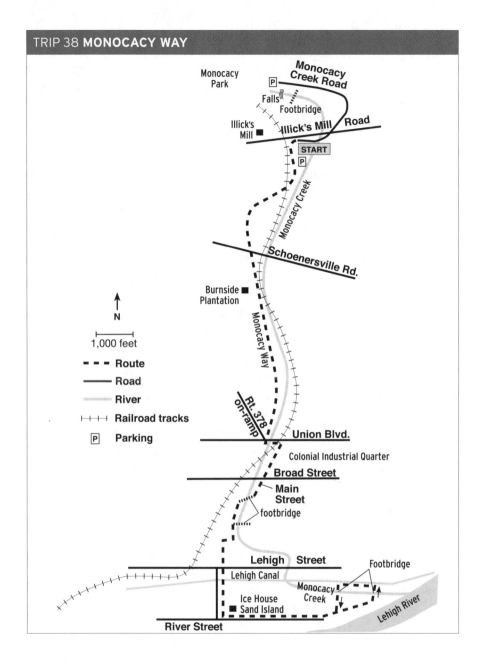

until 1915, one of seven on the creek. Surrounding the mill is Monocacy Park, built in the 1930s by the Civilian Conservation Corps (CCC).

From the parking lot, face away from Illick's Mill Road to enter Monocacy Way, a grassy path that parallels railroad tracks on the right and a brushy area along Monocacy Creek on the left. Monocacy Creek is fed in part by springs flowing from underground beds of limestone. The rock is naturally alkaline, and the springs remain at a constant temperature of 55 degrees Fahrenheit. The combination of cool temperature and low acidity creates conditions that support a complex aquatic food web, including a naturally reproducing wild brown trout population. The name "Monocacy" is said to derive from the Lenape word for "stream with several large bends."

Monocacy Way winds through floodplain woods for about 0.25 mile then crosses the railroad tracks. (Caution: This is an active railway.) After crossing, bear left and follow the trail along a wide open area for 0.6 mile. You'll reach an intersection with busy Schoenersville Road; cross it. The trail merges with the driveway to Burnside Plantation, an eighteenth-century farm that was the homestead of James Burnside, a Moravian missionary. Today it is a living history museum. You can take a self-guided tour of the gardens and buildings, including a farmhouse built in 1748 by the Moravians (a German Protestant sect) who founded Bethlehem on the banks of the Monocacy Creek in 1741. The other side of the creek is an industrial area.

The trail is a grassy path as it passes behind Burnside Plantation. It hugs the creek for 0.6 mile on a red shale surface with some wooden walkways. At Union Boulevard, turn left and continue on the sidewalk. At the first traffic light, turn right and cross Union Boulevard to pick up the trail. Follow the red shale surface along the creek and walk through Johnston Park. Here the creek's pools and riffles provide an excellent habitat for trout, as evidenced by the ubiquitous anglers. The attractive walls were built by the CCC.

Follow the paved path and pass under the Broad Street Bridge. To your left, just before Spring Street, is the Colonial Industrial Quarter, a group of restored historic buildings managed by Historic Bethlehem Museums & Sites. Here you'll find the Waterworks (built in 1762), the site of America's first town water-pumping system, a tannery (built in 1761), and Luckenbach Mill (built in 1869), as well as ruins of other early manufacturing buildings. Take the stairs up to Main Street, where you'll find the Historic Bethlehem Visitor Center at 505 Main Street. If you'd like to walk around historic downtown Bethlehem, this is a good place to start.

Follow the Main Street sidewalk to Spring Street; turn left and continue on Main Street, passing an old railroad depot that has been converted into the Main Street Depot restaurant. Cross a bridge over Lehigh Canal and Towpath (D&L Trail). You are now on Sand Island. Turn left onto River Street. Continue onto a gravel trail. Cross under the New Street Bridge and pass a footbridge on your left. Continue to the end of the trail. Here is the mouth of the Monocacy Creek at its confluence with the Lehigh River. Across the river is an iconic view of the mighty, now-stilled blast furnaces and rolling mills of Bethlehem Steel Corporation, once the second largest steel producer in the United States. The

A great blue heron pauses midstream in Monocacy Creek, a haven for many species of migratory birds. Photo by Jim, Creative Commons on Flickr.

mill ceased operations in 1995. In 2009 it was converted into a casino. You have now completed your journey through industrial history along Monocacy Creek.

Turn left to cross the small steel footbridge. Turn left again and walk along the Lehigh Canal on the gravel towpath, with the creek on your left. The towpath reaches a footbridge at a historic canal lock. Turn left over the bridge and retrace your steps through Bethlehem and along Monocacy Creek to return to Illick's Mill.

MORE INFORMATION

Restrooms are available in Illick's Mill Park and at Sand Island. Illick's Mill Park also features pavilions and picnic tables. The multiuse Monocacy Way is managed by Bethlehem Parks and Recreation. For more information: 10 East Church Street, Bethlehem, PA 18018; 610-841-5831; bethlehem-pa.gov/parks.

39

NEVERSINK MOUNTAIN PRESERVE

Neversink Mountain Preserve is hugged on the south by the Schuylkill River and on the north by the city of Reading. Its trail network allows hikers to feel far from the city, exploring 500 acres of protected land and taking in scenic vistas of Mount Penn and Reading.

DIRECTIONS

From I-76 take Exit 298 to merge onto I-176 north toward Reading/Morgantown. Take Exit 11A to merge onto US 422 east for 1 mile. Take the Mount Penn exit. Turn left at East Neversink Road. Take the first left onto Hearthstone Drive and continue straight for 0.7 mile. Turn left onto West Neversink Drive then immediately right onto Klapperthal Road. Follow the road 0.4 mile until it reaches a dead end at the trailhead for Klapperthal Trail. There is space for four to five cars. Alternative parking can be found in the back of Forest Hills Cemetery (adjacent to Klapperthal Road), near Forest Hills Pond. *GPS coordinates:* 40° 18.882′ N, 75° 53.577′ W.

TRAIL DESCRIPTION

Although Neversink Mountain's name derives from the Lenape word "Navesink," meaning "fishing ground," it is valued today for its forested slopes, the views from its summit, and its abundant plants and wildlife, including numerous species of butterflies and moths. Of its 900 acres, 500 are owned by Berks Nature (formerly Berks County Conservancy), which has established a 9-mile trail system that also connects the mountain to other area trails.

In the late nineteenth century, a number of resort hotels on the mountain drew summer visitors from Philadelphia seeking cooler air, with railways running on the mountain

LOCATION
Reading, PA (Berks County)

RATING
Easy to moderate

DISTANCE
4 miles

ELEVATION GAIN
525 feet

ESTIMATED TIME
2.5 hours

MAPS
USGS Reading; berksnature.org/ wp-content/ uploads/2015/09/ NeversinkTrailMap-2.pdf

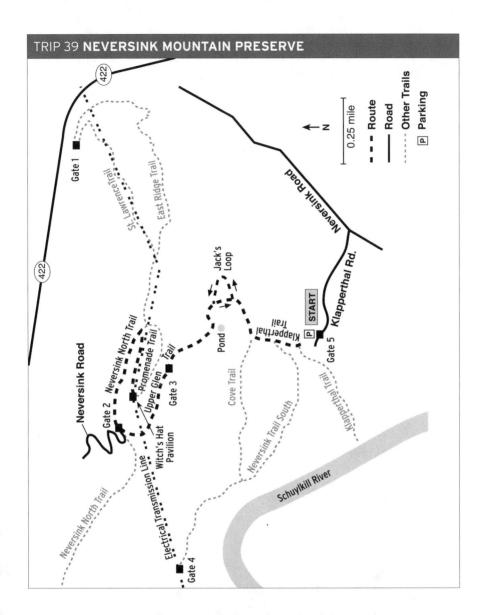

to serve the guests. When the hotels were razed in the 1930s and railbeds turned to trails in the 1960s the mountain returned to a quiet natural haven within the urbanized area of greater Reading.

This hike loops around the mountain to the Reading overlook and the Witch's Hat Pavilion before returning to the Klapperthal parking area. As you hike the preserve, be sure to follow the trail map above or the preserve map. Almost half of the mountain is still privately owned. Some of the trails are on private property; while hiking is permitted, stay on the marked routes to respect the rights of property owners.

From the Klapperthal parking area, walk uphill on the purple-blazed Klapperthal Trail, past the Berks Nature sign, to enter the forest. You can hear the gentle sound of a stream to the right. (Ironically, "Klapperthal" means "booming valley," referring to an area where cannonballs were tested during the Civil War.) After about 225 feet, you'll come to a kiosk trail map and soon cross a bridge. Pass another bridge and note that the trail is now blazed purple and orange. Cross a third bridge then continue onto a boardwalk, passing Cove Trail to your left.

Bear right after the boardwalk, onto the purple-and-orange-blazed Upper Glen Trail. This is one of the sections of the trail running through private property. Two more boardwalks follow. At the sign for Jack's Loop, bear right to follow this red-blazed trail, continuing about 1 mile until the trail ends (note the three red blazes); continue straight onto Upper Glen Trail. Follow this trail as it climbs uphill through the woods. This section is particularly beautiful, filled with mature oak, beech, and birch trees, as well as forest wildflowers, such as wood asters and goldenrods.

At a gravel road, turn left to continue on Upper Glen Trail. This portion of the trail is sometimes used to access private landowners' driveways; watch for vehicles. At Gate 3, still on Upper Glen Trail, turn left. The trail passes under a transmission line and intersects with a macadam road. Turn right and follow the road downhill (watch for vehicles) to Gate 2, turning right onto the

Witch's Hat Pavilion makes for a striking landmark. Photo by Mim, Creative Commons on Flickr.

purple-blazed Neversink North Trail on a gravel road. In late May and early June, mountain laurel, Pennsylvania's state flower, blooms abundantly on this section of the mountain. A member of the heath family, pink-flowered mountain laurel is an evergreen.

Neversink Trail North intersects with a gravel road; turn sharply right onto the road and go past an electrical equipment station. At the next two forks, bear right; at the third, bear left to go slightly uphill, through a brushy area, to reach the Witch's Hat Pavilion. Local residents gave the pavilion its nickname due to its conical shape. Built in 1892 as part of a mountain hotel, it was constructed as a memorial to foundryman William McIlvain, for whom it was originally named.

The view of Reading and Mount Penn from here is spectacular. When you reach this spot, you may find yourself surprised that the city is so close to such a gem of a mountain. Mount Penn is easily identified by the 72-foot pagoda on its summit. William A. Witman Sr., a local quarry owner, built this pagoda in 1908. Abandoning the quarry after years of public criticism of its scarifying effects on Mount Penn, Witman built the unique structure with the intention of making it a luxury hotel, but the venture failed. The structure was sold, eventually becoming city property in 1911. From Witch's Hat Pavilion, return the way you came until you reach the intersection with the red-blazed Jack's Loop and Upper Glen Trail. Turn right here to follow the purple-and-orange-blazed Upper Glen Trail downhill and back to the parking lot.

To extend your hike on the return, continue on the purple-blazed Klapperthal Trail past the parking lot about 0.5 mile to a railroad underpass, where the trail opens onto a view of the Schuylkill River.

MORE INFORMATION

There are no restrooms. Limited hunting is permitted in season. Trails are maintained by Berks Nature. For more information: 575 Saint Bernardine Street, Reading, PA 19607; 610-372-992; berksnature.org.

40

NOLDE FOREST ENVIRONMENTAL EDUCATION CENTER

Welcome to a tree lover's paradise: Meander up and down hills under an ever changing canopy of thousands upon thousands of evergreen and deciduous trees.

LOCATION
Reading, PA (Berks County)

RATING
Moderate

DIRECTIONS

Take the Pennsylvania Turnpike (I-76) west to Exit 298 (Morgantown) (I-176); continue to Exit 10 (PA 724 west toward Shillington). Remain on PA 724 for 2.5 miles then turn left onto PA 625. The Nolde Forest trailhead is 1.7 miles ahead on the right. There is ample parking. *GPS coordinates: 40° 16.869′ N, 75° 56.903′ W.*

DISTANCE
8 miles

ELEVATION GAIN
500 feet

ESTIMATED TIME
3 hours

TRAIL DESCRIPTION

Nolde Forest's 665 acres are covered with trees; there are scores of species, with specimens ranging from young to old, planted and nurtured by dedicated foresters. As the trees have grown, they've twisted their intertwined branches toward sunlight and snaked their enmeshed roots toward water. The forest has become a dense matrix of shapes. Hiking through it is like walking through a community whose members silently converse with and accommodate one another.

The thousands upon thousands of trees that grow here are the result of the efforts of one man: Jacob Nolde. A hosiery baron, Nolde acquired this property south of Reading in 1904. The site, like many others in southeastern Pennsylvania, had been cleared of trees, primarily to burn for charcoal production. Nolde came across a single white pine in a meadow and was inspired to plant a forest of conifers. Nolde and an Austrian forester named William Kohout planted more than a million pines, spruces, and firs. Deciduous trees also sprouted.

Pennsylvania acquired the site from the Nolde family in 1966 and established the state's first environmental

MAPS
USGS Reading; trail map available onsite; dcnr.pa.gov/StateParks/ FindAPark/NoldeForest EnvironmentalEducation Center/Pages/Maps.aspx

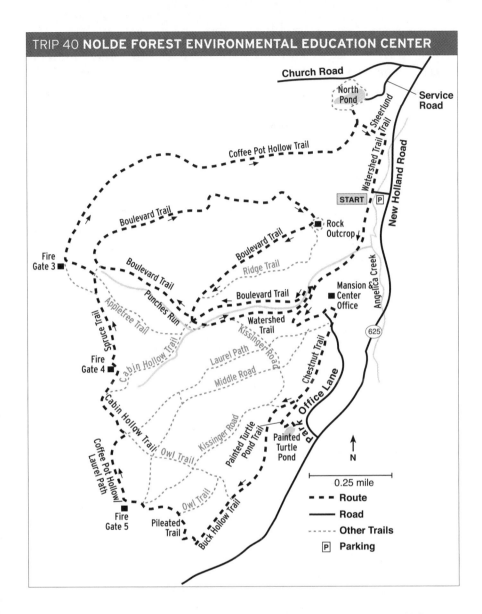

education center here in 1971. More than 10 miles of trails, mostly on old forest or colliers (i.e., charcoal-makers) roads, wind through the park. Because they were once roads, these trails are generally wide with good footing, and elevation gains are gradual. The trails are well maintained, in excellent shape, and stay dry even in wet weather. With few exceptions, trail intersections are well marked by posts indicating the names of the trails.

This hike consists of a 3-mile inner loop and a 5-mile outer loop. If you're short on time, select one of the loops. Beginning at the sawmill parking lot, head up the steps and over Angelica Creek onto a red gravel trail. Continue for 150 feet, turn left at a T intersection onto Watershed Trail, then bear left again onto Forester Road. The road heads uphill, along a stream at the bottom of a steep-sided ravine filled with hemlock and yellow birch. Bear right at the teaching station onto Boulevard Trail. Stay on Boulevard Trail for the remainder of this inner loop. The trail ascends to the ridgetop (there are fine winter views here) then descends about 0.75 mile.

Boulevard Trail bends right, but straight ahead via a short spur is a 15-foot-high rock outcrop. In contrast to the crumbly red shale and sandstone that dominate the park south of the main entrance, this rock is dark gray—almost black—and smooth. If it appears to have been squeezed up from the earth, that's because it has. This is an exposed chunk of intruded diabase, a volcanic rock (See "Black Rock, Green Forests," page 77). Some 200 million years ago, molten magma flowed into fractures in the sedimentary red shale and sandstone around it then hardened. Over time, the softer rock around the diabase eroded away, leaving the hard volcanic rock to stand alone. The diabase ridge falls off below the outcrop.

Shortly after Boulevard Trail leaves the outcrop, it becomes an arboreal neutral zone, the dividing line between a conifer plantation uphill and hardwood forest below. When Boulevard Trail crosses itself just past a restroom, bear left then turn right onto Cabin Hollow Trail; 150 feet later, turn left onto Watershed Trail and head back down into the ravine. The narrow Watershed Trail has a natural surface that parallels the wide Boulevard Trail, by which you ascended the ravine, and takes you into much more intimate contact with the trees, wildflowers, stream, and rocks. Continue to follow Watershed Trail as it crosses back and forth over Punches Run, and note the fine stone bridge that carries Boulevard Trail over the stream. Almost immediately after the stream, Watershed Trail joins Boulevard Trail and then makes a sharp right where it intersects a paved road.

Follow the road as it approaches the Nolde family home, which now serves as the park's main office. A good place for a lunch break, the stone Tudor-style mansion is worth a detour. Note its architectural details, including the delightful nursery tower, the imposing oak entrance door, and the stained-glass plaque depicting the single white pine that inspired Jacob Nolde to create a forest.

Head away from the mansion and bear right onto Chestnut Trail. There are quite a few American chestnut saplings on this trail, recognizable by their long, pointed leaves with jagged serrations. The early-twentieth-century chestnut blight killed off billions of these trees, which used to dominate eastern forests. The fungus culprit lives on. Although chestnut saplings continue to sprout from old stumps, they die before reaching nut-bearing age. (See "The King Is Dead; Long Live the King," page 194.)

After 0.25 mile, take a spur trail about 800 feet downhill to Painted Turtle Pond, a pretty little pool where basking turtles are common on sunny summer days. Return to Chestnut Trail; bear left onto Buck Hollow Trail. In just under 0.4 mile, turn right onto Pileated Trail; shortly, turn left onto Owl Trail.

At Fire Gate 5, turn right onto Laurel Path. Lining the trail are glossy-leaved, evergreen mountain laurels that are adorned with star-shaped white-and-pink

On Boulevard Trail in Nolde Forest, conifer needles and deciduous leaves touch each other.

flowers from late April to early May. Bear left onto Owl Trail, which descends through a lowbush blueberry patch, then left again onto Spruce Trail. Continue past Fire Gates 4 and 3.

After Fire Gate 3, there is a Y intersection; bear left onto Coffee Pot Hollow Trail. Continue on this trail for 1.25 miles then bear left onto Beech Trail and take it downhill to Pond Loop Trail. Follow this trail to the large, lily pad–covered North Pond; stop here as long as you like to enjoy pond wildlife and plants. Backtrack to Beech Trail, then turn left onto Sheerlund Trail, which terminates at Watershed Trail. Turn right to end at the sawmill parking lot.

MORE INFORMATION

The Nolde Forest office and mansion parking lot are open from 8 A.M. to 4 P.M. Monday through Friday. All other areas are open daily, sunrise to sunset. As in other Pennsylvania state parks, pets must be on a leash. Full restroom facilities are located at the C.H. McConnell Environmental Education Hall; dry toilets are located at the trailhead for Watershed Trail and at other locations along the route. For more information, contact Nolde Forest Environmental Education Center, 2910 New Holland Road, Reading, PA 19607; 610-796-3699; dcnr.state .pa.us/stateparks/findapark/noldeforest.

THE KING IS DEAD; LONG LIVE THE KING

Tall, durable, and long-lived, the oak is a beloved tree, prized for its lumber and its use in the landscape. Oaks dominate the forests in the Philadelphia area. Found in virtually every habitat, they are invaluable in the Delaware Valley, providing food, shelter, and cover for wildlife. It is hard to imagine our woods without oaks, but the story of another tree should caution us that a dominant species can disappear. The American chestnut once held a place in the pantheon of trees as great as the oak of today.

A century ago, there were 4 billion chestnuts on 200 million acres of eastern forests. Tall, straight, and fast growing, chestnuts created a continuous woods canopy. Wildlife relied on the nuts, which the trees produced annually (in contrast, oaks produce nuts every two to five years); the result was an abundance of game. People relished chestnuts too. Their sweetness contrasted with bitter acorns, which must be boiled before eating. Chestnut wood was renowned for its resistance to rot. Nuts, bark (for tanning), and lumber provided cash crops on which many rural Appalachian communities based their economies.

Chestnut blight, a fungus from Asia inadvertently introduced into North America, attacked American chestnuts in the late nineteenth century. First identified in 1905, the blight effectively wiped out the American chestnut within 50 years, altering the makeup of eastern forests, destroying rural communities, and perhaps (although research is lacking) reducing the abundance of wildlife. Oaks took over the role of dominant tree.

The American chestnut is not entirely extinct. Although most succumb to the blight when they reach maturity (but before they produce flowers and nuts), some trees continue to sprout from stumps or from old seedlings. The sprouts can grow to 8 inches in diameter. The chestnut's elongated, sharp-toothed leaves are common in healthy forests. You can get a sense of how dominant the chestnut was by observing the number of immature sprouts along a trail. Since 2008, volunteers conducting an annual survey along the Appalachian Trail have counted thousands within 15 feet of the trail in Pennsylvania.

Today, researchers are employing genetic engineering, cross-breeding the American chestnut with blight-resistant Asian chestnuts in an effort to reintroduce a hardier cultivar to the woods. Even if scientists succeed, however, regenerating a chestnut canopy will take another century or more. Perhaps one day, American chestnut trees will see the top of the forest, and future generations will know a different forest than we do.

41

BLUE MARSH LAKE

This varied and challenging hike follows wooded hillsides that surround an expansive lake set amid thousands of protected forest acres with abundant wildlife.

DIRECTIONS

Take the Pennsylvania Turnpike (I-76) to Exit 298 (I-176 north toward Morgantown). Drive 11.5 miles and take Exit 11B for US 422 west. After 4.6 miles, the road becomes US 222 north; continue 2.9 miles more and take the exit for PA 183 (Bernville Road/Strausstown). Turn left onto PA 183 north and drive 5.6 miles then turn left onto Old Church Road. Continue about 0.1 mile to the parking lot on the left, which has room for many cars. *GPS coordinates: 40° 24.429′ N, 76° 04.750′ W.*

TRAIL DESCRIPTION

Blue Marsh Lake is a gem of a recreational area, a mammoth sparkler in a lush setting. Situated in rural Berks County, northwest of Reading, the 8-mile-long lake's 1,150 acres are surrounded by another 6,000 acres of protected land. Its waters attract boaters, paddlers, swimmers, and anglers, but the recreational opportunities extend far beyond the lake's shoreline. For hikers, 30 miles of trails run through the Blue Marsh Recreational Area. This hike traverses the lake's wooded slopes and shores, incorporating several lake crossings to form a manageable loop that offers opportunities to see an abundance of birds and other wildlife.

The hike starts at the parking area. Turn your back to the lake and exit the parking lot. Turn left onto Old Church Road, stay on the left side of this actively traveled road, and cross the lake via a bridge. About 0.4 mile from the

LOCATION
Leesport, PA (Berks County)

RATING
Moderate

DISTANCE
7.5 miles

ELEVATION GAIN
960 feet

ESTIMATED TIME
4 hours

MAPS
USGS Bernville; trail map available onsite; nap.usace.army.mil/ Portals/39/docs/Civil/ Blue_Marsh/trail%20map.pdf

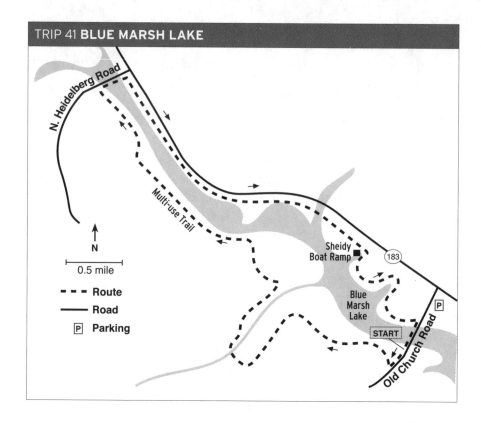

entrance, you'll see a trailhead kiosk on the left, beside the road. (Along the hike you will pass a number of named trailhead kiosks.) Instead of turning left here, carefully cross the road and take the trail slightly uphill on your right. This is the main multiuse trail, open to hikers as well as cyclists and horses. All along the trail, regularly placed markers on flexible brown posts and mile markers help gauge your progress. The hike starts just past mile marker 14, so expect to see marker 15 in a little less than 1 mile.

As you follow the narrow footpath through oak-hickory woods, you'll catch occasional glimpses of the lake below. After about 1.25 miles, you'll pass a pipeline crossing with views of the lake to the right. After another 0.15 mile, the trail forms a T intersection at an old road. To take a short detour that brings you to the lakeshore, turn right (away from the road) and head about 0.1 mile down to the lake, then return. To continue the hike, turn left at the T intersection, following arrows painted on the road surface. When the road ends, follow the trail as it becomes a footpath through meadows.

After about another 1.5 miles you will reach the Sheidy Trailhead, a T intersection. Turn right at the trail marker just before you get to the road. Continue on the trail and cross a wooden bridge over a stream that feeds into the lake.

Turn right at the next T intersection, follow a gravel drive, and pass an opening to the lake on your right. Continue through wet meadows, a pipeline crossing, and fields to marker 16, where the trail bends left (north) and uphill. At the ridgetop, enjoy views of the Reading hills to the east.

The trail turns left and winds past a hedgerow then turns right, opening up a view to the north. Turn right and then left to follow the well-marked trail past wildflower meadows. You'll eventually turn left (north) into the woods and go steeply downhill to the lake before following the trail away from the lake and entering a woods of tall tulip, maple, oak, hornbeam, and birch trees.

Bear right to cross a stream on a small footbridge, passing large leaves of skunk cabbage, which thrives in shady wetlands. Make a long climb out of the stream valley, passing mile marker 17, then descend the hill via some loose rocks. The trail follows an eroded path through the woods and bottoms out in a white pine grove then becomes an old woods road. Norway spruce and hostas mark the site where a homestead once stood. The trail continues downhill toward the lake, briefly leaving the old woods road and meeting it again. Shortly after mile marker 18, come to Heidelberg Road. Turn sharply right, following the arrows painted on the road, and cross the lake, being sure to watch for traffic.

You will soon reach the North Heidelberg trailhead at PA 183. Cross a stream via a footbridge and follow the trail along the lakeshore, with PA 183 above you and to your left. The trail passes through young woods and along brushy meadows. As you continue, the highway noises recede; eventually you're back

Hikers appreciate the many spots to pause and take in Blue Marsh Lake.

enjoying serene lake views and its quiet expanse. By mile marker 19, the trail is hugging the lakeshore on the right, with wildflower meadows cosseting the gentle hills on the left.

Just before mile marker 20, take a footbridge over a lake inlet. You'll shortly come to the access road for the Sheidy boat ramp, with a nice view of the lake on your right. Follow the trail markers and arrows to cross the road and then parallel the lakeshore. The trail turns away from the lakeshore into a woodsy area then skirts a dry streambed before returning to the shore at mile marker 21 for one final look at the lake. Linger here, enjoying the placid waters frequented by ducks, cormorants, and herons before following the trail away from the lake, through a meadow, up a hill, and across Old Church Road to the parking area, where you started.

MORE INFORMATION

There is a portable toilet at the parking area. Trails are open from 8 A.M. to dusk. Dogs are allowed but must be leashed at all times. Blue Marsh Lake is managed by the U.S. Army Corps of Engineers, which constructed the dam and the lake in 1979 to prevent flooding, to maintain the water supply and quality, and to create a place for recreation. For more information, visit nap.usace.army.mil/Missions/Civil-Works/Blue-Marsh-Lake.

42

LEHIGH PARKWAY

Hike along the scenic, wooded Little Lehigh Creek, which offers a multitude of historic, cultural, and natural sites to visit, including the Museum of Indian Culture and Lil'-Le-Hi Trout Nursery. This park is family-friendly, with flat, gravel-surfaced loop trails for both short and long hikes.

DIRECTIONS

Take the Pennsylvania Turnpike Northeast Extension (I-476) north to Exit 44. Continue north on PA 663 for 3.4 miles then turn left onto PA 309 north. After 9.2 miles, take I-78 west for 2 miles to Exit 57 (Lehigh Street). Head north on Lehigh Street for just under 1 mile and turn left on 15th Street, which becomes Jefferson Street. After 0.4 mile, make a sharp left turn onto Lehigh Parkway South and enter the park at the main entrance (Park Drive). Follow the road to its end, beside Klein's Bridge, adjacent to a maintenance shed and a stone barn. There is a parking lot on the right with space for twenty or more cars; additional parking lots are nearby. *GPS coordinates: 40° 34.756' N, 75° 29.617' W.*

TRAIL DESCRIPTION

Lehigh Parkway is one of Allentown's most prominent and picturesque parks. Wending through woods and open areas along both sides of Little Lehigh Creek, it provides nature enthusiasts with opportunities for scenic, family-ly-friendly hikes. Along the way are delightful creekside historic and cultural sites. Because several bridges cross the creek, hikers can create short or long circuit routes. From the starting point of the hike described here, there are options ranging from 4 to 6 miles in length.

LOCATION
Allentown, PA
(Lehigh County)

RATING
Easy to moderate

DISTANCE
6.5 miles

ELEVATION GAIN
125 feet

ESTIMATED TIME
2.75 hours

MAPS
USGS Allentown East;
allentownpa.gov/Portals/0/
files/Parks_Recreation/
maps/LehighPkwy-hr.pdf

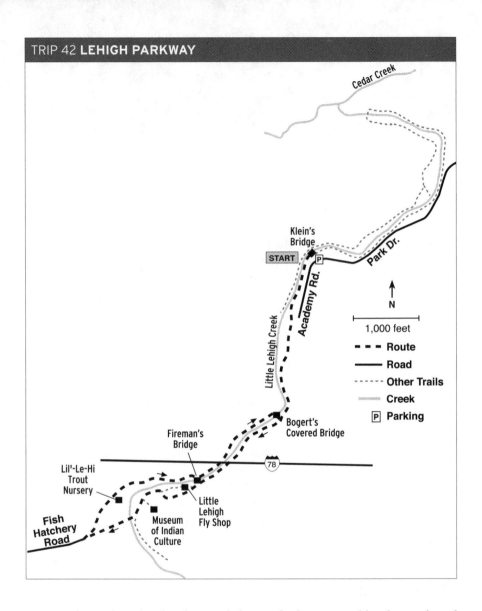

From the parking lot, head toward the crushed-stone trail by the creek and turn left, passing under Klein's Bridge. After the bridge, you'll see a series of signs marking the Rev. Dr. Ernest F. Andrews Memorial Planet Walk. This unique, 0.8-mile trail is a 1-foot-to-1-million-miles scale model of the solar system, designed to give hikers a true appreciation of the vastness of outer space. The trail leads past the Allentown Police Academy shooting range and into a mature oak-hickory woods. After the final sign (for Pluto), the trail passes Bogert's Bridge, one of seven covered bridges in the Lehigh Valley. Built in 1841, it is listed on the National Register of Historic Places. After following the trail

Feeding young trout at the fish hatchery on Lehigh Parkway.

past (not across) the bridge, walk uphill and steeply downhill before passing under I-78.

Continue another 0.6 mile, passing an old iron chimney stack on the left and Fireman's Bridge on the right. Little Lehigh Fly Shop is by the creek, just beyond the bridge in a nineteenth-century spring house, across from a stone barn (with a parking area and restrooms). Lessons in fly fishing, fly tying, and rod building are available at the shop. Fed in part by limestone springs, the creek's cool temperatures and its complex riffle-pool sequences—or shallow, fast-flowing, gravel-bottomed areas interspersed with deeper, calmer spots—help support a naturally reproducing population of wild brown trout.

From the shop, take the trail bearing left at the Y intersection. Down this path, you'll find a garden and the Museum of Indian Culture on your left. Exhibits at the museum are designed to educate both adults and children about the culture of the Lenape and other woodland Indians of the Northeast. Just 0.2 mile past the museum, the trail reaches Fish Hatchery Road. Turn right and walk along the road, crossing the creek and turning immediately right to take the grassy path next to the creek toward Lil'-Le-Hi Trout Nursery. The fish hatchery is owned by the city of Allentown and managed by several local sporting clubs. Brook, brown, rainbow, and golden rainbow trout are raised here. More than

25,000 trout are released annually to stock the city's waterways, including Little Lehigh Creek.

At the end of the grassy path is the White-Snyder House, where you can purchase food to feed the trout. The paved path to the left of the house leads to a gravel trail that heads uphill and sharply to the right. Follow this trail 0.4 mile to Fireman's Bridge but don't cross the bridge. Continue 0.6 mile to Hunter's Cabin, a restored structure dating from 1739 that is typical of an early German settler's dwelling. Pass under Bogert's Bridge then follow the trail as it bears left, passing a stone barn. Walk another 0.7 mile to return to Klein's Bridge. At this point, you have hiked about 2.6 miles. If you would like to end the hike here, cross Klein's Bridge to return to the parking lot. Otherwise, continue along the creek.

If you choose to continue, hike for about another 0.7 mile, where the trail reaches a parking area at a Y intersection. To end the hike here, follow the trail to the right and cross Robin Hood Bridge then turn right and hike the last portion of the trail back to the parking lot next to Klein's Bridge. To extend the hike another 1.5 miles, go left at the Y intersection. This paved loop passes old iron chimney stacks, a series of exercise stations along the parkway's Fitness Trail, a disc golf course, and a beautiful stone wall. When you reach the parking lot at the top of the loop, cross the Lehigh Parkway North Bridge over the creek and turn right onto the gravel trail. Follow this trail past Robin Hood Bridge and end at the parking lot next to Klein's Bridge.

MORE INFORMATION

Restrooms are located at the fly-fishing shop, at the White-Snyder House, and elsewhere along the route; portable toilets are at the trailhead and other parking areas. Dogs are permitted on leash. Fishing is allowed and encouraged at the park; children under 16 do not need fishing licenses in Pennsylvania. Horses are permitted on gravel trails. The Museum of Indian Culture is open Friday through Sunday from noon to 4 P.M. Museum admission is $5 for adults, $4 for seniors over 65 and children 12 and older; there is no fee for children under 12 (lenape.org). Lehigh Parkway is managed by Allentown Parks and Recreation. For more information: 3000 Parkway Boulevard, Allentown, PA 18104; 610-437-7757; allentownpa.gov/Parks-and-Recreation/Parks/Park-Inventory/Lehigh-Parkway.

43

SOUTH MOUNTAIN PRESERVE

Explore looping hillside trails that wind around boulders, all surrounded by nineteenth-century quarries and a mature forest of hardwood trees.

DIRECTIONS

Take the Pennsylvania Turnpike Northeast Extension (I-476) north to Exit 44. Take PA 663 north for 3.4 miles and turn left onto PA 309 north. Drive 9.2 miles and take I-78 west 0.2 mile to Exit 57. Drive south on Lehigh Street toward Emmaus for 0.3 mile. Turn left onto 31st Street and travel for 0.3 mile. Turn right onto Emmaus Avenue and continue for 0.5 mile, until Emmaus Avenue ends at a fork. Bear left at the fork onto Dalton Street. Turn left onto Alpine Street, a dead end. Parking is permitted along the street and in the parking lot to the left; there is room for more than ten cars. *GPS coordinates:* 40° 32.984' N, 75° 28.997' W.

TRAIL DESCRIPTION

South Mountain marks the southern edge of the Lehigh Valley, forming a cultural as well as geographical border. Sometimes called Lehigh Mountain, South Mountain is geologically part of a province of the Appalachian Range called the Reading Prong, a 45-mile-long region of low hills and ridges. It is composed of hard, billion-year-old metamorphic rocks—such as like granite, gneiss, and quartzite—that have been pushed up by forces from the southeast and now sit on 450-million-year-old sedimentary rocks (limestone and shale). The hard rocks are very resistant to erosion, so the hills and ridges stand markedly higher than the softer sedimentary rocks surrounding them. About 150,000 years ago, glaciers covered the northwestern slope of the mountain. Melting and refreezing water broke up

LOCATION
Emmaus, PA (Lehigh County)

RATING
Easy to moderate

DISTANCE
3.3 miles

ELEVATION GAIN
500 feet

ESTIMATED TIME
1.5 hours

MAPS
USGS Allentown East; wildlandspa.org/south-mountain-preserve/

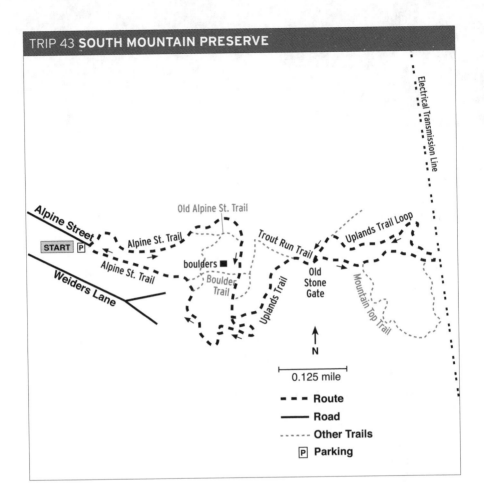

Old Alpine St. Trail

Alpine Street

START P

Alpine St. Trail

Alpine St. Trail

Weiders Lane

boulders ■

Boulder Trail

Trout Run Trail

Uplands Trail

Old Stone Gate

Uplands Trail Loop

Mountain Top Trail

Electrical Transmission Line

N

0.125 mile

--- **Route**

——— **Road**

...... **Other Trails**

P **Parking**

the hard rock; as the glaciers receded, they left huge boulders littering the slopes. The mountain's rocky soils were not conducive to farming, so the land was used for industry, its forests cleared of timber for charcoal production during the eighteenth and nineteenth centuries. The mountain also was a resource for iron ore, magnetite, and sandstone. Much of the stone used to construct the buildings at Lehigh University and Moravian College was quarried here. What's more, a hike through South Mountain Preserve affords the opportunity to enjoy the wilderness on the edge of a burgeoning metropolitan area.

From the parking lot at the end of Alpine Street, walk to the trailhead and turn left to proceed along Alpine Street Trail. As you hike through the preserve, follow the online preserve map; trails may not be consistently blazed or otherwise marked. You may encounter mountain bikers, as all trails are multiuse.

Alpine Street Trail enters a maturing, second-growth forest consisting mostly of tulip and oak trees, as well as black birch, shagbark hickory, red ash, and beech. A second-growth forest is a forest that has regrown after a major disturbance—in this case, the deforestation that occurred over a century ago when the charcoaling industry was thriving here. Due to the forest's fertile, moist soils, wildflowers such as black cohosh, Indian cucumber-root, liverleaf, rue-anemone, wild ginger, and wood geranium abound. The preserve also provides prime breeding grounds for reptiles and amphibians, as well as nesting habitat for more than 159 species of birds.

The area you're hiking through features vernal pools, or seasonal wetlands that fill with autumn and spring rain and snowmelt then dry out in the hot summer months. (See "Jump in the Pool," page 207.) The vernal pools on South Mountain provide a critical habitat for many types of amphibians. Species such as the wood frog, spotted salamander, Jefferson salamander, and marbled salamander breed in these temporary pools. Some of the pools are artificial, the pits having once been mined for jasper (by American Indians) or iron ore (by European settlers) before they were intentionally flooded. It is important to give the vernal pools a wide berth to avoid disturbing the amphibians, especially during spring breeding season.

Alpine Street Trail curves sharply to the right then passes the first of several massive boulder formations. These rock formations are popular climbing destinations for boulderers—and for taking a break to enjoy views of South Mountain Preserve and glimpses of Lehigh Valley.

After the boulders, continue past the intersection where Trout Run Trail turns sharply to the left. Take the second left onto Uplands Trail, at the edge of the mountain. After 0.3 mile, Uplands Trail passes an old stone gate to the right: evidence of a roadway that once ran perpendicular to the trail. Fragments of the stone gate are visible, as are some shallow, elongated grooves along sections of the roadway, which was once used by horse-drawn carriages to haul iron ore away from the mines.

Just past the old stone gate, Uplands Trail splits. Bear right at the Y intersection and continue 0.3 mile, passing both ends of the Mountain Top Trail loop, until the trail runs adjacent to a power line. Uplands Trail now loops back around to the old stone gate. After passing the gate, bear right at the Y intersection and hike downslope on Uplands Trail. Be careful, as this section of the trail is uneven. Continue on Uplands Trail until it meets up with Alpine Street Trail. Turn left and continue on Alpine Street Trail, gradually descending the slope of the mountain, crossing over intermittent streams and then over an elevated walkway that leads to the trailhead and the parking lot.

MORE INFORMATION

Trails are open from dawn to dusk. Dogs are permitted on leash. South Mountain Preserve is owned and managed by Wildlands Conservancy; its 350-plus acres, along with adjacent Allentown parkland, makes up the 750-acre Robert Rodale Preserve. Mountain biking and bouldering are permitted on South Mountain Preserve. A restroom is located near the parking lot at the Alpine Street trailhead. In the spring, some trails that approach or pass through the vernal pools are closed due to amphibian breeding season. Be sure to stay on the trails and respect boundary markers; the preserve is surrounded by private property. For more information, contact Wildlands Conservancy, 3701 Orchid Place, Emmaus, PA 18049; 610-965-4397; wildlandspa.org.

JUMP IN THE POOL

The late-winter sun rises higher and higher in the sky. In the woods, slowly warming air thaws the frozen soil, and water trickles into troughs, carving out a path downhill and collecting in a recess where a tree once stood. Frogs and salamanders arrive at these vernal pools to mate and lay eggs. The pools shrink over the course of the spring, giving the eggs room to hatch and the newborn amphibians time to mature. Before predators—fish, snakes, and turtles—can move in on their prey, the summer's heat has dried up the pools, and the young frogs and salamanders have moved on.

Wood frogs are typically the first to arrive at vernal pools, sometimes as early as mid-February. Leaf-brown with a black mask, they are terrestrial during most of the year, hence their name. To stay alive during their hibernation each winter, they burrow into the soil, their cells secreting special compounds that act like antifreeze. These frogs spend summer and fall hiding in leaf litter. Only in springtime do they attract attention with their distinctive calls. Following a chorus of strident quacks, hikers can find a pool alive not with ducks but with frogs swimming frantically to and fro—males on the hunt for an available female. Once she has mated, a female wood frog lays thousands of eggs in a mass that floats just under the surface of the pool and is often tinged green from algae.

In mid- to late March, the calls of spring peepers pierce the air. The tiny peeper, a thumbnail-sized frog, seems to be all voice. Its high-pitched peep, often mistaken for a bird call, seems to come out of nowhere yet be everywhere at once. When a chorus of peepers gets going, the noise can be deafening. A calling male perches on a waterside stem to attract a female. After mating, she lays hundreds of eggs underwater, around submerged vegetation.

Spotted salamanders remain silent in spring, much as they do the rest of the year. These 6- to 8-inch-long black, yellow-spotted amphibians stay hidden beneath leaves, rocks, or logs, or in underground burrows, emerging only at night. On warm spring nights, especially after it has rained, scores of salamanders make their way to the vernal pools to mate, traveling as far as hundreds or thousands of feet and even crossing roads. They return to the same pools year after year, perhaps drawn by familiar smells. The salamanders' distinctive, gelatinous, bloblike egg masses rise to the surface as the eggs grow. The young hatch, leave the pool, and find the woods—but they remember where they came from and return next spring.

44

APPALACHIAN TRAIL: PA 309 TO BAKE OVEN KNOB

This scenic, rugged stretch of the Appalachian Trail traces the crest of Kittatinny Mountain, providing a challenging ridge-top scramble over the Cliffs (a.k.a. the Knife Edge) and up Bear Rocks.

LOCATION
New Tripoli, PA
(Lehigh County)

RATING
Moderate to difficult

DISTANCE
11 miles

ELEVATION GAIN
200 feet

ESTIMATED TIME
5.5 hours

MAPS
USGS New Tripoli, USGS Slatedale; Pennsylvania Appalachian Trail Map, Section 3

DIRECTIONS

Take the PA Turnpike Northeast Extension (I-476) to Exit 56 (Lehigh Valley); take PA 309 north; after approximately 23 miles, PA 309 crests Blue Mountain. On the right is the State Game Lands 217 parking lot, where you will find space for twenty cars. If you miss it, turn around at the Blue Mountain Summit restaurant parking lot; there is an Appalachian Trail crossing here. *GPS coordinates:* 40° 42.474′ N, 75° 48.478′ W.

The hike can be done as a shuttle by parking a second vehicle at the Bake Oven Road State Game Lands 217 lot. To reach Bake Oven Road, drive south on PA 309 from the Blue Mountain Summit restaurant about 3 miles and turn left onto Mountain Road. Drive 2.8 miles and turn left again onto Bake Oven Knob Road (a gravel road); continue another 2.2 miles to the lot, where there is ample space for parking.

TRAIL DESCRIPTION

The Appalachian Trail (AT) in Pennsylvania has the exaggerated but not altogether unjustified reputation of being a long, green tunnel with a carpet of pointy rocks. The section of the AT stretching from PA 309 to Bake Oven Knob is a glorious exception, with splendid views and a few challenging scrambles up the rocks that more than make up for the bits in between—consisting of a long, green tunnel with a carpet of pointy rocks.

Start by heading east, downhill from the State Game Lands parking lot and toward PA 309, where a blue-blazed

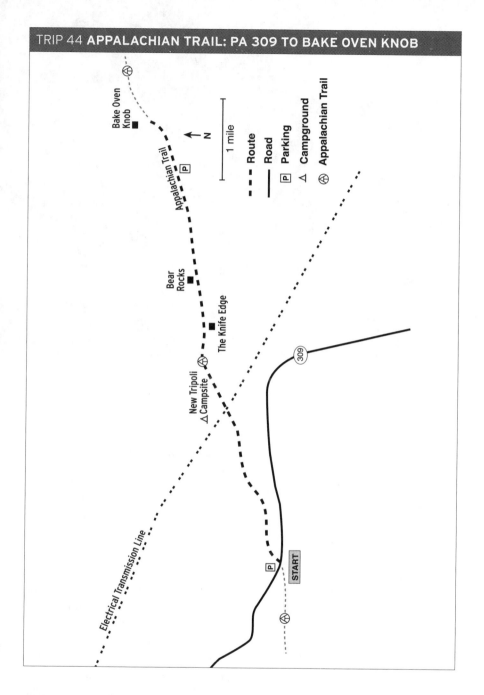

trail enters the woods. After just 60 feet it meets the AT, easily recognized by its distinctive rectangular white blazes. Turn left on the AT—and follow those blazes!

This is a typical Appalachian ridge-top woods, dry and full of chestnut and red oak, pitch pine, black gum, and hickory. Witch hazel, mountain laurel, mapleleaf viburnum, and blueberry and huckleberry shrubs also grow here, and

This Appalachian Trail scramble tests agility and strength, with a reward of fine views.

the ground is covered with teaberry. The forest is thick and healthy, a haven for birds and other wildlife.

The trail begins as a natural footpath, but after 0.25 mile it joins an old woods road, which is wide and rocky and offers south-facing views of the rural landscape to your right. At 1.8 miles, continue past a power line. You'll now be heading north. A trail leading to the New Tripoli campsite goes off to the left just beyond this point. Stay on the AT as it narrows and is studded with boulders (predominantly conglomerate). At 0.6 mile, it narrows further to become a rocky footpath.

At 2.6 miles, the trail crosses a 200-yard exposed section of rock atop the ridge, known as the Cliffs or the Knife Edge. Slabs of quartzite rock slope diagonally, like the side of a pitched roof, and the ridge drops off steeply on either side. This traverse requires agility. You have to hold on to the rocks while stepping across them, although there are plenty of footholds and handholds in the rocks to steady the course. If the rocks are wet or there is a wind, it is more challenging, but even a hiker averse to scrambling should be able to cross the Cliffs easily—and enjoy the exhilarating views on both sides—if he or she is attentive. As with other exposed rocks on the ridge, watch out for snakes.

After the Cliffs, the rocky trail continues through the woods, passing a blue-blazed trail to the Bear Rocks outcrop, immediately to the left at 3.6 miles. (You can take this detour now or wait until the return trip.) At 4.5 miles, turn right at the fork onto a grassy woods road, still following the AT. At 4.9 miles, you'll pass a metal gate and cross a gravel road (Bake Oven Knob Road); go through the State Game Lands parking lot and reenter the woods, proceeding uphill on a wide, rocky trail.

At 5.3 miles, you'll reach Bake Oven Knob, a flattish, open area with exposed conglomerate and quartzite rock outcrops on both sides of the ridge. There are beautiful vistas on either side of the valley and along the spine of Kittatinny Ridge. According to tradition, the name "Bake Oven" refers not to the outcrops (although on sunny summer days, they are indeed very hot) but to a depression resembling an oven in the rock face below the crest. Here you'll also find Bake Oven Knob Autumn Hawk Watch, where birders congregate in fall to observe and count migrating raptors as the winged creatures surf on thermal updrafts rising along the ridge.

Return the way you came, detouring to climb up Bear Rocks. This quartzite outcrop was formed over millions of years by a series of weathering processes that left the ridge in a serrated form with upturned edges. Water would freeze and expand, causing the edges to fracture vertically. Blocks then would break off and slide down the mountain, leaving standing towers lining the crest of the ridge like the crenellations of a ruined castle.

The Bear Rock scramble is strenuous, but the route across the rocks is well marked with blue blazes. If you can make it across the Cliffs, you can make it up Bear Rocks. At the top, enjoy a marvelous 360-degree view of the valley. Also note the fine weathered quartzite, which displays both horizontal layering and vertical fracturing. Return via the same route, carefully holding on to the rocks. Don't be embarrassed to slide on the seat of your pants.

Now that you have scaled the Cliffs and Bear Rocks, you may feel a little over-confident when approaching the return crossing. Be sure to exercise the same care as you did on the outbound leg. Follow the trail back to the blue-blazed access trail and onward to the parking area.

MORE INFORMATION

There are no restrooms. The AT is open 24 hours a day, 7 days a week. For overnight stays along the AT, Bake Oven Shelter and Campsite is 0.6 mile beyond Bake Oven Knob. This section of the AT is maintained by the Allentown Hiking Club (allentownhikingclub.org).

45

LEHIGH GAP NATURE CENTER AND APPALACHIAN TRAIL

This loop hike features long-range vistas from the north side of Blue Mountain into the Lehigh Valley, as well as close-up views of a grasslands restoration project at a once-barren Superfund site.

DIRECTIONS

Take the PA Turnpike Northeast Extension (I-476) to Exit 56 (Lehigh Valley); take PA 309 north toward Tamaqua for 5.8 miles. In Schnecksville, continue straight as the road becomes US 873. Follow it approximately 8.3 miles and turn right onto Paint Mill Road, where you'll see a sign for Lehigh Gap Nature Center. Follow the road about 0.5 mile to the Lehigh Gap Nature Center's Osprey House, on the left, where there is parking for about 30 cars. *GPS coordinates: 40° 47.002′ N, 75° 36.516′ W.*

TRAIL DESCRIPTION

On its southeasterly run to the Delaware River at Easton, the Lehigh River passes through a spectacular gap it has carved into Kittatinny Ridge. The V-shaped Lehigh Gap dramatically exposes Blue Mountain's rock layers and the 400 million years of geologic history that comes along with them—including many barren acres of rock that relate the most recent, human-made history of the gap.

A century's worth of pollution from zinc smelting in nearby Palmerton has caused extensive defoliation of the north-facing slopes of Blue Mountain on both sides of the gap. In 1980, the Environmental Protection Agency designated an 8-mile stretch, 5 miles east of the gap and 3 west, as a Superfund site, beginning a long process that has led to significant changes in the landscape. The Lehigh Gap Nature Center (LGNC) led efforts to restore the slopes west of Lehigh Gap by creating extensive prairies

LOCATION
Slatington, PA
(Lehigh County)

RATING
Moderate to difficult

DISTANCE
7.5 miles

ELEVATION GAIN
1,000 feet

ESTIMATED TIME
4.75 hours

MAPS
USGS Palmerton, USGS Lehighton; Pennsylvania Appalachian Trail Map, Section 2; trail map available onsite; lgnc.org/trail-map-and-guides/

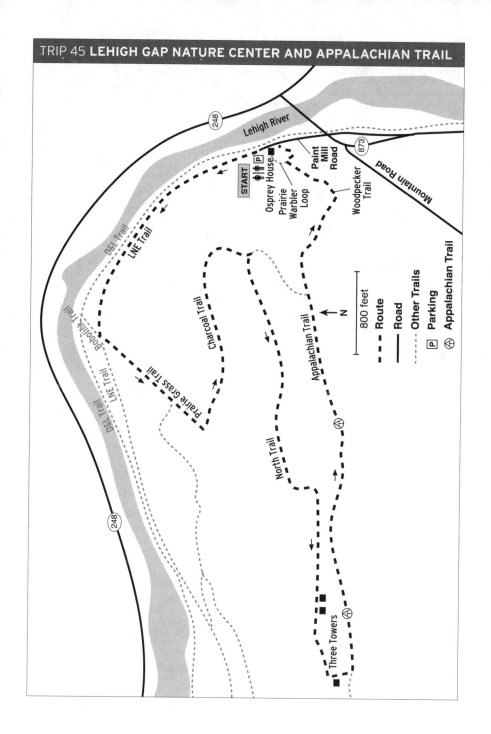

The scenic North Side Trail along Kittatinny Ridge (Blue Mountain), west of Lehigh Gap, offers expansive views of the valley below and a pleasant, relatively rock-free footpath.

of native grasses, which provide a habitat for an amazing variety of birds and other wildlife (see "Rebirth of a Mountain," page 243).

LGNC is the epicenter of a system of trails exploring the ecological and industrial history of Lehigh Gap. LGNC trails connect to the Appalachian Trail (AT) on the south face of the ridge, and to North Trail, a scenic route on its north face. This hike is a counterclockwise loop on parts of all three trail systems. It also can be hiked in a clockwise direction, depending on whether you prefer the uphill portion of the trip to be on the open, north side of the ridge, as it is on this hike, or on the shady, south side—a decision that may depend on the season.

The hike begins at LGNC. Follow signs downhill north of the Osprey House to pick up Lehigh & New England (LNE) Trail. (LGNC trails are marked with wooden signs at intersections.) After a short footpath, LNE Trail merges with an old railbed. The trail takes its name from the Lehigh & New England Railroad, which once made its way around the gap and crossed the river here, transporting anthracite coal from mines. Interpretive signage informs hikers about the railway's history, and the elevated footpath provides an intimate perspective on the long relationship between the rocks and water. The long-distance multiuse Delaware & Lehigh (D&L) Trail parallels LNE Trail 120 feet below. Above the railbed are the towering cliffs of Kittatinny Ridge, carved and weathered into sculptures. At the east end of the ridge is an especially striking rock formation called Devil's Pulpit.

LNE Trail begins to climb uphill as it rounds the gap. At the three-way intersection, where Bobolink Trail heads downhill to the right, take Prairie Grass Trail uphill to the left. The aptly named trail provides superb views of the beautiful warm-season meadow grasses that take over this face of the mountain, a process that began with deliberate plantings and has continued as the grasses spread naturally. The grasses are the foreground to the long-distance views across the Lehigh Valley. The trail is beautiful in all seasons.

Prairie Grass Trail climbs inexorably uphill in a straight line, meeting Charcoal Trail after about 0.5 mile. Where Prairie Grass Trail heads right, go straight onto Charcoal Trail, which continues to ascend the ridge. Charcoal Trail traverses areas of the north slope that were first deforested to produce charcoal used in iron ore smelting, decades before the Palmerton zinc smelter destroyed the second-growth forest. Look for flattened circular areas where logs were burned to create charcoal.

Charcoal Trail ends near the top of the ridge at the blue-blazed North Trail. From here, take in the splendid view of the bend in the Lehigh River then turn right to follow North Trail along the ridge. As the trail travels across bare rocks covered with scrubby growth, it may be challenging to follow. Look for cairns (rock piles) to guide your way. For the next 2 miles, North Trail hugs the north slope of the ridge. Lehigh Valley extends before you, its towns, highways, railroads, factories, hills, and—of course—the river all spread out below like a miniature train set.

In spring and summer, you'll be tempted to run your hands through the wavy native hairgrass as though trailing your fingertips through still waters. Lowbush blueberries cover the slopes here; from late June through July, the ripe berries make this a bear's paradise. Beware of snakes and listen for the distinctive calls of the towhee (*drink-your-teeeee!*), the indigo bunting (descending pairs of notes), and the prairie warbler (a rising trill), all of which frequent these slopes.

Note the first of three communications towers on the left. At the third tower (about 0.5 mile from the first), North Trail turns left over the ridge, heading into woods and joining the white-blazed AT. Turn left to follow the AT northbound. This trail is a typical "Rocksylvania" trail that challenges a hiker's agility. Under your feet are conglomerate and sandstone, both sedimentary rocks. The footpath traverses the south slope below the ridge crest, where white pine, oak, hickory, striped maple, and remnant chestnuts abound; fragrant hay-scented ferns grow in the understory. Smelter emissions did not affect this side of the mountain, but there are no scenic views from here, unless you count the continuous view of the beautiful forest.

The Kittatinny's forest of striped maple, black birch, and chestnut oak is accented occasionally by paper birch (or white birch), a New England species rarely found in Pennsylvania. The shade-intolerant paper birch is an early successional tree, indicating that this is a young forest. After 1.5 miles, pass the turnoff for Blue Trail; continue on the AT to descend the ridge. Pass the Outerbridge shelter, then a spring. After another 0.5 mile, turn left onto LGNC's Woodpecker Trail and follow it to Prairie Warbler Trail, which winds downhill to the Osprey House, where you started.

MORE INFORMATION

Restrooms are at the Osprey House (when open). The preserve and its trails are open from dawn to dusk, and the AT is always open. Leashed dogs are welcome on LGNC trails. LGNC is a superb regional environmental education center. The Bake Oven Knob Autumn Hawk Watch is a long-term LGNC project (see Trip 44). The Osprey House, which is staffed by volunteers, is typically open from 9 A.M. to 4 P.M. daily. Exhibits at the Osprey House provide information on the Lehigh Gap and the 750-acre Lehigh Gap Wildlife Refuge. (If your visit is dependent on the Osprey House being open, it's best to call ahead.) LGNC offers many other programs and outdoor recreational activities. For more information, contact Lehigh Gap Nature Center, 8844 Paint Mill Road, Slatington, PA 18080; 610-760-8889; lgnc.org. Note that, at presstime, a planned realignment of the AT that would switch North Trail and the AT had not yet begun.

TRAILSIDE FRUITS AND BERRIES

There is no food more local than the one growing beside the trail. And there is no finer-tasting food than one you've picked yourself. You can find many edible plants in the woods if you take the time to look and know what you're looking at. Picking out what's good to eat changes your relationship with the woods: They become as much a home as a place to visit. That said, it's crucial to show your outdoor home respect and to avoid overgrazing, leaving the woods in fruitful shape for the next hungry visitor, human or animal, who happens along. More on this below.

It's also essential to know what you're gathering. Unlike mushrooms, the edible and tasty fruits and berries you find by the trail are mostly easy to identify and to distinguish from inedible, distasteful, or occasionally toxic plants. The more you know, the more confident you'll feel. Get a good field guide, attend a presentation, or take a walk with an expert. If you're unsure, go foraging only with someone you trust. Learn to recognize all parts of edible plants and learn when fruits will be in season. (Elevation make a difference: Fruits appear earlier at higher elevations than in valleys.) If you recognize flowers, you can predict when the fruits will appear.

Tree fruits are a good place to start. There are few wild fruiting trees in the Philadelphia area, so it's hard to confuse them. The following trees are some of the more easily identified:

- Persimmons have dark, blocky bark. The round fruits ripen from an inedible, astringent green to a tropical orange-red and drop after ripening, typically in late summer or early autumn. What fun to gently shake the tree just enough to free a soft red globe and catch it in midair!

- Pawpaw fruit, shaped like bananas and tasting like nothing else, ripen in late summer under the broad, elliptical leaves of this small understory tree. The fruit can be gathered while green and left to brown and ripen. You'll find pawpaw patches in rich, moist, or wet soil, typically—but not always—south of Philadelphia. As noted in the trail description for Trip 10 (Alapocas Run State Park), picking pawpaws is illegal in Delaware state parks.

- Hackberries grow in moist, rocky soil. The bark of the tall hackberry tree forms corky furrows. Its dark berries, ripe in autumn, taste like very sweet raisins.

Berries on shrubs are so widespread, it is hard not to encounter them on a hike. The following are some of the most common:

- Blueberries, including their less familiar cousins huckleberries, can be found in many different habitats, including woods, mountains, and bogs, and can grow in sandy, rocky, wet, and dry soil. Blueberry shrubs have small, elliptical, toothless (or barely toothed) leaves; multiple short twigs; and white urn- or bell-shaped flowers. Shrubs can be knee-high (lowbush) or shoulder-height (highbush). The small berries are ripe when they're dark blue (or black, for huckleberries), and they separate from the stem with nary a tug. Depending on the variety, blueberries can be eaten from June to September. All blueberries are edible, although some—dewberries and deerberries—are not as sweet. Watch for bears in blueberry patches.

- With their numerous tiny globules of sweet, seedy pulp, blackberries and raspberries are so distinctive that even the most skeptical hiker will accept a freshly picked specimen. Look for the thorny canes—or stiff, curving stems—in sunny openings: fields, meadows, and railroad right of ways. (Be aware that these are often the same places where poison ivy can be found.) Black raspberries ripen in early summer, turning black as they sweeten; blackberries and bright red wineberries, an Asian fruit widespread in the Philadelphia area, are best in high summer.

- Serviceberries are shrubs or small trees; the only difference between the two forms is the relative height. Serviceberry, also called smooth shadbush, is common in rocky woods and thickets, as well as along roads. Its long-petaled, white flowers bloom in early spring, along with serrated leaves reddish when young. The sweet, juicy berries, which range in color from dark red to purple, arrive in June or July.

Don't pick the flowers? That's true. As a general rule, most parks do not permit picking or collecting plants (especially in large quantities). But most parks and public places do make an exception for fruits and berries. Gathering wild edibles is consistent with Leave No Trace ethics as long as you gather sustainably: Take no more than you can eat out of your hand; don't take rare or locally uncommon plants; and don't deplete the plant's ability to reproduce or deprive an animal of its food source. Provided the edibles are abundant, there's no harm in eating them—and there is plenty of pleasure. The best rule to follow is: "Gather ye blueberries while ye may, for tomorrow the bears may have eaten them all."

46

APPALACHIAN TRAIL: LEHIGH GAP EAST

This short but challenging hike begins with a steep scramble up and over a narrow, barren ridge. The stark landscape has a unique beauty, hosts unusual plants, and provides scenic views of the Lehigh Valley.

DIRECTIONS

Take the Pennsylvania Turnpike Northeast Extension (I-476) north to Exit 56 and then take PA 309 north toward Tamaqua. At 7.8 miles, bear right onto PA 873. Continue on 873 through Slatington (approximately 6 miles) and over the Lehigh River bridge. Turn right at the light onto PA 248 and bear left to stay on 248 where PA 145 bears right. After 300 feet, make a very sharp left onto an unmarked gravel road (note the National Park Service sign) going up the embankment to the parking lot, where you will find parking for 30 cars. *GPS coordinates:* 40° 46.984′ N, 75° 36.244′ W.

TRAIL DESCRIPTION

The east side of Lehigh Gap is a short but intense challenge for a hiker's courage, agility, and fortitude. It also exemplifies the effect that humans can have on the environment. Pennsylvania's mining and manufacturing industries have altered the landscape in many ways, leaving acidic mine drainage, slag heaps, slate hills, abandoned quarries, and underground coal fires in their wake. It's unusual for a hiker to be able to experience firsthand the effects of the still-vital mining sector. The trek up Lehigh Gap East evokes the barren desert beauty of the West, although the Gap's magnificent desolation is of human origin.

Nestled in the Blue Mountain valley northeast of the Lehigh Gap, Palmerton was home to a zinc smelting operation from 1898 to 1980. Prevailing winds carried sulfur

LOCATION
Slatington, PA
(Lehigh County)

RATING
Difficult

DISTANCE
2.75 miles

ELEVATION GAIN
900 feet

ESTIMATED TIME
2 hours

MAPS
USGS Palmerton;
Pennsylvania Appalachian
Trail Map, Section 2

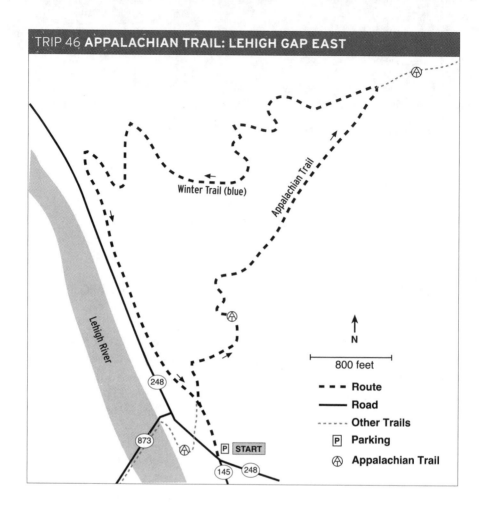

across the valley, defoliating Blue Mountain and depositing heavy metals that settled in the soil, preventing natural revegetation. In 1980, the Environmental Protection Agency designated Blue Mountain a Superfund site. While restoration projects have begun to yield partial success in reforesting the ridge, defoliation has left the nose of the Lehigh Gap's east side permanently bare, exposing the blocks of sandstone, conglomerate, and shale that compose the Shawangunk Formation.

This hike begins at the parking lot, once part of a railbed. The Appalachian Trail (AT) climbs the embankment, from the north side of the parking lot. Look for the AT sign then follow the AT's white rectangular blazes. The blue-blazed Winter Trail branches left from the AT; you will take this on the return leg.

The narrow, rocky trail climbs steeply uphill, traversing a scrubby area of hemlock, sassafras, chestnut oak, pitch pine, and the unusual paper (white) birch. The Lehigh River, hidden below the embankment, slowly appears on your left as the trail ascends. At 0.4 mile, the trail begins to traverse exposed boulders.

Follow the white blazes, which mark the best route. Continue up the rock face, using the ledges as handholds and footholds. Look down if you dare; this is not a place for those with a paralyzing fear of heights. Take it one step at a time and know where you are heading before taking each step, but don't be reluctant to stop and enjoy the view.

Although it is not a knife edge, the crest of the ridge is narrow. The weather on the north side can be surprisingly different from that on the south, as it is from here that wind and storms approach and collide with the great mass that is the ridge. Clamber down the rock face then begin a long scramble over boulders (not as steep as the south side). There are long views of the northwest side of the valley. At 0.65 mile, the trail flattens out along the crest, and scrubby vegetation reappears.

The north side hosts several plants that seem to thrive in contaminated soil. Lehigh Gap's east ridge is the only place in Pennsylvania where sandwort, a low-growing plant with ebullient sprays of tiny white flowers, can be found. Thrift (sea pink), a garden flower with a chive-like appearance, spreads over the bare rocks in great drifts. Wild bleeding-heart, an endangered plant with pink, heart-shaped flowers, grows more profusely around both sides of the gap than anywhere else in the state. Blueberries are abundant as well. Lehigh Gap hemlocks are reported to have developed resistance to the hemlock woolly adelgid, an insect that feeds on and kills the trees. Scientists are studying whether the

Lehigh Gap East features a challenging rock scramble.

unusual growth patterns are due to the presence of metals, nutrients in amended soil added during restoration projects, or some other factor(s).

The trail proceeds along the crest, a wide boulder field occasionally marked by cairns rather than blazes. At 1.4 miles, the blue-blazed Winter Trail branches off to the left. The AT continues, and the hike can be lengthened as far as you please by continuing north. (The northern endpoint, at Katahdin in Maine, is only 928 miles away.)

Follow the Winter Trail along the crest via a grassy trail with easy footing. It heads through a grove into a sea of wavy hairgrass, an elegant, ruddy-stemmed native plant that flourishes on dry, rocky sites. The Winter Trail descends into shady woods and follows a ridge cove around to the north. At several points there are good views of the bare ridge to the south. Emerging from the woods, the trail descends down a wide, exposed rock path. Near the bottom it passes a double-decker spring. After 1 mile, the trail meets an old railbed that parallels the road below. Turn left. The trail is occasionally muddy or swampy here, as water from the spring above sometimes spills down the ridge.

The trail passes through the gorge carved out by the river and augmented by roadcuts made during railway and highway construction, giving you a river's-eye view of the spectacular rock strata and the bare nose of the ridge above. The hike ends at the junction with the AT at the parking lot.

MORE INFORMATION

The Winter Trail is aptly named: Ice, snow, and wind make the main trail treacherous, so the blue-blazed trail is the only reasonable route in winter. This is not a four-season hike, although it can be an out-and-back over the Winter Trail; however, the Winter Trail is also exposed during storms. The Keystone Trails Association (kta-hike.org) maintains this section of the AT. There are no restrooms. Note: At presstime, a partial reroute of this leg of the AT was still in the planning stages. When completed, the route will be modified but will retain its signature ascent over the exposed rock.

47

HICKORY RUN STATE PARK

This long but rewarding hike explores numerous rich forests with diverse wildlife, climbs across ridges with fine views of the Lehigh Valley, and ends with a creekside trek down a beautiful ravine filled with rhododendrons.

LOCATION
White Haven, PA
(Carbon County)

RATING
Difficult

DISTANCE
12 miles

ELEVATION GAIN
550 feet

ESTIMATED TIME
5 hours

MAPS
USGS Hickory Run; trail maps available onsite; dcnr.pa.gov/StateParks/FindAPark/HickoryRunStatePark/Pages/Maps.aspx

DIRECTIONS

Take the Pennsylvania Turnpike Northeast Extension (I-476) to Exit 95, proceed west on PA 940 for 3 miles, and turn left on PA 534 east. Drive 6 miles to the parking lot indicated by the park sign on the left. You will find ample parking. *GPS coordinates:* 41° 01.473′ N, 75° 42.588′ W.

TRAIL DESCRIPTION

This hike is the northernmost—and, at 12 miles, the longest—in the book. Its rewards, however, make the effort more than worthwhile. This hike concentrates on Hickory Run State Park's western section, but eastern trails, including the celebrated Boulder Field, are just as enjoyable. There are more than 15,500 acres and more than 43 miles of trails in the park, and the massive, healthy forests support a great variety of wildlife. Birds that call the forest interior home, such as veery, scarlet tanager, and Swainson's thrush, reside here in spring and summer. Black bears are not uncommon, although you're more likely to encounter a porcupine, a wood frog, or a chipmunk.

Hickory Run also shows the influence of glaciers on the landscape. The hike primarily traverses a terminal moraine, or a pile of debris left by glaciers that covered portions of the park 20,000 years ago. It is characterized by sand, gravel, and loose rocks (glacial till); conifer forests; boggy, swampy soil; and steep-sided valleys.

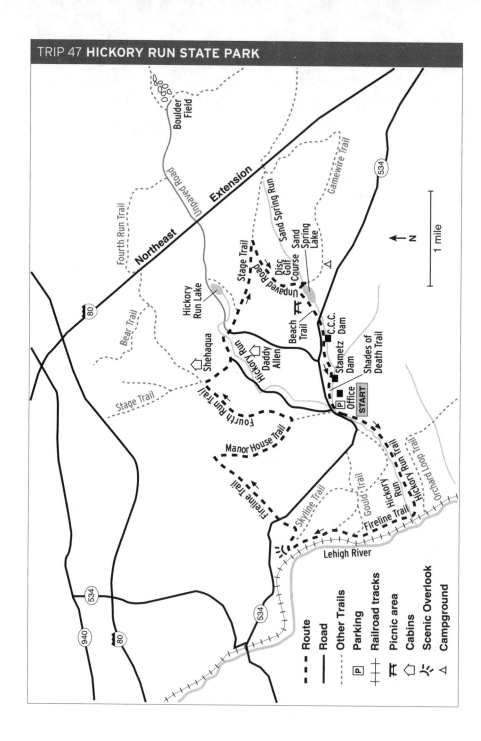

N

1 mile

Boulder Field

Gamewire Trail

534

Fourth Run Trail

Unpaved Road

Northeast Extension

Sand Spring Run

Stage Trail

Disc Golf Course

Sand Spring Lake

△

Bear Trail

80

Hickory Run Lake

Unpaved Road

Beach Trail

C.C.C. Dam

Shades of Death Trail

Shehaqua

Hickory Run

Daddy Allen

Stametz Dam

Stage Trail

Fourth Run Trail

Office

P

START

Manor House Trail

Gould Trail

Hickory Run Trail

Hickory Run Trail

Orchard Loop Trail

Fireline Trail

Skyline Trail

Fireline Trail

Lehigh River

534

534

940

80

Legend:
- - - **Route**
—— **Road**
······· **Other Trails**
P **Parking**
+++ **Railroad tracks**
⊼ **Picnic area**
⌂ **Cabins**
⚎ **Scenic Overlook**
△ **Campground**

Although this lengthy hike follows a series of trails, it's not complicated. Note, though, that the trails are blazed with colors to indicate their permitted uses (e.g., hiking, skiing), not to distinguish them from one from another. Carry a trail map to avoid getting lost.

Start the hike by heading south along PA 534 from the parking lot, keeping to the left and staying behind the guardrail. After 0.25 mile, bear left and follow Hickory Run Trail along the stream and down into a boggy meadow adorned with a fine display of summer wildflowers. Hickory Run Trail comes close to the creek and, at 0.75 mile, it enters the woods along the bottom of a steep ravine. This is a moist woods with big trees—yellow birch, hemlock, red maple—accompanied by an understory of ferns. Rhododendrons are abundant here. Continue to follow the wide, flat trail. (Caution: Although it has become common for hikers to walk along the railroad tracks ahead, the tracks are private property and actively used. It is neither permissible nor wise to walk on them.)

Turn right onto Fireline Trail, which after about 2 miles climbs uphill to an overlook. Climb steadily for another 0.25 mile past a field speckled with meadowsweet, along with white birch and blueberries, and toward a much larger open meadow affording views of the hills surrounding Lehigh Gorge. The trail continues alternating between open areas and woods. Cross the stream on rocks; you'll pass by stone walls and foundations indicating this was once a settlement. In the open areas, blueberries and blackberries are abundant in season. At a bend in the trail, an old spring flows downhill to a vanished cove. At about 3 miles from your start, there are fine north-facing views of Kittatinny Ridge. Pay attention to the rocks in and around the footpath, noting the change in type and orientation. About 0.75 mile later, you can see a view of the Lehigh Gorge.

At 4.2 miles, cross PA 534 to Manor House Trail, another old road that steadily climbs uphill. Here the rocks in the trail are granitic boulders. There are many fungi in this section of successional woods. Beech and striped maple dominate overhead. Manor House Trail goes downhill, crossing Irishtown Run, a stream, several times. At the bottom of the hill (6.4 miles), take Fourth Run Trail to the left. This trail follows a power line clearing where highbush blueberries and huckleberries ripen in summer. Another plant growing here is sweet fern. Despite its name, it's not a fern but rather a shrub that grows on dry, sterile soils and produces aromatic, fernlike leaves. Fourth Run Trail returns to the woods; at 7.75 miles, you'll reach Stage Trail. Turn right onto this old, red gravel road. The trail is flat, wide, and shady.

At 8 miles, you'll pass Camp Shehaqua then the Saylorsville Dam. Mallows line the small lake. About 0.5 mile after you pass Camp Daddy Allen but before a stop sign, the trail breaks away from the road. Cross the road to stay on Stage Trail,

Although the trail following the dramatic, rhododendron-filled ravine surrounding Sand Spring Run is called Shades of Death, it is full of life's wonders.

passing through a pine-hemlock woods with many mountain laurels. At 9.5 miles, you'll reach a gravel road; the trail turns right and passes a well-hidden water tower. At 9.75 miles, the trail enters the Sand Spring Lake day-use area and passes by a disc golf course. Keep the disc course on your left and head for either the restrooms across the field (if needed) or the lake bathhouse to the far left (to stay on the trail). Pass by the lake and go below the dam to the right, where you'll pick up Beach Trail, a red gravel road. Continue on this trail, with the stream to your left.

At 10.8 miles, cross the road to enter Shades of Death Trail, marked with a sign. While colorful legends purporting to explain the trail's name abound, the truth seems shrouded in a fog as mysterious as the one that often rises from the ravine here. The trail, blazed yellow, is the most beautiful and most challenging on the hike, although it is not nearly as difficult as the park's literature suggests. Shades of Death Trail goes along the edge of Sand Spring Run as the stream tumbles down a gorge. This deep hemlock ravine is studded with numerous falls and rock pools. Overhanging the trail are masses of rhododendrons. There are many spots where you can stop, sit on the rocks, and take in the drama.

The roaring creek quiets as it nears a dam, installed long ago to power a sawmill. The dam has a pretty spillway. At about 12 miles, get to PA 534; follow it to return to the parking lot.

MORE INFORMATION
A portable toilet is located at the parking lot. Full restroom facilities are available at Sand Spring Lake. For more information, contact Hickory Run State Park, 3613 State Route 534, White Haven, PA 18661; 570-443-0400; dcnr.state .pa.us/stateparks/findapark/hickoryrun.

48

GLEN ONOKO FALLS AND LEHIGH GORGE STATE PARK

Climb a rugged, steep ravine with numerous waterfalls and enjoy a bird's-eye view of the Lehigh Gorge from Broad Mountain before descending along a misty mountain creek.

DIRECTIONS

Take the Pennsylvania Turnpike Northeast Extension (I-476) to Exit 74 (Mahoning Valley/US 209). Follow US 209 south to Jim Thorpe. Turn right to take PA 903 north across the river. At the stop sign, continue straight. Turn left at the signs for Glen Onoko, where you will find ample parking. *GPS coordinates: 40° 53.017' N, 75° 45.604' W.*

TRAIL DESCRIPTION

Lehigh Gorge State Park's Glen Onoko Run plunges 860 feet from the top of Broad Mountain to the Lehigh River below, generating a series of cascading waterfalls in its wake and making Glen Onoko Falls one of the most spectacular hiking sites in eastern Pennsylvania. On summer weekends, it attracts a steady stream of locals who come to cool off in the splash and spray. Many seem content to climb only partway up the gorge, and others seem frightfully unprepared for the steep and slippery path—especially coming down. The 1-mile-long trail up to the highest part of the falls is challenging, but there are great rewards in store for the hiker who continues across the crest, down the mountain, and along the river. This long circuit hike offers a wealth of forested ridge and riverside experiences.

From the state park parking lot, follow the signs for "Glen Onoko Access." The trail descends to the river, passes beneath some railroad tracks, and climbs steeply up a wooded hill. Follow the stone steps, remnants of a nineteenth-century resort hotel, and bear left at all trail

LOCATION
Jim Thorpe, PA
(Lehigh County)

RATING
Difficult

DISTANCE
10 miles

ELEVATION GAIN
950 feet

ESTIMATED TIME
4.5 hours

MAPS
USGS Weatherly,
USGS Christmans

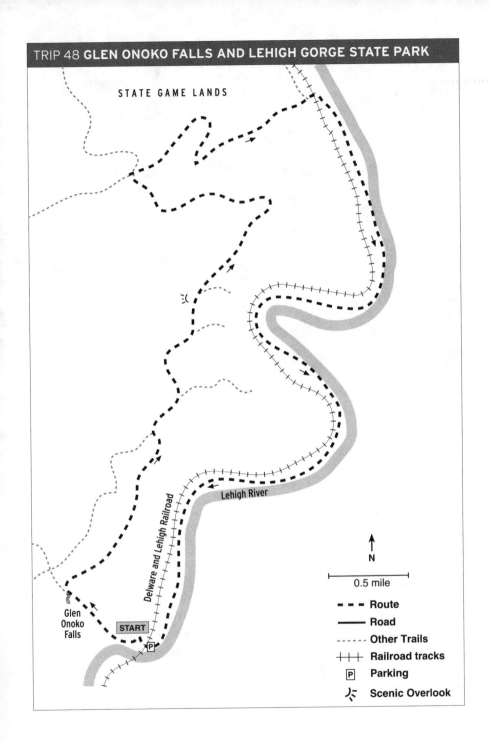

STATE GAME LANDS

Delware and Lehigh Railroad

Lehigh River

Glen
Onoko
Falls

START

P

N

0.5 mile

- - - Route
—— Road
---- Other Trails
+++ Railroad tracks
P Parking
⌇ Scenic Overlook

From the top of Glen Onoko, where the falls begin, the water seems to disappear into the abyss.

forks. The trail enters Pennsylvania State Game Lands 141 and is blazed red or orange. Follow the trail up the canyon, scrambling over large boulders along the way.

On the left, the water falls in sheets, tumbling over boulders to rest in quiet pools. A cool mist hangs over the glen. Mountain laurel, rhododendron, yellow birch, hemlock, mosses, and ferns cling to the rock ledges. Huge fallen trees tossed here and there like matchsticks among the boulders testify to the power of falling water. A cataract falling before a wide, concave rock face creates a veil of water that you can walk behind. At the top of the canyon, the water spills lazily over a table ledge and seems to disappear into the sky high over the valley.

The trail turns to the right, entering the woods and ascending to the hillcrest. The dry, rocky woodland here is a far cry from the moist glen, with completely different types of vegetation: chestnut oak, black birch, pitch pine, blueberry, and sheep laurel. After 0.3 mile past the turn, you'll pass stone steps leading to an overlook on the right. These steps—additional remains of the defunct hotel—lead to a trail that descends the mountain, enabling a route for the return trip that is much less treacherous than a descent of the falls would be, should you prefer to shorten your hike.

Continue north along the ridge on the rocky, flat trail. You can take in fine views of the valley to the southeast (right) in winter. At about the 4.3-mile mark, there is an excellent overlook of the Oxbow Bend of the Lehigh River. This is the perfect place to take a rest and enjoy the free entertainment. At eye-level or below, turkey vultures habitually soar, spiral, and glide along the 1,500-foot-high sheer cliffs of the gorge.

Continue on the crest trail as it bends left; about 750 feet farther on, turn right onto a 10-foot-wide, unpaved fire road; soon you'll pass under a power line. The flat, open ridge-top terrain continues. About 1 mile past the overlook (5.3 miles in), the fire road splits at a Y intersection. Just before this intersection, turn right onto a narrow, rocky trail leading into a thick woods. Mountain laurel and blueberry abound.

After proceeding through this dry woods for roughly 0.5 mile, the trail descends the mountain through a beautiful, intimate ravine. The grade declines gradually but becomes steeper; your footsteps will be accompanied by the sound of rushing water as the creek and trail descend the mountain in parallel. Eventually the trail meets up with the creek and follows it closely, crossing it once. The trail may be muddy and slippery. Here you'll find rhododendron, hemlock, yellow birch, and hornbeam. Look for shade-loving native wildflowers, such as foamflower and wild ginger.

At the bottom of the ravine, the trail emerges from the woods in front of a railway. Stop, look, and listen! These tracks are active. Take care as you cross and descend quickly by way of the embankment. (About 50 feet to the right of the trail, the embankment becomes more level and easier to pass.) Turn right at the paved trail.

The last 3.5 miles of the hike takes you down the Lehigh Gorge Trail, a 21-mile multiuse trail between White Haven and Jim Thorpe. This trail is part of the D&L Trail, a planned 165-mile route from Wilkes-Barre to Bristol that traces an old shipping route that conveyed millions of tons of anthracite coal to ports via canals and railways until the 1930s. The multiuse D&L Trail runs along the Lehigh River, passing through Allentown (see Trip 38) and Lehigh Gap (see Trip 45), as well as the Delaware Canal (see Trip 32). Although scenic, flat, and quiet, with the exception of the occasional train, this long, level, paved section of the hike nevertheless can be fatiguing. You might want to bring along a pair of light-weight shoes to replace your heavy hiking boots, especially in hot weather. Continue down the trail toward the Glen Onoko parking lot.

Glen Onoko Falls from underneath.

MORE INFORMATION

Restrooms are located at the Glen Onoko parking lot. State parklands, including the parking lot, are open from sunrise to sunset. State Game Lands and D&L Trail are always open. For more information, contact Lehigh Gorge State Park, c/o Hickory Run State Park Complex, 3613 State Route 534, White Haven, PA 18661; 570-443-0400; dcnr.state.pa.us/stateparks/parks/lehighgorge .aspx. For map of Glen Onoko access see docs.dcnr.pa.gov/cs/groups/public/ documents/document/dcnr_003767.pdf. For more on the D&L Trail, visit delawareandlehigh.org.

49

APPALACHIAN TRAIL:
THE PINNACLE AND THE PULPIT

Climb through rich woods and up and over rugged, steep mountain trails to take in stunning views of the Appalachian Mountains and the bucolic valley below. This is the best-known vista on the Pennsylvania Appalachian Trail.

DIRECTIONS

Take the Pennsylvania Turnpike Northeast Extension (I-476) to Exit 56 (Lehigh Valley); continue on I-78 west to Exit 35 (Lenhartsville). Turn right at the off-ramp then turn right again onto West Penn Street (Old US 22) in Lenhartsville. Drive 2 miles then turn right on Reservoir Road. Continue 1 mile to the parking area, where you will find parking for twenty cars. *GPS coordinates:* 40° 34.987′ N, 75° 56.515′ W.

TRAIL DESCRIPTION

The view from the Pinnacle is the most celebrated on the 229-mile-long Pennsylvania segment of the Appalachian Trail and one of the most renowned of any trail in the state. The hike to the Pinnacle is a must for any collection of day hikes in southeastern Pennsylvania. Indeed, there are hikers who will tell you they could do this hike every day and never be bored by it. Some know and love it so much they hike it in moonlight. That said, it is a challenging hike, with steep trails and boulders to climb. In addition, this popular stretch can become so crowded on nice weekends that the view may be obstructed. Nonetheless, this is a hike that makes people fall in love with hiking—and hiking in Pennsylvania.

Head from the parking lot past a yellow gate and continue uphill along a gravel road (blue blazes) about 0.5 mile until it reaches an unpaved road. Note the wooden

LOCATION
Hamburg, PA (Berks County)

RATING
Difficult

DISTANCE
9.25 miles

ELEVATION GAIN
1,300 feet

ESTIMATED TIME
5.5 hours

MAPS
USGS Hamburg;
Pennsylvania Appalachian
Trail Map, Section 4

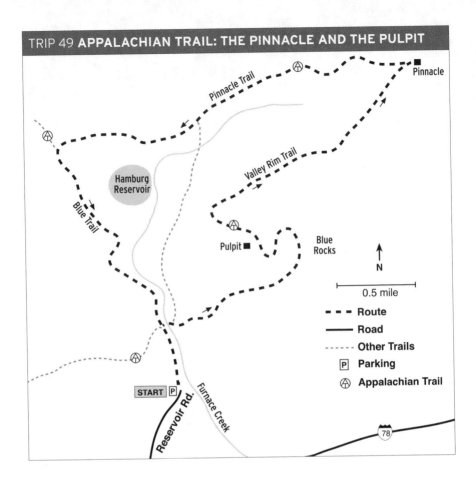

Pinnacle Trail

Pinnacle

Valley Rim Trail

Hamburg Reservoir

Blue Trail

Pulpit ■

Blue Rocks

N

0.5 mile

- - - Route
—— Road
····· Other Trails
P Parking
Ⓐ Appalachian Trail

START P

Reservoir Rd.

Furnace Creek

78

Appalachian Trail (AT) sign straight ahead, indicating an AT crossing: The southbound AT is to your left, the northbound AT to your right. (AT convention is that the Maine-bound trail heads north and the Georgia-bound trail heads south, even though "AT north" here is actually heading east, according to the compass.) Turn right, onto the road, following the AT north. As with all sections of the AT, the trail is marked with white rectangles. Double blazes indicate turns; sometimes the upper blaze may be offset in the direction of a turn.

The AT crosses Furnace Creek via a short footbridge then bends right and into the woods, where it quickly narrows to a footpath. The trail begins to climb the hill. Continue past a blue-blazed spur trail to the Windsor Furnace shelter and turn right to follow Valley Rim Trail, which runs concurrently with the AT. The trail is narrow, natural surfaced, and rocky.

This is a rich, dense forest. At the height of the growing season, the woods are so thick from canopy to ground that you cannot see through them. Red and white oak, hickory, tulip, ash, and striped maple trees predominate; you'll also see many chestnut saplings. Witch hazel, dogwood, rhododendron, pinxter flower (a native azalea), and viburnum shrubs form a middle layer. Cinnamon fern, wood ferns, mayapple, and a variety of wildflowers are common at ground level, as are greenbrier and Virginia creeper vines. Mountain laurel, the state flower, is also abundant, blooming on evergreen shrubs from late May to mid-June.

The number of tree seedlings indicates a healthy woods that can regenerate itself, unlike woods ravaged by deer. "Healthy" does not necessarily mean "ancient," however. This is not an old-growth forest. As indicated by nearby places with the word "furnace" in their names, it was cleared for charcoal production in the nineteenth century. Now it is part of a 13,000-acre protected area that includes Hawk Mountain Sanctuary, the AT corridor, Pennsylvania State Game Lands 106, the Hamburg Borough watershed, and Weiser State Forest, making up one of the largest protected tracts of contiguous forest in southeastern Pennsylvania. The forest's vitality and sheer size attracts diverse wildlife, including the many songbirds you may hear in spring and summer.

The trail bends left after about 1 mile from where you entered the AT and climbs a long hill, then bends sharply left and climbs steeply to the crest of the ridge. Near the crest, the rocks in the trail increase in size until the entire trail is composed of rock. Mountain ash shrubs greet you, letting you know you are in the mountains now.

Climb the rock steps then make a sharp right toward an exposed expanse of rock. As with all exposed rock on this trail, watch carefully for basking snakes. Pass this outcrop then cross a short, grassy opening to reach the Pulpit Rock overlook, at 1,582 feet in elevation. The Pulpit is more than just a preamble to the Pinnacle. The views here are marvelous.

Continue on the AT as the trail traverses the dry, rocky ridge. Chestnut oaks predominate, and the woods are scattered with hemlocks. Lowbush blueberry is abundant here, as is sarsaparilla, with its distinctive clusters of three spherical flower heads.

Shortly after the Pulpit, you'll pass a communications tower on the left. The AT continues along the rocky ridge, dipping down and then up again. About 1.8 miles after the Pulpit, continue past a yellow-blazed trail on the right that leads down to the privately owned Blue Rocks Family Campground.

In another 0.4 mile, you'll reach a spur trail leading to the Pinnacle. Take it, heading past a huge hiker-made cairn to the right. The Pinnacle overlook is about 250 feet from the AT. To the northeast is Kittatinny Ridge (or Blue Mountain), the southeastern edge of the Pennsylvania Appalachian Mountains. "Kittatinny" means "endless hills," and from here the ridge does seem to stretch without end along the horizon, broken only by water gaps (such as the Lehigh Gap and, much farther in the distance, the Delaware Water Gap) and wind gaps (long-vanished waterways). Views to the east and southeast are of the Great Valley. Blue Mountain is composed of hard, blocky quartzite, a sedimentary rock.

The Pinnacle offers the most celebrated views along Pennsylvania's Appalachian Trail.

In the valley below, you can see a "river" of rocks: boulders that tumbled from the ridgetop and ended up in a course of rocks as a result of frost heaves in the soil as the last glaciers (far to the north) retreated. Turkey vultures soar above and below you on the breezes that rise and fall along the cliffs.

After you've given the view its due, head back to the AT and continue past the cairn. Although you are traveling on the northbound AT, you are actually heading west. After about 0.5 mile, the rocky trail becomes a wide woods road with easy footing and a gentle descent and continues in this fashion through the end of the hike. After another mile, you'll pass a flat, grassy expanse on the right called the Helipad. To your left is a blue-blazed trail that descends along the east side of the reservoir via Furnace Creek. This is an alternative return route approximately 1 mile shorter than the one described below.

Continue on the AT and pass (or detour down-and-back on) a spur trail to the pretty Gold Spring, 100 feet off the trail. In another mile, you'll reach a T intersection with another woods road. The AT turns right here, heading toward Eckville, but you'll want to turn left and follow the blue blazes. Continue to descend, passing the west side of Hamburg Reservoir on the left after about 1.25 miles. In another 0.5 mile, you'll reach the road you came in on; follow it back to the parking lot.

MORE INFORMATION

There are neither seasonal nor daily time restrictions on the AT and its blue-blazed alternatives. Hunting is permitted Monday through Saturday at Hamburg Reservoir; wear orange in season. Bikes are not permitted on the AT. Although children may delight in the rock climbing and the beautiful vistas, these are dangerous cliffs, and young hikers must be closely supervised. Given that, this hike may not be suitable for very young children. There are no restrooms. The AT portion of this hike is maintained by the Blue Mountain Eagle Climbing Club (bmecc.org).

Four miles north on the AT from the turnoff to the Hamburg Reservoir is a blue-blazed trail that connects to Hawk Mountain Sanctuary, a site that is more feasibly reached in a separate trip, but eminently worth a visit. The sanctuary is a world-renowned center for raptor migration research and conservation. The entrance fee is $10 for adults, $7 for seniors 65 and older, $5 for children ages 6 to 12, free for children younger than 6.

SONG OF THE ETERNAL MORNING

This is the only bird whose note affects me like music, affects the flow and tenor of my thought, my fancy and imagination. It lifts and exhilarates me. It is inspiring. It is a medicative draught to my soul. . . . It changes all hours to an eternal morning.

—Henry David Thoreau on the wood thrush

Its song is arrestingly beautiful: a trill followed by a flutelike *ee-oh-lay* and a bubbling coda. The song may be distinctive, but the singer is not. The robin-sized wood thrush is not spectacularly colored: brown, with a white breast speckled with brown spots. It spends the spring and summer breeding seasons in the deciduous woods of the eastern United States. During those months, the male can be heard singing from treetops in remote forests, parks, and even suburban backyards all over the Delaware Valley.

What it seems to require above all else is woods. That does not mean trees. Trees alone do not make a woods. A woods requires three layers: a high canopy of mature trees; an understory, or middle layer, of shrubs and medium-sized trees; and a ground layer of leafy plants (vines, wildflowers, and ferns) and plenty of leaf litter (decaying organic matter). A healthy woods has rich soil to provide nutrients, a balance between old and young growth, and a diversity of scales to accommodate creatures of many sizes.

One reason wood thrushes need woods is their diet. In spring and summer, they eat spiders, caterpillars, beetles, ants, and flies, all of which proliferate in areas with diverse shrubs and wildflowers and a rich bottom layer of soil and leaf litter. In fall, they eat fruits and berries produced by small trees, shrubs, and vines. Because the birds nest close to the ground, in shrubs or the trunks of short trees, a dense layer of vegetation provides cover from predators.

The wood thrush is the poster bird for the decline of neotropical migrant songbirds. Although it is not endangered, its numbers have been decreasing rapidly since the 1970s. Loss and fragmentation of its habitat—both in Central America, where it winters, and North America, where it breeds—are the most probable culprits, along with cowbird nest parasitism.

When you hear a wood thrush singing, you're hearing the sound of a relatively healthy, intact woods. The birdsong is the sound of the natural world in harmony.

50

SAND SPRING TRAIL AND TOM LOWE TRAIL

Hemlock ravines, rocky creeks, and an unusual walled, sand-bottomed spring greet hikers on these remote mountainside trails.

LOCATION
Shartlesville, PA
(Berks County)

RATING
Moderate

DIRECTIONS

Take PA Turnpike Northeast Extension I-476 to Exit 56 (Lehigh Valley); take I-78 West to Exit 23 (Shartlesville) and drive north on Mountain Road for 0.3 mile. Bear left onto Forge Dam Road and continue 1.5 miles to Northkill Road. Turn right to find the State Game Lands 110 parking lot, with space for twenty cars. *GPS coordinates:* 40° 32.266′ N, 76° 07.405′ W.

DISTANCE
5.25 miles

ELEVATION GAIN
500 feet

ESTIMATED TIME
2.75 hours

TRAIL DESCRIPTION

The Appalachian Trail (AT) traverses the crest of Kittatinny Ridge (Blue Mountain) in eastern Pennsylvania, offering valley views, peaceful woods, and a demanding footpath. Although you will certainly want to hike the AT, other rewarding hikes in the area beckon, such as this one. Below the AT, on Blue Mountain's south slope, streams tumble over rocks; thick forests harbor multitudes of wildlife; and the humanmade trail melds into wilderness. The Sand Spring Trail–Tom Lowe Trail loop skirts the AT, never meeting it. Those who hike this footpath will feel they've spent time getting to know the mountain instead of merely making their way across it.

Blue Mountain stretches across the landscape like one of summer's ubiquitous (and harmless) black rat snakes. Its luscious green forests conceal an inner structure: layers of rock deposited when ancient continents were drifting and colliding, oceans forming and disappearing, muddy currents swirling. Blue Mountain's top layer is light-colored quartzite, sandstone, and conglomerate; the band below, dark mudstone.

MAPS
USGS Friedensburg,
USGS Auburn; Pennsylvania
Appalachian Trail Map,
Section 5

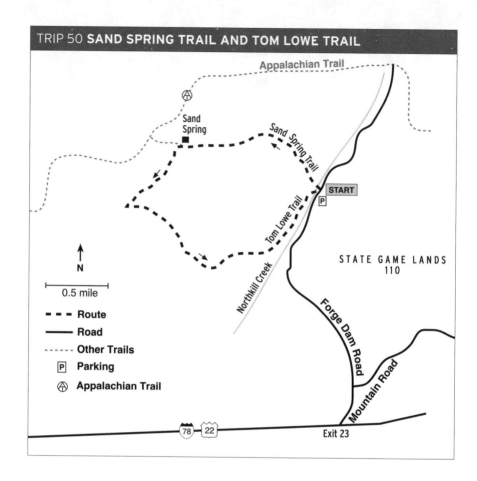

Water and rock tell the continuing story of the mountain, with Sand Spring Trail following the course of a stream that cuts into the rock layers. This hike begins in a hemlock ravine, a deeply incised valley formed by Northkill Creek tumbling down the mountain, breaking the rock into pieces and carrying sediment away. Hemlocks and rhododendrons thrive in the cool, moist, rocky environment of these ravines, as do ferns and fungi.

From the parking lot, head past the gate and up the road 0.1 mile; the well-marked and blue-blazed Sand Spring Trail begins to the left. The rocky trail follows a tributary of the Northkill, crossing it many times and even running up the stream's center. (Use caution, as the rocks may be slippery.) Over the sound of rushing water, the thick, extensive forest resounds with the calls of birds that thrive in deep woods: veery, pewee, and scarlet tanager. Chipmunks are everywhere, chirping and scampering over the mossy rocks. Along the forest floor run partridgeberry, wood strawberries, trailing arbutus, and teaberry. Pink lady's slippers abound in spring, ghostly white Indian pipes in summer. In sunlit openings, butterflies bask and dragonflies hunt.

A simple log bridge crosses a stream in a hemlock ravine on the Tom Lowe Trail.

Sand Spring Trail climbs the ravine steadily but, for the most part, gently. There are light- and dark-colored boulders and pebbles in the stream, eroded from one of the two rock layers. At 2 miles, the trail reaches eponymous Sand Spring. Surrounded on three sides by low walls, the spring percolates silently, bubbling into a clear, sand-bottomed pool before flowing down the ravine. The fine white sand comes from the underlying quartzite and sandstone that caps the ridge and is slowly being eroded by the water.

Sand Spring Trail continues 600 feet north to join the AT, but you'll turn left here to take the orange-blazed Tom Lowe Trail, which heads southwest. Tom Lowe Trail ascends gradually for 0.2 mile through a dry, deciduous woods; flattens briefly over a hillcrest; then steeply descends for 0.2 mile into another quiet, cool, shady hemlock ravine. The trail follows the stream gently downhill for 0.5 mile then crosses it via a two-log bridge. (Walking upright on this narrow bridge may be disconcerting; either scooch along it or walk on the stones below, using one of the logs as a railing.) A few more fords follow—some that are easily stepped over, others that require more difficult balancing acts. The trail veers away from the creek; at 3.8 miles, it crosses a small, open, marshy area, formerly a gravel pit. Note the catalpa trees, which indicate that humans once lived here and planted these ornamental trees to enjoy their cooling shade. Watch carefully

Indian pipe, common in rocky woods in summer, lacks chlorophyll and obtains nutrients by partnering with underground "mycorrhizal" fungi that feed from roots of green plants.

for a faded blaze at 3.9 miles. The trail turns left here and heads back uphill into the woods.

From here, Tom Lowe Trail twists and turns uphill and downhill, continuing in a counterclockwise direction around the lower slope of a mountainside bulge. At 4.9 miles, Northkill Road comes into sight through the trees, and the rushing Northkill Creek is audible. The trail follows the creek, crossing it at 5.1 miles. Be prepared for wet feet: The creek sometimes swells, covering the stepping-stones, and the alternative crossing—leaping over the foundations of an old dam—is challenging. In another 0.2 mile upstream along the creek, Tom Lowe Trail ends at a road, just below the parking lot.

MORE INFORMATION

Hunting is not permitted on Sundays; wear blaze orange at all other times. There are no restrooms. Several other trails can be accessed from this location. You can continue on Sand Spring Trail past the spring itself to reach the AT, or you can follow the State Game Lands access road past the Sand Spring trailhead to the AT, taking that north to Auburn Lookout. The Blue Mountain Eagle Climbing Club (bmecc.org) maintains these trails.

REBIRTH OF A MOUNTAIN

They called it the Dead Zone. Eight miles of Blue Mountain in Pennsylvania, on both sides of the Lehigh Gap, bare of soil, plants or trees: a moonscape seemingly dropped from space onto the Kittatinny Ridge. For over 80 years, beginning in 1898, the smelters of New Jersey Zinc Company belched fumes from Palmerton into the mountain air, creating localized acid rain from sulfuric acid, and depositing lead, cadmium, and zinc onto the steep forested slopes. By the time the smelters stopped the forest was gone.

In 1983, the U.S. Environmental Protection Agency (EPA) designated 3,000 acres of the mountain a Superfund site, along with a 2.5-mile-long slag bank along the Aquashicola Creek, a tributary of the Lehigh River. Crowning a prominent ridge that straddles a major river, the mountaintop site is visible for miles. Thousands of vehicles pass it daily and thousands of hikers walk through it every year.

Since 1980, the Superfund program has enabled the EPA to clean up sites, compelling the parties responsible for contamination to perform the cleanups or reimburse the government for cleanups.

The scale and visibility of the Palmerton Zinc Superfund site was matched by the complexity of relationships among project participants. In addition to the EPA, interested parties included (among others) the U.S. Fish & Wildlife Service, National Park Service, NOAA, and PA Departments of Environmental Protection and Conservation & Natural Resources, Pennsylvania Game Commission, Pennsylvania Fish & Boat Commission, Lehigh Gap Nature Center, Horsehead/Viacom/CBS (successors to the New Jersey Zinc Company), and residents of Palmerton, many of whom were former employees of New Jersey Zinc.

Palmerton was a company town, built in 1912 by New Jersey Zinc for its employees: a diverse and vibrant community whose jobs ranged from manufacturing to research and engineering. Palmerton was named for the executive who established the town—Stephen S. Palmer, then-president of New Jersey Zinc. Its location was selected because of geography: it was close to rail and river transportation, and near population centers. But geography made it the worst possible location for smelters. The mountain trapped pollutants that otherwise would have blown away.

When the Superfund project began, there were two overarching environmental goals. One was to fix contaminants in place so they would not disperse by air or water. The second was to restore damaged natural resources.

At first the idea that the dead mountain could be resurrected was almost unimaginable.

Today, the mountain is alive again. Where bare rocks reigned, green grasses and sturdy trees are taking hold. Wildlife is rediscovering the slopes above the Lehigh River and Aquashicola Creek. Hikers are enjoying radically new views.

And the residents of Palmerton are looking up at a mountain landscape last known by their great-grandparents.

People accomplished the seemingly impossible task through creativity, partnership, and scientific expertise.

The restoration proceeded differently on the two sides of the Gap because of differences in ownership. On the west side, Lehigh Gap Nature Center led restoration efforts beginning in 2003 that focused on establishing zinc-tolerant native grasses. The grasses, some of which grew naturally on disturbed areas there, quickly established themselves and continue to thrive today. Many species of birds nest in the grasslands. Over time, as new soil accumulates, grass may be replaced in part by trees and shrubs, the beginnings of a new forest.

On the east side, change was slower. The EPA and partners eventually implemented a successful plan beginning in 2011 to revegetate the rocky slopes using aerial reseeding with a mixture of grass, shrub, and tree seeds. In addition, blight-resistant American Chestnut saplings were planted in several protected areas, with the objective of creating viable nodes from which the chestnuts might reestablish themselves in the forest.

Today the green slopes of Blue Mountain stand in testament to the resilience of nature—and to the residual power that humankind retains to do good work for the benefit of the environment and for future generations, who, perhaps will only know the horror of environmental disasters from the pages of history books, not the mountains they hike.

APPENDIX A
HIKING CLUBS IN THE
PHILADELPHIA AREA

Joining a hiking club is a great way to learn about local recreation areas and to meet others who share your interest in the outdoors. Most hiking clubs also maintain trails, which can include activities as diverse as building bridges, steps, and shelters or brush clearing. Many clubs welcome volunteers without requiring them to join.

Appalachian Mountain Club's
Delaware Valley Chapter
outdoors.org
amcdv.org

Allentown Hiking Club
allentownhikingclub.org

Batona Hiking Club
batona.wildapricot.org

Blue Mountain Eagle Climbing Club
bmecc.org

Chester County Trail Club
cctrailclub.org

Lancaster Hiking Club
lancasterhikingclub.com

Outdoor Club of South Jersey
ocsj.org

Wilmington Trail Club
wilmingtontrailclub.org

York Hiking Club
yorkhikingclub.com

ALSO SEE
Keystone Trails Association,
a statewide association
kta-hike.org

New Jersey Trails, trail
maintenance association for
central New Jersey
njtrails.org

APPENDIX B
FURTHER READING ON NATURAL HISTORY OF THE DELAWARE VALLEY

Barnes, John H. and W.D. Sevon. *The Geological Story of Pennsylvania.* 4th ed. Harrisburg: Pennsylvania Geological Survey, 2014.

A good general introduction to the geological processes that shaped the state and the physiographic provinces. Available online at docs.dcnr.pa.gov/cs/ groups/public/documents/document/dcnr_014597.pdf

Boyd, Howard P. *A Field Guide to the Pine Barrens of New Jersey.* Medford, NJ: Plexus Publishing, 1991.

A guide to the flora, fauna, ecology, and history of the Pine Barrens.

Collins, Beryl Robichaud, and Karl H. Anderson. *Plant Communities of New Jersey.* New Brunswick, NJ: Rutgers University Press, 1994.

This book describes the plants that are typically found together in specific habitats throughout the Delaware Valley.

Delaware Geological Survey. *The Geology of Delaware.* Newark: University of Delaware, 2017.

Online publication describing the physiographic provinces of Delaware. dgs.udel.edu/delaware-geology

Fergus, Charles. *Wildlife of Pennsylvania and the Northeast.* Mechanicsburg, PA: Stackpole Books, 2000.

Comprehensive nontechnical reference for birds, mammals, amphibians, and reptiles.

Harper, David P. *Roadside Geology of New Jersey.* Missoula, MT: Mountain Press Publishing Company, 2013.

An excellent guide to New Jersey's geologic history, with profuse illustrations.

New Jersey Geological and Water Survey. *Bedrock Geology of New Jersey.* Trenton: New Jersey Department of Environmental Protection, 2016.

Includes a summary of New Jersey geology and physiographic provinces. Available online at state.nj.us/dep/njgs/enviroed/freedwn/psnjmap.pdf

Rhoads, Ann Fowler, and Timothy A. Block. *Trees of Pennsylvania*. Philadelphia: University of Pennsylvania Press, 2005.

> An illustrated reference to native trees.

Van Diver, Bradford G. *Roadside Geology of Pennsylvania*. Missoula, MT: Mountain Press Publishing Company, 1990.

> Out of print but worth tracking down. A bit more technical than *The Geological Story of Pennsylvania*, this book enables a more specific focus on rocks in southeastern Pennsylvania.

INDEX

ABOUT THE AUTHOR

Susan Charkes writes frequently about the outdoors, nature, and the environment. An avid hiker and paddler, she is also a volunteer maintainer of the Appalachian Trail and Horse-Shoe Trail. She works in the land conservation field. Learn more at susancharkes.com.

AMC'S DELAWARE VALLEY CHAPTER

AMC's Delaware Valley Chapter offers a wide variety of hiking, backpacking, climbing, paddling, bicycling, snowshoeing, and skiing trips each year, as well as social, family, and young member programs and instructional workshops. The chapter also maintains a 15-mile section of the Pennsylvania Appalachian Trail between Wind Gap and Little Gap, as well as trails at Valley Forge National Historical Park.

To view a list of AMC activities in Pennsylvania, Central and South Jersey, Northern Delaware, and other parts of the Northeast and Mid-Atlantic, visit outdoors.org/activities.

AMC BOOK UPDATES

AMC Books strives to keep our guidebooks as up-to-date as possible to help you plan safe and enjoyable adventures. If after publishing a book we learn that trails are relocated or route or contact information has changed, we will post the updated information online. Before you hit the trail, check for updates at outdoors.org/bookupdates.

While hiking or paddling, if you notice discrepancies with the trail description or map, or if you find any other errors in the book, please let us know by submitting them to amcbookupdates@outdoors.org or in writing to Books Editor, c/o AMC, 10 City Square, Boston, MA 02129. We will verify all submissions and post key updates each month.

AMC Books is dedicated to being a recognized leader in outdoor publishing. Thank you for your participation.

APPALACHIAN MOUNTAIN CLUB

At AMC, connecting you to the freedom and exhilaration of the outdoors is our calling. We help people of all ages and abilities to explore and develop a deep appreciation of the natural world.

AMC helps you get outdoors on your own, with family and friends, and through activities close to home and beyond. With chapters from Maine to Washington, D.C., including groups in Boston, New York City, and Philadelphia, you can enjoy activities like hiking, paddling, cycling, and skiing, and learn new outdoor skills. We offer advice, guidebooks, maps, and unique lodges and huts to inspire your next outing. You will also have the opportunity to support conservation advocacy and research, youth programming, and caring for 1,800 miles of trails.

We invite you to join us in the outdoors.

YOUR CONNECTION
TO THE OUTDOORS

AMC's Best Day Hikes near Washington, D.C., 2nd Edition
Beth Homicz & Annie Eddy

Discover 50 of the best hikes that can be completed in less than a day in and around the nation's capital, including Maryland and Virginia—from wilderness experiences to close-to-home immersions in nature, with an increased focus on Annapolis and Baltimore.

$18.95 • 978-1-62842-037-1

AMC's Best Sea Kayaking in the Mid-Atlantic
Michaela Riva Gaaserud

This new guide features 50 coastal paddling adventures from the New York City Water Trail to beautiful Virginia Beach at the mouth of the Chesapeake River, with an at-a-glance trip planner, descriptions and maps of the routes, and information on launches, tide and currents, and nearby attractions. It's your indispensible guide to kayaking on the Mid-Atlantic seaboard.

$18.95 • 978-1-62842-031-9

AMC's Best Backpacking in the Mid-Atlantic
Michael R. Martin

Within hours of New York, Philadelphia, and Washington, D.C., thousands of miles of trails cross a wide variety of wild terrain. Whether you're looking for a two-day loop or a challenging weeklong trek, this three-season guide is an essential tool for finding the most exciting Mid-Atlantic backpacking experiences.

$19.95 • 978-1-934028-86-5

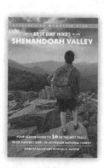

AMC's Best Day Hikes in the Shenandoah Valley
Jennifer Adach & Michael R. Martin

Bounded on the east by the Blue Ridge Mountains and on the west by the Appalachians, the Shenandoah Valley is a region of exceptional natural beauty. This guide offers 50 of the best hikes that can be accomplished in the region in less than a day, from easy saunters of a few miles to longer treks through rugged terrain.

$18.95 • 978-1-62842-017-3